FAIRNESS IN INTERNATIONAL TAXATION

This book explores the thorny normative issues raised by the changing landscape of international tax policy.

Proposals for taxation of the digital economy and the OECD/G20 BEPS framework promise fundamental changes in the international tax system. The book features perspectives from legal scholars, political theorists, and political philosophers on international corporate and individual taxation. Contributors advance new theories of international tax justice, develop theoretically informed reform proposals and critique influential approaches to international tax reform. Key themes include justice in bilateral and multilateral international tax agreements, the taxation of cross-border workers, fair division of tax revenue from multinational corporations, and the fairness of the international tax policy-making process.

This book provides new perspectives on leading international tax policy debates, analyses the intersection between international distributive justice and contemporary tax policy, and proposes innovative ways to meet the demands of tax justice in a global context.

Fairness in International Taxation

Edited by
Ira K Lindsay
and
Benita Mathew

·HART·
OXFORD · LONDON · NEW YORK · NEW DELHI · SYDNEY

HART PUBLISHING

Bloomsbury Publishing Plc

Kemp House, Chawley Park, Cumnor Hill, Oxford, OX2 9PH, UK

1385 Broadway, New York, NY 10018, USA

Bloomsbury Publishing Ireland Limited, 29 Earlsfort Terrace, Dublin 2, D02 AY28, Ireland

HART PUBLISHING, the Hart/Stag logo, BLOOMSBURY and the Diana logo are trademarks of Bloomsbury Publishing Plc

First published in Great Britain 2025

A catalogue record for this book is available from the British Library.

Library of Congress Cataloging-in-Publication data

Names: Lindsay, Ira K, editor. | Mathew, Benita, editor.

Title: Fairness in international taxation / edited by Ira K Lindsay and Benita Mathew.

Description: Oxford ; New York : Hart Publishing, 2025. | Includes bibliographical references and index. | Summary:
"This book explores the thorny normative issues raised by the changing landscape of international tax policy. The book
features perspectives from legal scholars, political theorists, and political philosophers on international corporate and
individual taxation. Contributors advance new theories of international tax justice, develop theoretically informed reform
proposals and critique influential approaches to international tax reform. This book provides new perspectives on leading
international tax policy debates, analyses the intersection between international distributive justice and contemporary tax
policy, and proposes innovative ways to meet the demands of tax justice in a global context"—Provided by publisher.

Identifiers: LCCN 2024047142 (print) | LCCN 2024047143 (ebook) | ISBN 9781509968077 (hardback) |
ISBN 9781509968114 (paperback) | ISBN 9781509968084 (Epub) | ISBN 9781509968091 (ebook)

Subjects: LCSH: International business enterprises—Taxation—Law and legislation. | Double taxation. |
Corporations—Taxation—Law and legislation. | Income tax—Foreign income. | Taxation—Law and
legislation. | Fairness. | Conflict of laws—Taxation—Europe. | International and municipal law—Europe.

Classification: LCC K4475 .F35 2025 (print) | LCC K4475 (Ebook) | DDC 343.06/7—dc23/eng/20241008

LC record available at https://lccn.loc.gov/2024047142

LC ebook record available at https://lccn.loc.gov/2024047143

ISBN: HB: 978-1-50996-807-7
         ePDF: 978-1-50996-809-1
         ePub: 978-1-50996-808-4

Typeset by Compuscript Ltd, Shannon

For product safety related questions contact productsafety@bloomsbury.com

To find out more about our authors and books visit www.hartpublishing.co.uk. Here you will find extracts,
author information, details of forthcoming events and the option to sign up for our newsletters.

CONTENTS

PART IV
INDIVIDUAL TAXATION ACROSS BORDERS

NOTES ON CONTRIBUTORS

Laurens van Apeldoorn is Assistant Professor of Tax Law at Leiden University, the Netherlands. His research within the research programme 'Limits of Tax Jurisdiction' concerns the philosophical foundations of taxation. He is the co-author of *Tax Cooperation in an Unjust World* (Oxford, Oxford University Press, 2021).

Dirk Broekhuijsen is Associate Professor of Tax Law at Leiden University, the Netherlands. Before his appointment as Associate Professor, he was a tax inspector at the Amsterdam Office of the Dutch Tax and Customs Administration for several years. Dirk teaches in courses on international and personal income tax law.

Peter Dietsch is a Professor in the Department of Philosophy at the University of Victoria, Canada. His research focuses on questions of economic ethics, including theories of just income, tax justice, climate justice, and the normative dimensions of money and monetary policy.

Bastiaan van Ganzen is a Lecturer and PhD candidate at the Institute of Tax Law and Economics of Leiden University, the Netherlands.

Vasiliki Koukoulioti is a Lecturer in Tax Law at the Centre for Commercial Law Studies, Queen Mary University of London, UK. Prior to joining Queen Mary, she was a Lecturer in Digital Law, Policy & Society at Newcastle University, UK, and a tax consultant in accounting and law firms. Her research focuses on international taxation and its interaction with technology and sustainability.

Ira K Lindsay is Associate Professor of Law at the University of Surrey, UK, where he serves as Head of Surrey Law School and Associate Head of the School of Social Sciences. He holds a J.D. from Yale Law School and a Ph.D in Philosophy from the University of Michigan.

Benita Mathew is an ACCA and ACGP Affiliate from PwC Academy. She holds an MSc in Accounting and Taxation from the University of Exeter, UK. Her PhD project at the University of Surrey proposes international tax policy reform by rethinking the role of digitalisation in business tax planning. Her research interests lie at the intersection of AI, digital business models, tax policy, e-administration and compliance.

Doron Narotzki is an Associate Professor of Tax at the University of Akron College of Business, US, Daverio School of Accountancy, and the Director of the Master of Taxation Program, where he teaches and writes about international tax and corporate tax issues.

Amanda Parsons is an Associate Professor at the University of Colorado Law School, US. Prior to joining Colorado Law, she was a fellow at Columbia Law School and an associate at Skadden Arps. She holds a JD from Yale Law School, an MPhil from Oxford, and a BA from Columbia University.

Natalia Pushkareva is a PhD Candidate in Global Studies at University of Urbino, Italy. She has degrees in Law and Finance from Lomonosov Moscow State University and University of Oxford, and has been working on tax policy issues for a decade as a tax policy practitioner and a researcher.

Thomas Rixen is Professor of International and Comparative Political Economy at the Otto Suhr Institut of Political Science, Freie Universität Berlin, Germany. His research interests and teaching are in (de-)globalisation, institutionalist theory and economic policies, in particular taxation and financial regulation. More info: www.thomasrixen.eu.

Bernard Schneider is Senior Lecturer in International Tax Law and Director of the Institute of Tax Law at the Centre for Commercial Law Studies, Queen Mary University of London, UK. His main research interests are taxation in emerging and developing countries, taxation of individuals, the politics of taxation and tax administration and procedure.

Tamir Shanan is a Senior Lecturer at the Haim Striks Faculty of Law, at the College of Management Academic Studies, Israel, where he teaches and writes about public finance, personal tax, partnership tax, corporate tax and international tax issues.

Henk Vording is a Professor of Tax Law at Leiden University, the Netherlands. His main fields of interest include tax history, philosophical foundations of taxation, and effective taxation of wealth also in relation to the ongoing redesign of international tax law. He participated in Dutch government advisory committees on letterbox companies, labour market and general tax reform. His teaching focuses on topical issues in international tax, esp. Pillars 1&2.

TABLE OF CASES

TABLE OF LEGISLATION

Canada

Singapore

United States of America

European Union

International Treaties and Conventions

Introduction

IRA K LINDSAY AND BENITA MATHEW

The international tax policy landscape has changed dramatically in recent years. It has transformed from one in which international co-operation was limited in scope, with most matters of substance left to the discretion of national governments, to one with much greater ambitions for limiting tax competition, avoiding double non-taxation of income, and allocating tax revenue between nations.[1] Issues, such as corporate tax rates, traditionally left for national governments to decide, are now within the purview of international tax policy. Proposals that might have been considered unrealistic or perhaps just short of utopian a few years ago are now on the international agenda. Most prominently, the Organisation for Economic Co-operation and Development (OECD)/G20 Inclusive Framework on Base Erosion and Profit Shifting (BEPS) seeks to undermine incentives for multinationals to shift profits to low tax jurisdictions and to better align the allocation of taxable profits with the location of economic activity. The recent BEPS Pillar 1 and Pillar 2 agreements aim to reallocate a portion of profits to market jurisdictions and to impose a global minimum corporation tax rate of 15 per cent.[2] This negotiation plays out against the background of a dispute over how to tax the digital economy, with many European nations threatening to impose new taxes on US tech giants that gather user data and sell advertising overseas. How this dispute and the OECD's proposed solution evolve will have large implications for the global economy. Regardless of the ultimate fate of the BEPS project, it is clear that we are in a new era.

Twentieth-century international tax policy was largely concerned with the avoidance of double-taxation, implemented through double-taxation agreements that allocate the right to tax income from cross-border transactions so that a single increment of profit is not taxed in two separate jurisdictions.[3] These

---

[1] R Mason, 'The Transformation of International Taxation' (2020) 114 *American Journal of International Law* 353.

[2] C Noonan & V Plekhanova, 'Compliance Challenges of the BEPS Two-Pillar Solution' [2022] *British Tax Review* 512, 523–24.

[3] eg, 'Convention Between The Government Of The United Kingdom Of Great Britain And Northern Ireland And The Government Of The United States Of America For The Avoidance Of Double Taxation And The Prevention Of Fiscal Evasion With Respect To Taxes On Income And On Capital Gains'. Entered into force 31 March 2003.

bilateral agreements seek to remove barriers to foreign investment and secure the fair treatment of taxpayers engaging in cross-border economic activities. A second form of international cooperation involves information exchange between nations to reduce the chances that an internationally mobile taxpayer can evade taxes. International information exchange has expanded notably in recent years.[4] But in essence, it is international co-operation aimed at enforcing national tax laws. Neither of these forms of international tax co-operation encourages a robust analysis of international tax in terms of distributive justice because key distributive questions are left to national governments. The initial model conventions for double tax agreements focused on the division of tax rights over international business activity in ways often justified by economic efficiency, administrative convenience, or a perceived relationship of economic activity to a particular jurisdiction. The distributive consequences of international agreements thus often followed from rules adopted for other reasons.

The status quo of the twentieth-century international tax policy, built upon narrowly focused bilateral double-taxation agreements, is under severe pressure for several reasons. First, the shameless exploitation of international tax rules by multinational corporations to manufacture 'stateless income' that escapes taxation entirely has made it clear that ineffective international tax rules are a threat to the tax bases of many nations, including powerful countries with sophisticated tax administrations.[5] As a result, governments around the world are taking a more aggressive position against tax avoidance and states that appear to facilitate it. Second, the traditional categories of international taxation, such as residence and source, are under pressure as cross-border investment grows, economic activity becomes more geographically mobile and cross border transactions are increasingly embedded in digitalised business models. As a consequence, the identification of profits with particular jurisdictions, never a matter that lent itself to great precision, has become even more nebulous. Third, fiscal deficits, the challenges of funding welfare states with older populations, and the smaller proportion of working age adults create a need for greater tax revenue while reducing the scope for collecting it from workers. Fourth, disputes over taxation of the digital economy have provided strong incentives to agree on new multilateral rules for taxation of profits from international business. Credible threats by European nations to impose new taxes targeting US tech companies and the possibility of US retaliation give both sides an interest in reaching agreement on how to divide the taxable profits of multinational companies between jurisdictions in order to avert a potentially ugly conflict between otherwise friendly nations.

The incipient wave of international tax agreements seems likely to be very different in terms of scope, substance, and procedure. The substance of international tax

---

[4] eg, The Foreign Account Tax Compliance Act 'FATCA', codified at 26 U.S.C. ss 1471–1474; Council Directive 2014/107/EU of 9 December 2014 amending Directive 2011/16/EU as regards mandatory automatic exchange of information in the field of taxation [2014] OJ L359.

[5] E Kleinbard, 'Stateless Income' (2011) 11 *Florida Tax Review* 699.

policy is now as much concerned with avoiding double-non-taxation of income as it is with avoiding double-taxation of income. Preventing double-non-taxation requires not only a system of rules to allocate various kinds of income between jurisdictions, but also a way to backstop the international tax system by imposing taxes on revenue that otherwise would fall between the cracks of these rules and an allocation of this new source of revenue among jurisdictions. The focus on double-non-taxation and harmful forms of tax competition will require restricting the policy choices of national governments in ways that limit fiscal self-determination. International tax policy agreements now include matters such as corporate tax rates that were previously the prerogative of national governments. This in turn poses a much starker conflict between the benefits that can be obtained from international co-operation to limit tax competition and the interest of national governments in maintaining autonomy to set policy. Some nations may believe that a larger tax base is not sufficient compensation for losing the ability to use low tax rates to attract inbound investment,[6] while others may worry that the prospect of tax competition limits their ability to raise sufficient revenue.[7] As the scope of international tax policy has changed, the locus of international tax policy making has shifted from bilateral agreements to multilateral agreements negotiated in fora such as the OECD. This raises the stakes for questions about the fairness of international decision-making procedures and the extent to which some nations have disproportionate power in institutions that make rules for a much larger group of nations. The tension between the interests of developed and developing nations is one fault line, but, as the recent conflict between the US and EU demonstrates, it is far from the only one. Finally, the increased mobility of high-skilled labour makes the tax treatment of cross-border workers a very important policy question for many nations. The basic framework for taxing internationally mobile workers was created when they accounted for a far smaller fraction of economic output and has not fundamentally changed for many years. Current policies in this area are also ripe for reconsideration.

The policy stakes are thus very high. As international tax policy has begun to aim at far more ambitious goals, there is an urgent need for normative theories adequate to this agenda. There is a deep, rich, and venerable literature on fairness in taxation at the level of the nation state.[8] However, theories of tax fairness at the

---

[6] M Desai, CF Foley & J Hines, 'The Demand for Tax Haven Operations' (2006) 90 *Journal of Public Economics* 513; M Marques, C Pinho & T Menezes Montenegro, 'The Effect of International Income Shifting on the Link between Real Investment and Corporate Taxation' (2019) 36 *Journal of International Accounting, Auditing and Taxation* 100268.

[7] P Dietsch, *Catching Capital: The Ethics of Tax Competition* (New York, Oxford University Press, 2015).

[8] eg, A Smith, *An inquiry into the nature and causes of the Wealth of Nations* (Oxford, Clarendon Press, 1979); JS Mill, *Principles of Political Economy* (London, Longman, Green & Co, 1909, reprinted Fairfield, Augustus M Kelley, 1976), Book V, ch II; R Musgrave, *The Theory of Public Finance: A Study in Public Economy* (New York, McGraw-Hill, 1959); JM Buchanan, *The Limits of Liberty* (Chicago, The University of Chicago Press, 1975); J Rawls, *A Theory of Justice* (Cambridge MA, Harvard University Press, 1999); L Murphy and T Nagel, *The Myth of Ownership* (New York, OUP, 2002).

national level are insufficient for the evaluation of international tax policy. The latter concerns not only the distribution of burdens among individuals in the same nation, but also the distribution of benefits among states, the duties that states owe to one another, the duties that states owe to their own citizens, and to the citizens of other states. What may appear to be a fair result from the perspective of distributive justice at the national level may undermine distributive justice at the international level or may not be practical in a world in which policy emerges from negotiation between states. For these reasons, political theorists in the past three decades have been increasingly focused on developing theories of global distributive justice.[9]

Despite the increasing importance of the topic in the public arena, the division of tax revenue among nations has been a less prominent part of the global distributive justice literature until recently, at least relative to international trade, climate change, international migration, and foreign aid.[10] Although tax law scholars have raised alarm about the distributive implications of profit shifting for many years,[11] scholarship that examines fairness in international taxation from the perspective of political philosophy or political theory has only recently emerged.[12] In part, this may reflect the challenge of applying insights from highly abstract political theory literature to a fairly technical area of international policy with a complex institutional context. In part, it may reflect the relatively lower public profile of international tax policy prior to the recent BEPS agreement.

This volume brings together tax scholars and political theorists to examine the thorny normative issues raised by the international conflict over taxation rights. The authors, who include both leading contributors to the international tax justice debates and new voices, engage with high-level theoretical questions about the nature of fairness in international taxation, proposals to reform international business and personal taxation, and questions about the institutional and regulatory structure of international tax policy. In each of these domains, contributors strike out in new directions, introducing new theories of fairness in international taxation, advancing original proposals to reform the taxation of business income and cross-border workers, exploring the questions raised by recent attempts to

---

[9] eg, T Pogge, 'An Egalitarian Law of Peoples' (1994) 23 *Philosophy & Public Affairs* 195; J Rawls, *The Law of Peoples* (Cambridge, MA, Harvard University Press, 1999); S Caney, *Justice Beyond Borders: A Global Political Theory* (Oxford, OUP, 2005); T Nagel, 'The Problem of Global Justice' (2005) 33 *Philosophy & Public Affairs* 113; G Brock, *Global Justice: A Cosmopolitan Account* (Oxford, OUP, 2009).

[10] eg, A James, *Fairness in Practice* (Oxford, OUP, 2012); J Broome, *Climate Matters: Ethics in a Warming World* (New York, W. W. Norton and Company, 2012); J Carens, 'Aliens and Citizens: The Case for Open Borders' (1987) 49 *The Review of Politics* 251; H Shue, *Basic Rights: Subsistence, Affluence, and US Foreign Policy* (Princeton, Princeton University Press, 1980).

[11] eg, R Avi-Yonah, 'Globalization, Tax Competition, and the Fiscal Crisis of the Welfare State' (2002) 113 *Harvard Law Review* 1573.

[12] eg, A Christians and L van Apeldoorn, *Tax Cooperation in an Unjust World* (Oxford, OUP, 2022); T Dagan, *International Tax Competition: Between Competition and Cooperation* (Cambridge, CUP, 2017); Dietsch (n 7).

coordinate international tax policy through the EU, and exploring the possibility of using corporate disclosure requirements to improve tax compliance.

This volume has four parts. The first part explores theories of justice in international taxation at a foundational level, mapping the existing literature and contributing new perspectives on what fairness requires in bilateral and multilateral international tax policy agreements. Peter Dietsch and Thomas Rixen provide a fitting opening to the volume in their chapter, 'Global Justice and International Taxation', which schematises existing theories of global tax justice. Diestch and Rixen classify theories of justice as either idealist or realist on the one hand and as either associativist or humanist on the other. The former distinction concerns the extent to which a theory takes features of the status quo as given. An idealist theory will aim at a theory of a maximally just order, even if this requires abstracting away from some features of the status quo, whereas a realist theory takes more aspects of the status quo as given and recommends improvements from a baseline of the existing state of affairs. The latter distinction concerns whether global tax justice addresses duties owed to individuals, such as the citizens of foreign states, or to collective entities, such as other states. A humanist theory of international tax justice regards policy as just if it is adequate to the moral relations between individual citizens in the various nations that are party to an agreement. States acquire rights and obligations from the moral rights and duties of the citizens that they represent. Associativist theories, by contrast, take states as bearers of moral rights and duties to one another that are not merely derivative of the rights and duties of citizens. These pairs of distinctions allow Dietsch and Rixen to map existing theories against a two-by-two matrix, categorising them as Realist-Associativist, Realist-Humanist, Idealist-Associativist, or Idealist-Humanist. In addition to helping to make sense of the current literature, their analysis yields a number of insights. One is that some apparent disagreements between theorists may reflect differences in approach rather than disagreement about the content of justice. Realist and idealist theories of justice have different aims and depart from different assumptions about the function of a theory of justice. They may be best viewed not as competing theories of the same phenomenon, but rather as separate projects. A second implication of Dietsch and Rixen's argument is that humanist theories of global tax justice are under-represented in the literature in both their realist and idealist guises. It is hoped that future authors will develop these theories in greater detail.[13]

The next two chapters develop new lines of analysis of the fairness of international tax agreements. Bastiaan van Ganzen, Dirk Broekhuijsen, and Henk Vording appeal to the rich and well-developed literature in contract theory to explore the fairness of tax treaties or double taxation agreements, especially those

---

[13] One recent example of humanist theorising about global tax justice is Adam Kern's 'Progressive Taxation for the World'. A Kern, 'Progressive Taxation for the World' (forthcoming 2025) *Tax Law Review*.

between nations with unequal bargaining power. Double taxation agreements are bilateral agreements designed to prevent situations in which both states seek to tax the same increment of income. The appeal to contract theory is a seemingly promising approach because double taxation agreements share important features with contracts, but one that has been seldom explored in existing literature. Many of the normative concerns about tax treaties – unequal bargaining power between the parties, asymmetric information, adverse effects on third parties, coercive imposition of terms – arise in contractual relationships as well and have been analysed by contract theorists in great detail. Van Ganzen, Broekhuijsen, and Vording use the theoretical apparatus developed in private law theory to analyse analogous issues with the substance and procedure of double taxation agreements. They conclude that, notwithstanding the clear parallels between contracts and double taxation agreements, contract theory has only limited success in elucidating the bounds of fair dealing when it comes to tax treaties. It is very helpful in diagnosing the ways in which double taxation agreements raise issues of fairness both between the parties to the agreement and between the parties to the agreement and third parties. But it is less adequate to the task of providing guidance when, as is often the case, tax treaties have significant effects on nations that are not parties to the treaty. For this, Van Ganzen, Broekhuijsen, and Vording argue, we will need a normative theory that is designed for multilateral relationships and can account for the normative significance of the interests of parties to tax policy agreements *and* of states that are not parties but are affected by the agreements.

In 'Justice as Mutual Advantage in International Taxation', Ira Lindsay turns to a venerable but slightly out of the mainstream strand of political philosophy to provide a new framework for evaluating the fairness of international tax agreements. Justice as mutual advantage represents one aspect of the social contract tradition dating back to Thomas Hobbes and David Hume. It provides a middle path between the altruism required by egalitarian and utilitarian theories of justice and the unbridled pursuit of self-interest. Lindsay argues that justice as mutual advantage is well-suited for analysing international negotiations between states that are expected to pursue the interests of their citizens but may realise benefits from co-operating with other states. According to justice as mutual advantage, fair rules are those that divide the gains from cooperation in a way that benefits all co-operators and provides each party with a reason to support the cooperative scheme. In the international tax context, fair agreements should give each nation some combination of higher tax revenue and greater investment than they would otherwise enjoy and divide these gains in a way that does not give any nation incentive to undermine the agreement in hopes of renegotiating a better deal. What is fair will thus depend upon the antecedent interests of various countries, their degree of bargaining power, and the scope of potential gains from tax co-operation. Justice as mutual advantage may require that nations that otherwise might benefit from tax competition, including many developing countries, receive compensation for agreeing to rules that restrict their right to use tax incentives to attract inbound investment. Justice as mutual advantage differs from more ambitious theories in permitting pre-existing inequalities in entitlements and bargaining power to influ-ence the outcome of agreements. But precisely because it is limited in ambition and parsimonious in its moral commitments, it is well-suited to identifying agree-ments that partisans of greatly differing moral theories can agree are unjust.

The second part turns from theories of fairness in the abstract to concrete proposals for reforming international business taxation. In 'The Shifting Economic Allegiance of Capital Gains', Amanda Parsons proposes a new approach to the taxation of capital gains from the sale of shares of multinational corporations. At present, capital gains from the sale of shares in a company are typically taxed by the jurisdiction where the shareholder resides. This means that the right to tax capital gains has no relation to the location of the business activities of the company. Parsons proposes that tax rights over capital gains from certain multina-tionals should instead be allocated across the jurisdictions in which the company conducts business, including both where it produces goods and services and where it makes sales. This approach has advantages over the status quo along multiple dimensions. Parsons' proposal would make the distinction between capital gains and income from dividends matter less for tax purposes and thus better align the taxation of these two ways in which passive investors realise income from their investments. It better reflects the current nature of multinational corporations, which in the digital age often derive income from activities across the world, and is responsive to the claims of market jurisdictions that their consumers of goods and services and their users of digital platforms create value for multinationals. It also reflects the contemporary nature of business investment, which is often made by passive investors with no practical involvement in corporate decisions who hold a range of small, diversified investments in a large number of public companies. Parsons' solution responds to these facts by greatly reducing the significance of the residence of shareholders and increasing the tax entitlements of market juris-dictions. In addition to being a more attractive way to tax the value created by multinational corporations, Parsons' proposal may have distributive advantages. It would also reallocate tax revenue from the jurisdictions in which equity investors reside, which are disproportionately in the developed world, to the jurisdictions in which multinationals operate, which are relatively more likely to be in less devel-oped nations. This would respond simultaneously to the concerns of developing nations and of market jurisdictions for digital platform businesses that they do not receive a fair share of corporate tax revenue from multinational corporations.

In 'Destination-based Taxation, Incentive Compatibility and International Justice', Laurens van Apeldoorn analyses one of the most interesting recent proposals for wholesale reform of the international tax system, the destination-based cash flow tax proposed by Michael Devereaux, Alan Auerbach, Michael Keen, Wolfgang Schön, and John Vella.[14] The destination-based cash flow tax

---

[14] M Devereux, A Auerbach, M Keen, P Oosterhuis, W Schön, and J Vella, *Taxing Profit in a Global Economy* (Oxford, OUP, 2021).

imposes a tax on net revenue derived from a jurisdiction rather than on corporate profits. This is economically equivalent to replacing taxes on corporate profits with a VAT imposed on corporate revenue and an equivalent reduction in the rate of tax on salaries and wages of corporate employees.[15] Its proponents claim that the destination-based cash flow tax would greatly reduce the scope for corporate tax avoidance, improve economic efficiency, and reduce the complexity of tax administration relative to the current tax on corporate profits. For a short time in 2017 it seemed as though this proposal might be adopted by the United States, although ultimately the US Congress decided to pursue a much less radical reform of US international taxation instead.[16] Van Apeldoorn analyses Devereux et al.'s proposal from the perspective of international distributive justice, revealing the normative commitments implicit in their arguments. Van Apeldoorn focuses on their appeal to incentive compatibility as a criterion for sound international tax policy. A body of rules is incentive-compatible if, when the rules are in force, each agent to whom the rules apply has an incentive to comply with them.[17] Van Apeldoorn shows that incentive compatibility is attractive as a criterion of tax justice because it allows both international cooperation on tax policy *and* fiscal sovereignty for states despite the prima facie tension between the two. Incentive-compatible international tax rules do not require an external enforcement mechanism and thus allow each state to make free choices concerning their tax policy against the background of this common framework of rules. While this feature of the destination-based cash flow tax is attractive, it is not necessarily enough to justify the policy if the distributive consequences turn out to be undesirable. Van Apeldoorn argues that much will depend on whether enforcement mechanisms for alternative international tax policies are feasible. His analysis thus clarifies both how the destination-based cash flow tax might be justified and what justificatory burden the incentive compatibility argument must meet.

The third part turns from reform proposals to the procedures through which international tax policy is made and the context in which corporate taxpayers decide how to respond to these policies. It explores the procedural fairness of international tax policymaking and the scope for using sustainability reporting to influence corporate tax compliance decisions. In 'Globalisation, Taxation and the Essence of Europe' Natalia Pushkareva investigates the problem of multilateral international tax policymaking. The legitimacy of international tax policy-making institutions and the disadvantaged position of many developing countries in international tax policy negotiations are widespread concerns.[18] Pushkareva approaches

---

[15] ibid 274.

[16] A Auerbach, 'Demystifying the Destination-Based Cash Flow Tax' (Fall 2017) *Brookings Papers on Economic Activity* 409, 429.

[17] M Devereux, A Auerbach, M Keen, P Oosterhuis, W Schön, and J Vella, *Taxing Profit in a Global Economy* (Oxford, OUP, 2021) 55.

[18] eg, M Hearson, *Imposing Standards: The North-South Dimension to Global Tax Politics* (Ithaca, Cornell University Press 2021) 5; I Ozai, 'Institutional and Structural Legitimacy Deficits in the International Tax Regime' (2020) 12 *World Tax Journal* 53.

the issue of power inequalities from a different angle by considering inequalities in the context of intra-European negotiations. She examines the case of Hungary, which held out for some time against the EU's approval of the global minimum corporate tax in Pillar 2 of the BEPS project. This conflict has implications for the nature of European cooperation and the principle of 'sincere cooperation' between Member States as well as for the broader question of how to design multilateral policymaking institutions. The experience of Hungary suggests that smaller states and those with weaker economies are susceptible to pressure to consent to policies that they oppose, despite the ostensibly co-operative nature of multilateral governance. Pushkareva also shows that universal consent rules for adopting new policies are vulnerable to what she calls 'the unilateralist's curse'. When the desirability of a policy requires making estimates of its effects, a universal consent rule allows the actor with the most extreme views to determine policy. Because of the deficiencies of universal consent mechanisms and the inequalities introduced by any voting mechanism that weighs economic influence, Pushkareva favours a qualified majority voting system in which each country, regardless of size or economic power, has one vote.

In 'Sustainability Reporting and Corporate Taxation', Vasiliki Koukoulioti examines the role that tax metrics can play in corporate sustainability reporting. This topic is important both from the perspective of whether tax metrics can encourage better corporate citizenship on the part of corporations and of whether they can usefully supplement other sustainability indicators to give socially conscious investors a better understanding of corporate social responsibility. Tax metrics could provide a means to influence corporate tax compliance separately from and complementary to legal sanctions. They also might allow socially responsible investors to encourage better tax compliance by multinational corporations operating in jurisdictions with poor administrations or limited bargaining power with foreign investors. As Koukoulioti shows, despite real promise, the hurdles for implementing effective tax sustainability metrics are considerable. Given the wide range of contexts in which multinational corporations operate, tax metrics need to be tailored to the specific features of particular industries and jurisdictions. But there must also be uniform reporting standards so that investors can easily compare the tax behaviour of different companies, thereby enabling competition for investment from socially responsible investors. Harmonising tax reporting metrics will require cooperation between governmental, non-governmental and corporate actors to establish a framework that is accepted by companies, investors and tax-focused NGOs.

The fourth part of the volume turns away from the corporate sector to consider the other main policy question of international taxation: the taxation of internationally mobile individuals. It features contrasting proposals for the taxation of workers that move abroad for employment in a new jurisdiction or split their professional activities between multiple jurisdictions. This topic is of increasing importance as international migration reaches new heights and as the digital economy opens new opportunities for workers to move between jurisdictions while retaining the same job.[19] It raises questions of fairness both in terms of how tax rights should be divided between states and in terms of the treatment of internationally mobile taxpayers relative to each other and to non-mobile taxpayers. In 'Taxation of Cross Border Migrations: Re-evaluating the Allocation between Home Country and Host Country' Tamir Shanan and Doron Narotzki examine the 'brain drain' problem and consider how the tax system might respond to it. Shanan and Narotzki point out that the flow of skilled workers from less developed countries to wealthier countries has only increased since Jagdish Bhagwati proposed taxation as a response to the 'brain drain' problem fifty years ago.[20] Bhagwati suggested that host nations impose a surtax on skilled migrant workers and remit this tax to the worker's country of origin. This would compensate countries of origin for their costs in training the worker and the loss to their economy from the worker's emigration. Because asking host nations to give up a significant portion of their tax base might be politically unpalatable, Shanan and Narotzki instead propose a system of information exchange between host and origin jurisdictions that would allow origin jurisdictions to impose taxes on emigrant workers. This tax would be imposed until the worker establishes a domicile in the host country and might exempt a sufficiently large amount of income that it would only fall on the most well-compensated migrants. The scheme would thus compensate less developed countries for their loss of skilled workers without imposing undue burdens on migrants or making excessive demands on host jurisdictions.

In 'Caught Between Two Sovereigns: The International Taxation of Cross-Border Individuals', Bernard Schneider considers a different conundrum related to cross-border workers. This is the problem of apportioning tax rights over income earned by individuals who work in multiple jurisdictions in a single tax year. Although this challenge is not new, it might have been considered something of an edge case for many jurisdictions when highly paid employees were less mobile. Today, however, highly paid workers often work in multiple jurisdictions in a single year and the possibility of remote work allows a significant number of workers to live as 'digital nomads' if they so choose.[21] This raises complex questions of fairness, both concerning which states have the best claim to tax an individual's income and to what extent states' overlapping claims over the same income can be justified. These questions are complicated by the fact that different states have different rules for determining tax residence. Possible factors include nationality, immigration status, domicile, location of one's family, place of residence, financial accounts, or physical presence as evidenced by the number of days present in a

---

[19] T Makimoto and D Manners, *Digital Nomads* (Chichester, John Wiley & Sons, 1997).

[20] J Bhagwati and K Hamada, 'The Brain Drain, International Integration of Markets for Professionals and Unemployment: A Theoretical Analysis' (1974) 1 *Journal of Development Economics* 19; J Bhagwati and K Hamada, 'Domestic Distortions, Imperfect Information and The Brain Drain' (1975) 2 *Journal of Development Economics* 265.

[21] R Avi-Yonah, 'Taxing Nomads: Reviving Citizenship-Based Taxation for the 21st Century', in T Dagan and R Mason (eds), *Taxing People: The Next 100 Years* (Cambridge, CUP, forthcoming 2024).

year. As Schneider observes, there are reasonable arguments in favour of many of these rules. It is preferable, however, for states to coordinate on a uniform set of rules for residency to minimise conflicting claims over the same increment of income or situations in which highly mobile taxpayers may escape taxation on some increments of income altogether. After considering the advantages and disadvantages of the various possible approaches, Schneider ultimately concludes that tax residence should be determined by the number of days that a taxpayer spends in a jurisdiction over the course of a year. This objective test minimises the chances the two states will claim the same individual as a resident in a given year and gives both taxpayers and tax authorities certainty about which individuals are tax residents. Even in the face of new circumstances, simple old-fashioned rules are sometimes best.

Drafts of the chapters in this volume were presented at the Fairness in International Taxation workshop at the University of Surrey School of Law on 23–24 June 2022. This workshop was generously supported by the Institute of Advanced Studies at the University of Surrey and by the Surrey Centre for Law and Philosophy. In addition to feedback from the contributors to this volume, the work here greatly benefited from comments by David Elkins, Adam Kern, and Henry Ordower.

PART I

Theories of Justice

1

Global Justice and International Taxation

PETER DIETSCH AND THOMAS RIXEN*

When analysing the relationship between justice and taxation, we intuitively think of taxation as the main policy instrument to implement our ideal of distributive justice by adjusting the market distribution of income and wealth. However, there is another, perhaps less obvious dimension to the relationship between the two concepts. In the context of multiple jurisdictions and cross-border economic activity, the question arises: which jurisdiction should be granted the right to tax which portion of this activity? In different terms, this is the question of how the global tax base should be allocated or distributed between jurisdictions.[1]

This chapter focuses on this second dimension of global tax justice, which has recently received renewed and growing attention. Commentators view the way global tax justice is addressed under the status quo as deficient and unjust in two ways. First, the capacity of states to effectively tax the portion of the global tax base they have been assigned has been hollowed out by tax evasion and tax avoidance. In the former case, individuals who are supposed to pay their taxes in their country of residence fail to declare income made abroad; in the latter case, multinational enterprises (MNEs) shift the profits generated by economic activity in high-tax jurisdictions to countries with lower tax rates. Both cases represent instances of *poaching*, with low tax jurisdictions appropriating parts of the global tax base that actually belong to someone else. Second, even if everyone paid their nominal tax rates, it is obvious that economic activity will gravitate towards lower tax jurisdictions, some of which actively use their fiscal laws to lure individuals and MNEs to their shores. The normative question in this context is whether justice requires any limits to this practice of *luring*.[2]

* The chapter is a shortened and modified version of P Dietsch and T Rixen (2024), 'Dimensions of Global Justice in Taxing Multinationals.' *Moral Philosophy and Politics*, https://doi.org/10.1515/mopp-2023-0062. We thank de Gruyter for transfer of copyright.

[1] The two dimensions of the relationship between justice and taxation may of course overlap. At the extreme, for instance, one might think of allocating taxing rights as a purely instrumental question that serves the broader goal of global distributive justice. In this chapter, we focus on the normative question of how to allocate the global tax base without making this limiting presumption.

[2] The OECD uses the term 'poaching'. For the distinction between 'poaching' and 'luring', see P Dietsch and T Rixen, 'Tax Competition and Global Background Justice' (2014) 22 *Journal of Political Philosophy* 150.

Several factors have pushed these issues up the political as well as the intellectual agenda in recent years. Pressure on public finances in the wake of the financial crises, the sovereign-debt crisis in the Eurozone, and post-Covid-19 public deficits gave governments increasing motivation to look for tax revenue; increased media attention and, in particular, the efforts of investigative journalism to uncover particularly egregious cases of tax evasion and tax avoidance have stoked public outrage; and even the Organisation for Economic Co-operation and Development (OECD) as the main international tax regulator has acknowledged that tax competition can be harmful and raises questions of justice.[3]

These policy developments have spurred a wave of theoretical contributions to global tax justice over the course of the last ten years in particular. At first, their goal was, in part, to bring the issue of tax base allocation to the attention of global justice theorists. With time, a number of distinct normative positions have emerged. The goal of this chapter is to survey the philosophical literature on international taxation. We distinguish idealist and realist accounts of global tax justice on the one hand and associativist and humanist conceptions on the other. The resultant 2×2-matrix serves as a taxonomy to situate recent contributions to the global tax justice literature. Further, it illuminates the debates *between* the contributions and the objections they raise against one another. The taxonomy helps to diagnose the respective strengths and weaknesses of the contributions to the debate and to detail specific avenues for mutual improvement and learning in future research.

We first discuss the distinctions between humanism and associativism on the one hand, and between idealism and realism on the other hand in the philosophical literature on global justice (section I). We then apply these distinctions to construct our taxonomy of global *tax* justice and situate different contributions to the literature in it (section II). In section III, we discuss the implications of our taxonomy for future research. Section IV concludes.

I. Global Justice in Two Dimensions

To develop our taxonomy, we borrow two distinctions from the literature on global justice more generally. The first refers to the justification of duties towards people in other countries. We distinguish *humanist* versus *associativist* theories of global justice, where the former ground duties in our shared humanity, whereas the latter ground them in some relationship that we have with people in other states. Second, we rely on a specific interpretation of the distinction between *ideal* versus

---

[3] OECD, *Harmful Tax Competition. An Emerging Global Issue* (Paris, OECD 1998); OECD, International Community Strikes a Ground-Breaking Tax Deal for the Digital Age (2021) web-archive. oecd.org/2021-10-20/612898-international-community-strikes-a-ground-breaking-tax-deal-for-the-digital-age.htm (last accessed 29 March 2024).

non-ideal theory, namely one that reflects the different degrees to which theories of global justice rely on idealist *versus* realist assumptions. We have no ambition to settle the normative and methodological debates between these approaches, but instead want to suggest that they can illuminate our understanding of the relationship between different theories of global tax justice.

A. Humanist versus Associativist Theories of Global Justice

According to humanist theories of global justice, states have obligations towards other states in virtue of the fact that the members of those other states are fellow human beings.[4] The basic moral duty in this case holds between *individuals* in different countries, and their respective states are merely presumed to be the entities through which to most effectively discharge these duties. Importantly, no interaction is required between the individuals in question for the moral duty to exist.

By contrast, associativist theories of global justice hold that states have obligations towards other states in virtue of the relations they entertain with those states and their members. Associativist positions come in different flavours depending on the kind of association they deem relevant for triggering the obligations of justice in question.[5] For present purposes, we shall limit ourselves to one particular approach, based on the idea that obligations between states arise from various kinds of connections between them. Young calls this approach the *social connection model*.[6] Some associativist theories of global justice focus their attention on one particular kind of connection between states such as trade,[7] the climate[8] or, as we shall see in more detail in section III, taxation.

---

[4] S Caney, *Justice Beyond Borders: A Global Political Theory* (Oxford, OUP 2005); K-C Tan 'Luck, Institutions, and Global Distributive Justice: A Defence of Global Luck Egalitarianism' (2011) 10 *European Journal of Political Theory* 394.

[5] For instance, Gilabert distinguishes four families of associativist theories. P Gilabert, *From Global Poverty to Global Equality* (Oxford, OUP, 2012) 167–79. See also C Barry, and L Valentini, 'Egalitarian Challenges to Global Egalitarianism: A Critique' (2009) 35 *Review of International Studies* 485. Some theorists (eg, T Nagel, 'The Problem of Global Justice' (2005) 33 *Philosophy & Public Affairs* 113) consider that strong, that is, egalitarian duties of justice at the global level presuppose that an institution exists to discharge those duties; others argue that egalitarian duties are linked and limited to either the justificatory burden of states and their monopoly of power (M Blake, 'Distributive Justice, State Coercion, and Autonomy' (2001) 30 *Philosophy and Public Affairs* 257) or the participation in a particular type of cooperative scheme, namely one of reciprocal provision of public goods (A Sangiovanni, 'Global Justice, Reciprocity, and the State' (2007) 35 *Philosophy & Public Affairs* 1). Finally, and this is the approach that will preoccupy us here, some scholars argue that 'obligations of justice arise between persons by virtue of the social processes that connect them'. IM Young, 'Responsibility and Global Justice: A Social Connection Model' (2006) 23 *Social Philosophy and Policy* 102, 102.

[6] Young (n 5).

[7] eg, A James, *Fairness in Practice – a Social Contract for a Global Economy* (New York, OUP, 2012); M Risse and G Wollner, *On Trade Justice. A Philosophical Plea for a New Global Deal* (Oxford, OUP, 2019); J Christensen, *Trade Justice* (Oxford, OUP, 2017).

[8] eg, SM Gardiner, 'A Perfect Moral Storm: Climate Change, Intergenerational Ethics and the Problem of Moral Corruption' (2006) 15 *Environmental Values* 397.

B. Idealist versus Realist Theories of Global Justice

Thinking about justice in an unjust world involves a trade-off in terms of the methodology one adopts.[9] An idealist theory has the goal of highlighting the shortfall of the status quo compared to an ideally just institutional arrangement, whereas a realist theory is prepared to take some unjust features of the world as given in order to raise the probability that its normative recommendations will lead to effective change.[10] If one focuses on formulating an ideal of justice, one will risk losing the connection to our world here and now and, as a consequence, the practical leverage for making the world more just. If, on the other hand, in focusing on improving relative to the status quo, one takes on board unjust features of the world, one will risk tolerating injustice and losing the claim to defending a theory of justice at all.

Consider the following example. If your theory of global justice calls for a world without states, then it might run into trouble when formulating recommendations for reforms in the actual world, which is one dominated by states. By contrast, if your theory of global justice takes the political division of the world into states for granted, it might also take on board some of the unjust structures of domination of some existing states by others that we observe today.

Even if this example is formulated at a high level of abstraction, it suggests two dimensions in which idealist and realist theories of justice differ. First, as already mentioned, they tend to have different goals. The goal of idealist theory is to provide an outline of what a just world would look like and to point out where and how the status quo differs from this ideal. The goal of realist theory is to identify ways of making our current world more just or, put differently, to improve the status quo. The more unjust the status quo, the more pronounced the difference between idealist and realist theories of justice will be.

Second, it is worth highlighting that the methodological choice between an idealist versus a realist approach will have consequences for what one considers to be the problems of injustice that need to be solved in the first place. In an ideally just world, some of the features that give rise to injustices in the real world will not even exist and thus obscure the latter from view. For example, if your theory of trade justice presents an ideal in which there is no World Trade Organisation, then it might prove tricky to use it to formulate principles on how to reform the existing WTO. Conversely, taking unjust elements of the status quo for granted can limit the alternatives one might consider in the name of justice. Imagine you are thinking about international monetary reform, and you take for granted the fact that the dollar plays the role of global reserve currency. Some have argued that the latter confers an 'exorbitant privilege' on the United States.[11] If that is a correct

---

[9] P Gilabert, *From Global Poverty to Global Equality* (Oxford, OUP, 2012) 95.

[10] L Valentini, 'Ideal Vs. Non-Ideal Theory: A Conceptual Map' (2012) 7 *Philosophy Compass* 654, 660.

[11] B Eichengreen, *Exorbitant Privilege: The Rise and Fall of the Dollar and the Future of the International Monetary System* (Oxford, Oxford University Press, 2010).

assessment, then taking this feature of international monetary arrangements as given not only amounts to implicitly accepting an unjust feature of the status quo, but also means that – by construction – one will not consider more radical reform proposals that will get rid of this injustice.

II. A Taxonomy of Global Tax Justice

We use the two distinctions to identify four approaches to global tax justice, represented in the two-by-two matrix in Table 1.1 below. Not only can recent contributions to the global tax justice literature be situated in the four categories of this table, but it is also a useful tool for understanding the debates *between* the contributions as well as the objections they raise against one another.

But before we turn to this exercise, it is necessary to briefly explain the mechanics of international tax base allocation. The key concept in this respect is the notion of *nexus*. Nexus is usually understood as '(1) some notion of what is going on where and (2) a concept of who has what right to share in the fruits of international economic activity'.[12] The traditional nexus rules are based on the idea of 'economic allegiance'.[13] While this idea is based on complex arguments about the types of income and activities that create an economic allegiance, the main intuition is that the right to tax is granted to the country where a taxpayer is resident. Individuals are considered residents of the country they live in. Corporations are considered residents of the country of incorporation or where their management is located.[14] Specifically, the source country can tax foreign (corporate) active business income, whereas the residence country (eg, the country where the headquarter is located or where shareholders reside) is given the primary (or exclusive) right to tax passive investment income of the corporation, such as interest, dividends, or royalties that a multinational corporation pays out.[15] Overall, these rules ensure that individuals are taxed in the country in which they reside and corporations are taxed in the jurisdictions in which they are active. To implement this allocation, international

---

[12] RM Bird, and JM Mintz 'Sharing the International Tax Base in a Changing World' in S Cnossen, and H-W Sinn (eds), *Public Finance and Public Policy in a New Century* (Cambridge, MIT Press, 2003) 421.

[13] League of Nations, *Report on Double Taxation. Submitted to the Financial Committee by Professors Bruins, Einaudi, Seligman and Sir Josiah Stamp* (Geneva, League of Nations E.F.S.73.F.19, 1923).

[14] However, for dependent (ie, non-incorporated) foreign branches of a corporation, liability to tax is created through the concept of permanent establishment (PE). If some economic activity passes the permanent establishment threshold, this creates the necessary nexus to warrant taxation by the country where that activity is located. Basically, factories, offices, warehouses, depots, but also construction sites of more than 3, 6 or the full 12 months of the tax year (depending on domestic rules and bilateral double tax treaties) are considered PEs and thus subject to tax in the respective country.

[15] One of the contributions to this volume challenges the idea that the separation of active versus passive business income still makes sense today. Parsons argues that, contrary to current practice, source countries should be granted taxing rights to passive income, notably to capital gains, as well as active business income. A Parsons, 'The Shifting Economic Allegiance of Capital Gains' in I Lindsay & B Mathew (eds), *Fairness in International Taxation* (Oxford, Hart Publishing, 2024).

tax law defines a series of constructs, such as residence tests for individuals, separate entity accounting, and arm's length transfer pricing for corporations.[16]

This allocation of the transnational tax base and the legal constructs on which it is based are enshrined in various multilateral model conventions, bilateral tax treaties, and domestic rules. While the specific concepts have been subject to gradual adjustments in reaction to taxpayers' successful attempts to evade or avoid taxes, the basic principles are valid to this day. Two observations on this established understanding of nexus can be made: First, it defines tax *nexus* essentially in terms of economic value creation. The rules define a link between a specific act of value creation and a given state to justify granting this state the right to tax. The ambition is for taxation to track the geography of value creation. Second, established nexus rules preserve *de jure sovereignty*.[17] Driven by the desire to retain fiscal autonomy, governments crafted the rules in a way that retains independent authority over all elements of their tax law – namely, the tax base, tax rate, and system of taxation. Governments highly value their *fiscal self-determination* to navigate politically salient domestic tax policy choices that involve distributive conflict between different societal interests. In this sense, the term 'international tax' 'is a misnomer, since there is no overriding international law of taxation',[18] but only rules of allocation that operate at the interfaces of different national tax systems. The idea is that of territorial disentanglement of different tax systems.[19]

According to many analysts, nexus rules have become dysfunctional and incapable of securing efficient and just taxation under conditions of deep economic globalisation.[20] As the following discussion will show, the question of how one defines nexus is indeed crucial for the grounds and scope of one's theory of global tax justice.

---

[16] The classic residence test in the case of individuals states that one is considered a resident of a country if one lives there for at least 183 days a year. Separate entity accounting and arm's length transfer pricing proscribe that parent companies, subsidiaries or permanent establishments are treated as independent units for tax purposes and that the intermediary services and products they exchange have to be priced at market values (arm's length). These rules are often subject to manipulation by taxpayers and especially transfer mispricing to 'optimize' (avoid) tax has received a lot of attention in the literature on tax justice. A detailed discussion of nexus rules, their rationale and implementation can be found in T Rixen, *The Political Economy of International Tax Governance* (Basingstoke, Palgrave/Macmillan, 2008) 57–81.

[17] Rixen (n 16) 63–65; P Dietsch, *Catching Capital – the Ethics of Tax Competition*, (New York, Oxford University Press, 2015) ch 4.

[18] J Li, *International Taxation in the Age of Electronic Commerce: A Comparative Study* (Toronto, Canadian Tax Foundation, 2003) 31.

[19] T Rixen, 'From Double Tax Avoidance to Tax Competition: Explaining the Institutional Trajectory of International Tax Governance' (2011) 18 *Review of International Political Economy* 197.

[20] eg, E Saez and G Zucman, *The Triumph of Injustice: How the Rich Dodge Taxes and How to Make Them Pay* (New York, Norton, 2019); M Hearson and T Rixen, 'The Politics and History of Global Tax Governance' in L Hakelberg, and L Seelkopf (eds), *Handbook on the Politics of Taxation* (Cheltenham, Edward Elgar, 2021).

A. Realist Associativism

For international tax practitioners, associativism has intuitive appeal because it aligns well with the traditional interpretation of the *nexus* they take to underpin and justify the right of a state to a certain share of the tax base.

Realist associativists are united behind the idea that states have a right to tax the economic activity occurring in their respective jurisdictions, because they implicitly accept one of several versions of a more fundamental principle of justice that arguably justifies this arrangement. Kern labels this principle the 'capture principle',[21] and critically discusses three candidate notions to underpin it: fair play, compensation, and contribution. We shall here focus on the last, which is presented by Kern as the strongest possible argument in favour of the capture principle. In a nutshell, the idea is that states have a right to tax the economic activity in their jurisdiction, because this activity provides a proxy for the contribution from their jurisdiction to the global division of labour and productive output.

Independently of the precise way in which they give substance to the idea of an economic nexus, what unites realist associativists is an explicit or implicit normative commitment to fiscal self-determination, ie, national sovereignty.[22] In other words, they maintain that once we have come up with a definition of nexus that carves up the global tax base, then states have a right to tax this base as they see fit and in line with the political preferences of their citizens.[23]

However, a number of complications emerge within the realist associativist picture, notably with regards to the historical contingency and potential bias in both the way today's *distribution* of tax base has come about and the varying fiscal *capacity* of different states to tax it effectively.

As a concrete example of the first of these dimensions, a lot of the world's production and investment capacities tend to be concentrated in developed economies such as the US or the Eurozone, and the way this concentration has come about has involved major injustices – think of colonialism as one important example. Therefore, it would be unjust to jump from the observation that what we have defined as the tax base is distributed in a certain way to the conclusion that states have an entitlement to 'their' share. One potential remedy in corporate taxation may be *progressive formulary apportionment*, which aims to correct for past

---

[21] According to the capture principle, '[e]ach state ought to have a package of rights, R_i, to tax income generated from economic activities within its borders. The value of R_i ought to be proportionate to the amount of income generated from the economic activities hosted by i.' A Kern, 'Illusions of Justice in International Taxation' (2020) 48 *Philosophy & Public Affairs* 151, 155.

[22] eg, Dietsch and Rixen (n 2); Dietsch (n 17); A Cassee, 'International Tax Competition and Justice: The Case for Global Minimum Tax Rates' (2019) 18 *Politics, Philosophy & Economics* 242; L van Apeldoorn, 'BEPS, Tax Sovereignty, and Global Justice' (2018) 21 Critical Review of International Social and Political Philosophy 478. Christians & van Apeldoorn's 'entitlement principle' also falls into this category. A Christians & L van Apeldoorn, *Tax Cooperation in an Unjust World* (Oxford, Oxford University Press, 2021) 14–16. By contrast, their 'equal benefit principle' does not. ibid 12–14.

[23] This is what motivates, for instance, the *membership principle* in Dietsch & Rixen (n 2).

injustices that introduced a bias into the distribution of the global corporate tax base.[24] Another example in this category from the domain of taxing individuals is the issue of how cross-border migration should or should not affect taxing rights. For example, if a doctor was trained in the Global South, but then moves to and works in the Global North, should their country of origin retain certain taxing rights? In this volume, Shanan and Narotzki propose that taxing rights should be allocated on a domiciliary basis rather than based on residence.[25] One advantage of this concept is that it avoids individuals not meeting residence requirements, and thus avoiding taxation, anywhere.

Turning to the second dimension – the fiscal capacity of states – a similar observation applies. Rich developed countries dispose of the administrative means to levy taxes in ways that poorer countries find difficult. Thus, if one values fiscal self-determination, one also has to acknowledge that significant inequalities exist between states when it comes to *exercising* their self-determination and that, more often than not, these inequalities will be the result of past injustices.[26] Once again, corrective measures may be called for.

Two further complications deserve mention here, this time emanating from the question of whether a state's autonomy over its tax base should be absolute or limited in some way. Some accounts of global tax justice have argued that reducing the challenge of international tax competition to corporate tax base erosion through profit-shifting results in an incomplete analysis. They maintain that it is not just the dissimulation of economic activity by MNEs that raises questions of tax justice but also their shifting of real economic activity from one jurisdiction to another.[27] For instance, it is not just that huge volumes of MNE paper-profits get routed through Ireland that are problematic, but also that the relatively low Irish tax rate of 12.5 per cent induces MNEs to shift real assets and employment to the country. In other words, accounts in this category argue that the remit of global tax justice should include both the *poaching* from another jurisdiction's tax base and the *luring* of parts of another jurisdiction's tax base to one's own, that it should protect fiscal self-determination not just from *virtual* but also from *real* tax competition.[28] This implies that the fiscal self-determination of one state is limited by its duty to respect the fiscal self-determination of others.[29]

The second issue in this category pertains to the most effective means to protect states from real tax competition. Some have argued for a test to determine whether a state's policies represent an authentic exercise of fiscal self-determination in order to eliminate strategic uses of the tax system to attract

---

[24] Kern (n 21) 27–28.

[25] T Shanan and D Narotzki, 'Taxation of Cross Border Migrations – Re-Evaluating the Allocation of Tax Collection of Immigrants Between Home Country and Host Country' in I Lindsay & B Mathew (eds), *Fairness in International Taxation* (Oxford, Hart Publishing, 2024).

[26] Van Apeldoorn (n 22).

[27] eg, Dietsch and Rixen (n 2).

[28] eg, ibid 160.

[29] cf Dietsch (n 17) ch 4.

taxpayers or capital from abroad.[30] Others have criticised this approach on feasibility grounds and defended a global minimum tax rate instead.[31] Both of these proposals limit the fiscal self-determination of states. The latest OECD reform package on corporate taxation has adopted the latter route.

Importantly, all of these complications can be interpreted as steps towards ideal theory. They all point to ways in which the current institutionalisation of associativism turns a blind eye to certain unjust features of global fiscal arrangements. The reason we chose to list these approaches in the non-ideal theory category here is that making these kinds of adjustments seems feasible within the current paradigm of international taxation. We accept that where exactly we draw the line between ideal and non-ideal theories might seem somewhat contingent or ad hoc, but we believe that this represents a feature rather than a bug of this distinction. After all, the feasibility constraints to address different types of injustices evolve over time.

B. Idealist Associativism

As we have just seen, *realist* associativists maintain that states have a right to tax the economic value creation that occurs in their jurisdiction. Their approach is in sync with the standard interpretation of nexus described in section I. *Idealist* associativists have formulated a powerful critique of this idea.[32] They show that taking the economic activity within a given jurisdiction to be a proxy for that jurisdiction's economic contribution rests on a fundamental misunderstanding of international economic cooperation. How so? As Adam Smith's example of the pin factory emphasised, in any division of specialised labour, the increased productivity of all participants *depends* on the cooperation of everyone else.[33] This insight also applies internationally. For instance, several accounts of the ethics of trade emphasise that it is impossible and would be misleading to attribute the gains from trade to any particular nation, because there is no such thing as 'their' contribution but only a joint cooperative surplus.[34]

The implications of this insight in the fiscal context are plain to see. Accepting any traditional proxy of the contribution to the global economy by a particular jurisdiction misses the point that this activity could not even take place without international cooperation and is therefore as much a product of everyone else's contribution. To take a concrete example, the economic activity happening in

---

[30] Dietsch and Rixen (n 2) 161–66.

[31] eg, Cassee (n 22).

[32] Kern (n 21).

[33] *cf* also P Dietsch 'Distributive Lessons from Division of Labour' (2008) 5 *Journal of Moral Philosophy* 96; P Dietsch, 'Just Returns from Capitalist Production' (2023) 26 *Ethical Theory and Moral Practice* 785.

[34] eg, James (n 7).

Canada is not in any meaningful sense a proxy for the Canadian contribution to the global economy, but simply the share of the global cooperative surplus that happens to fall under Canada's jurisdiction. This is insufficient to ground a Canadian right to tax this activity.

Kern provides the clearest formulation of this critique of the capture principle, although he interestingly does not end up endorsing the perspective of idealist associativism on which this critique is based.[35] Risse and Meyer's critique of what they call the Independence Fallacy makes a similar point.[36] However, the remedy Risse and Meyer propose leaves behind the conceptual framework we use here, because they switch from an analysis of global tax justice in the narrow sense to an analysis of global tax justice in the broad sense: for them, whether or not specific tax policies are justified or not depends on whether they promote overall global justice, not just global tax justice as defined and used in this chapter. The 'equal benefit principle' defended by Christians and van Apeldoorn could also be interpreted in a similar vein.[37] The complication that arises in their formulation is that they seem to limit the cooperative practice that the equal benefit principle applies to, to 'international investment' only.[38] The motivation for this limitation in the scope of the principle and its implications for their view remain unclear.

Generally, relying on the capture principle and our standard measures of economic allegiance will benefit developed countries, where the components of these measures tend to be concentrated. Conversely, taking on board the idealist associativist's point would plausibly lead to a considerably more egalitarian distribution of tax base globally.

In short, idealist associativists accuse their realist cousins of getting the economics underlying international taxation wrong. The misunderstanding they point out is certainly relevant from the perspective of justice, and so one might wonder whether any plausible response is open to realists at all. Here is one possibility: While the idealists' observation is correct, it represents such a radical departure from how we conceptualise international taxation today that its chances of instigating reform here and now – for instance, by giving each state the right to tax a share of the global cooperative surplus that is proportionate to its working population – seem close to zero. In other words, the politics of international taxation stand in the way of rethinking its economics.

If reform here and now is the goal, so the realist might argue, one is better off taking an admittedly unjust feature of the world – the application of the

---

[35] Kern (n 21).

[36] M Risse and M Meyer, 'Tax Competition and Global Interdependence' (2019) 27 *Journal of Political Philosophy* 480.

[37] Christians & Van Apeldoorn (n 22) 12–14.

[38] ibid 19.

capture principle – as given, on two conditions. First, one has to be aware of this non-ideal aspect of one's theory and, second, one has to ensure that taking it as given will not move us further away from an ideally just world. We shall come back to these constraints later in the chapter. For now, let us conclude this discussion of the idealist variant of associativism by observing that it makes a convincing case that the conventional way of defining nexus in international taxation is myopic.

C. Realist Humanism

Realist humanism attacks realist associativism from a different angle. Suppose we adopt any of the variants of realist associativism. Within the constraints elaborated there – eg, adjustments for past injustices or global minimum tax rates – realist associativists propose to grant states a right to tax 'their' tax base and spend the proceeds as they see fit. Now suppose that under such an institutional arrangement, and despite the incremental improvements in the name of justice compared to the status quo that it might entail, some individuals in some countries continue to live in absolute poverty and die of curable diseases. In such a scenario, attributing a right to states over 'their' tax base seems hard to justify. Doing so would expose one to an instance of what Caney has called the *wrong priorities objection*, mistakenly valuing a state's autonomy more than the attainment of a certain minimal level of social outcomes globally.[39]

What distinguishes the humanist response from the associativist one is that it suggests a different interpretation of *nexus*. On this account, what connects people across borders and grounds a jurisdiction's right to a certain share of the global tax base is *not, or at least not primarily*, economic allegiance but common humanity. In the case of the *realist* humanist, the nexus of common humanity imposes a constraint on the nexus of economic allegiance. This constraint is expressed by Dietsch's *global justice constraint*[40] and by Christians and van Apeldoorn in the idea that their entitlement principle[41] – the idea that states have a right to tax their tax base – is conditional on the respect of subsistence rights deficits elsewhere in the world. Realist humanism in fact proposes a hybrid view: until a sufficientarian level of well-being is attained for everyone, the relevant nexus underpinning states' right to tax is our common humanity;

---

[39] Caney (n 4) 732. You might say that this is the kind of consideration that we seem to have set outside the scope of this chapter when we chose to analyse global tax justice in the narrow sense as defined in section I. But this would be a misunderstanding. The realist humanist concern here falls under the central question of global tax justice in the narrow sense: Which state(s) should have the right to tax which part of the tax base and why?

[40] P Dietsch 'The State and Tax Competition – a Normative Perspective' in M O'Neill, and S Orr (eds), *Taxation – Philosophical Perspectives* (Oxford, Oxford University Press, 2018) 203–223.

[41] Christians & Van Apeldoorn (n 22) ch 3.

beyond that threshold – the realist concession of this version of humanism, if you like – the relevant nexus is economic allegiance. One interpretation of this realist concession is to view it as an acknowledgement that, in our current world dominated by states, it is unrealistic to expect anything more than a sufficientarian version of humanism.

We need to add one important qualification here. While humanist realism makes a realist concession to associativism in virtue of its sufficientarian component, it also clearly makes an idealising assumption of a different kind. It takes for granted that giving taxing rights to states with populations that live in absolute poverty will actually result in improvements for the latter. Independently of any worries one might have about the political feasibility of humanist views – which we will come back to – one might challenge this assumption and worry about the effectiveness of humanism in achieving its declared aims.[42]

D. Idealist Humanism

This position adopts common humanity as the relevant nexus for allocating taxing rights and combines this normative commitment with a thoroughgoing idealism that does not make any concessions to the geopolitical interests of states in formulating its policy recommendations. We think it is fair to say that this conceptual position, while certainly prominent in the literature on global justice broadly conceived, has received less attention in the debate on global tax justice.

What follows from a humanist commitment in terms of allocating tax rights? One intuitively plausible formula might be to grant states taxing rights to shares of the tax base that are proportional to the size of their population. Another option would be to understand humanism in a prioritarian fashion and, for instance, call for an allocation of taxing rights that is inversely proportional to the GDP of the country in question.[43] Other possibilities to operationalise the humanist commitment in practice are certainly conceivable. Whatever they are, they will all share the departure from one feature at the core of today's framework of international taxation, namely that states should have 'proportionate opportunities to tax income derived from the economic activities that they host.'[44]

Table 1.1 summarises the insights above and classifies a number of recent contributions to the literature in the four categories we introduced.

---

[42] This worry applies, *mutatis mutandis*, to idealist humanism, too.

[43] RA Musgrave and PB Musgrave, 'Inter-Nation Equity' in RM Bird, and JG Head (eds), *Modern Fiscal Issues: Essays in Honour of Carl S. Shoup* (Toronto, University of Toronto Press, 1972) 74.

[44] Kern (n 21) 7. Kern, having considered and rejected idealist associativism, is clearly sympathetic to a humanist idealism, though his article is short on the details of what that position entails.

Table 1.1 A taxonomy of global tax justice theories

	Realist	**Idealist**
Humanist	Global justice constraint (Dietsch 2018, n 40) Subsistence constraint on entitlement principle (Christians & van Apeldoorn 2021, n 22)	Taxing rights inversely proportional to GDP (Musgrave & Musgrave 1972, n 43)
Associativist	Membership principle & fiscal policy constraint (Dietsch & Rixen 2014, n 2; Dietsch 2015, n 17) Effective tax sovereignty (van Apeldoorn 2018, n 22) Global minimum tax rate (Cassee 2019, n 22) Progressive formulary apportionment (Kern 2020, n 21) *Entitlement principle* (Christians & van Apeldoorn 2021, n 22) Justice as mutual advantage (Lindsay 2025, this volume) *Domiciliary taxation* (Shanan and Narotzki 2025, this volume)	Critique of Independence Fallacy (Risse & Meyer 2019, n 36) Critique of capture principle (Kern 2020, n 21) *Equal benefit principle* (Christians & van Apeldoorn 2021, n 22)

III. Lessons for Future Global Tax Justice Research

If our taxonomy and the distinctions underpinning it are appropriate, this refines our understanding of how different theories of global tax justice relate to one another.

Prima facie, one might be tempted to view all of the theoretical contributions as being engaged in the same exercise of formulating a global theory of tax justice in the narrow sense and, therefore, as presenting rival answers to one and the same question. We submit that this would be a mistake. Granted, the horizontal dimension of the table, ie, the choice between a humanist and an associativist foundation for global tax justice, does indeed present us with a choice between two different answers to the same question.[45] However, the same is not true for the vertical dimension of the table. As already indicated in the presentation of the distinction

---

[45] Having said that, as we have seen in the discussion of non-ideal humanism, it is possible to *combine* these two answers by combining a sufficientarian threshold justified on humanist grounds with an associativist justification above that threshold.

between idealist versus realist theories of justice in section II.A, these two kinds of theories tend to have different *goals* altogether.

Idealist theories have the goal of presenting an ideal institutional arrangement. Imagine we could redesign the rules of global tax justice and even the context in which they operate, such as, for instance, the size and power of states. From scratch, what set of global tax institutions would we choose? By contrast, the goal of realist theories of tax justice consists of improving the status quo. In order to do that, shooting for the moon might be unfeasible or even counterproductive. In order to effect change, one plausibly has to proceed incrementally, which means that one might have to tolerate *some* unjust features of current global tax arrangements in order to make progress on reforming others.

When advocates of idealist and realist theories of global tax justice ignore these differences in their respective objectives, they run the risk of talking past one another. Importantly, this does not imply that they have nothing to learn from each other. Specifically, while an ideal of justice might fail to yield action-guiding political recommendations for a realist approach to global tax justice, it can and should serve as a constraint on potential reforms in the following sense: Reforms recommended by realist theories of global tax justice should always move us *closer* to an ideal situation than further away from it, and they should do so not just today but also when taking into account the potential path dependencies[46] of reformed systems. For example, if we introduced formula apportionment tomorrow, this would still be vulnerable to the fundamental objections from associative idealism, but it would arguably make global tax governance *more just* rather than less just. Evaluating whether or not any particular reform proposal satisfies this constraint will not always be straightforward to assess, but this does not undermine its plausibility in principle. Advocates of realist theories of global tax justice, including ourselves,[47] have arguably paid insufficient attention to this constraint to date.

Conversely, idealist theories of global tax justice might benefit from thinking about incremental steps through which the status quo could be brought into closer alignment with their ideal. While idealist theories have the virtue of reminding us how unjust the world we live in is, they can arguably learn something from realist theories when it comes to translating their theoretical insight into reform action. One image that comes to mind here is that of identifying 'stepping stones' in making global tax arrangements more just.[48]

In sum, these considerations suggest that we should take more seriously the diverging objectives pursued by different contributions to the growing literature on global tax justice. Both idealist and realist theories yield important insights, but putting them on the same footing risks comparing apples with oranges. The field

---

[46] T Rixen and LA Viola, 'Putting Path Dependence in Its Place: Toward a Taxonomy of Institutional Change' (2015) 27 *Journal of Theoretical Politics* 301.

[47] Dietsch and Rixen (n 2).

[48] We borrow this image from Risse and Wollner, who use it in the context of global trade justice. Risse and Wollner (n 7) 246–47.

of global tax justice is still in its infancy. Moving forward, we encourage scholars to acknowledge and make explicit the distinctions drawn in Table 1.1 as well as some of their implications that we have tried to highlight here.

IV. Conclusion

The literature on global tax justice has expanded rapidly in recent years. Not all contributions to this literature start from the same conceptual premises, and this chapter has tried to shed some light on the most salient differences in this regard. The result is a taxonomy that categorises different theoretical contributions with the help of two distinctions and that serves as an interpretive lens through which to read the fast-growing literature on global tax justice.

The first of these refers to the normative criterion or nexus that grounds any state's right to a particular share of the global tax base. Whereas associativist theories tend to argue that the right to tax should track economic value creation, humanist theories maintain that our common humanity and some interpretation of an equal right to human flourishing are what should inform the allocation of taxing rights between jurisdictions. While certain forms of associativism have dominated global tax practice for the last 100 years, it is instructive to acknowledge that such an arrangement is not without alternatives.

The second dimension of the taxonomy distinguishes between two different goals that theories of global tax justice might pursue. Idealist theories, on the one hand, enquire what the institutional arrangement should be in a world without feasibility constraints; realist theories, on the other hand, take some unjust parameters of the status quo as given and then enquire how we can make the world *more* just within those constraints.

We have worked to match specific contributions to the literature to these categories. Independently of whether our interpretation of the individual approaches in question is correct, we hope that the taxonomy of theories of global tax justice will serve to avoid confusion and misunderstandings in the future development of this important field. In addition to the remarks made in section III, we would like to highlight one additional observation: there are very few contributions to the debate that take a humanist position, be it in the idealist or the realist variant. While this may be unsurprising given that the theory of taxation, both in the domestic and international domains, relies on notions such as 'ability to pay', benefit taxation, and economic allegiance, it is regrettable from the perspective of exploring the full spectrum of the meaning of tax justice. It would seem worthwhile to more fully explicate what global tax justice demands from a humanist perspective. At the very least, such accounts would provide a powerful and arguably necessary corrective to the dominant associativist views.

2

Contract Theory as a Guide to Fairness in Tax Treaties

BASTIAAN VAN GANZEN, DIRK BROEKHUIJSEN
AND HENK VORDING

Whereas most theories of international tax justice take a normative stance on the fairness of unilateral tax policy, the realm of international taxation is dominated by bilateral treaties. Those raise fairness issues of their own: to what extent do developing as well as developed countries benefit from tax treaties; how does the relative negotiating power of those countries impact treaty content; are existing Organisation for Economic Co-operation and Development (OECD) treaty standards renegotiable; are countries under economic and/or political pressure to sign; do both countries oversee the treaty's consequences; and does the treaty generate spill-over effects on third countries? The answers to these questions have considerable implications for international tax justice and may possibly conflict with normative theories on unilateral tax policy.

A similarity between the abovementioned issues is that they can be regarded as international analogues of three much-examined problems in the theory of contracts, namely: externalities, which are spill-over effects imposed on third parties that are not involved in the agreement; coercion, whereby voluntary consent to the agreement is negated by severely constrained choices; and information asymmetry, whereby one of the contracting parties is inadequately informed about the contents and consequences of the agreement. In this chapter, we aim to investigate whether and how those aspects of contract theory can provide guidance in discussions of fair tax base distribution. Our aim is not to draw an analogy between the law of contracts and international tax law, as they are incomparable in many respects.[1] Instead, we base our analysis on the *theory* of contracts, which provides the philosophical underpinning for the norms that guide the conduct of

---

[1] Y Brauner, 'The True Nature of Tax Treaties' (2020) 74 *Bulletin for International Taxation* 28; A Rasulov, 'Theorizing Treaties: The Consequences of the Contractual Analogy' in CJ Tams, A Tzanakopoulos and A Zimmermann (eds), *Research Handbook on the Law of Treaties* (Cheltenham, Edward Elgar, 2014).

two autonomous parties entering into agreements. The contract analogy seems appropriate, as several theories of international tax justice compare the sovereignty of nation states to the concept of individual freedom as used in liberal political theory.[2] The axiom 'one's freedom ends where another's begins' then applies analogously to national sovereignty. The regulation of those conflicting spheres of individual freedom is the basis of contract law in our liberal democratic order.

This chapter is structured as follows. In section I, we highlight several issues of fairness raised by bilateral tax treaties. As shown in recent studies, developing countries do not necessarily benefit from treaties, but they feel pressure to sign and may be forced to accept poor treaty conditions. This has to do with competition for foreign direct investment (FDI), the dominance of the OECD Model in the tax policy community, and imbalances in countries' tax-technical expertise. We then use insights from contract theory to analyse those issues. Starting with externalities in section II, we argue that tax treaties have the potential to induce a 'race to the bottom' in treaty conditions accepted by developing countries. This policy spill-over is comparable to that caused by unilateral tax competition. But whereas the tax fairness literature has proposed several standards aimed at reducing the negative spill-overs of unilateral tax policy while leaving room for national autonomy, we show that such standards fail when applied to bilateral tax treaties. We illustrate this using Dietsch and Rixen's Fiscal Policy Constraint. We argue that the only workable solution is to significantly reduce the normative weight attached to national tax policy autonomy. This negates the value of freedom of contract. With respect to coercion (section III), contract theory appears equally unhelpful because the philosophical theories that underpin contract freedom are unable to provide a satisfactory criterion to determine whether a country has voluntarily consented to certain treaty conditions. We show that resultingly, existing remedies to imbalances in bargaining positions, including Christians and Van Apeldoorn's Equal Benefit Principle, may produce adverse outcomes. Only with respect to asymmetric information, which we examine in section IV, can contract theory provide some guidance. As a remedy to clear imbalances in knowledge and expertise, existing treaties could be interpreted in favour of the weaker party. However, when it comes to drafting new treaties, the question arises whether a country knows which treaty conditions are 'best', which makes it difficult to avoid value imperialism. Section V concludes.

I. Bilateral Tax Treaties and Fairness

It might be assumed that tax treaties, like contracts, are entered into for mutual benefit – that is, there is a net benefit and both parties perceive to get a share in

---

[2] eg, P Dietsch, 'The State and Tax Competition: A Normative Perspective' in M O'Neill and S Orr (eds), *Taxation: Philosophical Perspectives* (Oxford, OUP, 2018), 214–15.

that benefit. For instance, a contracting state's citizens may experience more tax certainty and fewer fiscal obstacles when engaging in economic activities in the other state. The government or the national community at large may benefit when enhanced cross-border economic activities increase tax revenues, GDP, welfare, employment, and/or human and financial capital inflow.

The assumption that bilateral tax treaties are beneficial for both parties was first challenged 50 years ago by Irish, who argued that treaties 'shift substantial amounts of income tax revenues to which developing countries have a strong legitimate and equitable claim from their treasuries to those of developed countries', which 'creates the anomaly of aid in reverse – from poor to rich countries'.[3] This is why Dagan calls the prospect that double tax relief will benefit all parties involved by facilitating free trade and generating allocative efficiencies, the 'tax treaties myth'.[4] Nowadays, it is broadly accepted that low- or middle-income countries do not necessarily, or even usually, obtain benefits from concluding tax treaties.[5]

For instance, Leduc and Michielse note that, for those countries, potential tax treaty gains break down into: (1) a positive impact on FDI inflows; (2) supporting tax administration functions; and (3) enhancing international relations. In reviewing these gains, they find little indication of success. Moreover, with respect to the first point, they argue that even if source-country tax incentives stimulate FDI and/or generate positive economic spill-overs that increase human and financial capital, 'the optimal policy would seemingly be to adopt this reduction unilaterally under domestic statutes (by legislating moderate-to-low statutory withholding tax rates, for example)'.[6] As Hearson notes, high-income countries' tax systems already offer relief for taxes paid in source countries routinely, such that 'the most significant effect of a [bilateral tax treaty] between a developed and a developing country is to shift the burden of doing so from the former to the latter'[7] – which is indeed the key finding of Dagan's 2000 article.[8]

With respect to the second point mentioned by Leduc and Michielse, we would underscore that technical tax assistance offered by high-income countries (or by the OECD) to lower-income countries can be, and is, supplied independent of any tax treaty context. Additionally, one wonders whether the recent tendency to add anti-avoidance rules to bilateral tax treaties (such as principle purpose tests) has much practical relevance to low- and middle-income countries.[9] In sum, as

---

[3] CR Irish, 'International Double Taxation Agreements and Income Taxation at Source' (1974) 23 *International and Comparative Law Quarterly* 292.

[4] T Dagan, 'The Tax Treaties Myth' (2000) 32 *JILP* 939.

[5] Overview in M Hearson, *Imposing Standards* (Ithaca, Cornell University Press, 2021).

[6] S Leduc and G Michielse, 'Are Tax Treaties Worth It for Developing Countries' in R de Mooij, A Klemm and V Perry (eds), *Corporate Income Taxes under Pressure: Why Reform Is Needed and How It Could Be Designed* (Washington DC, IMF, 2021) 143.

[7] M Hearson, 'When Do Developing Countries Negotiate Away Their Corporate Tax Base?' (2018) 30 *Journal of International Development* 233, 236.

[8] Dagan (n 4).

[9] Illustratively, few low-income countries have signed the MLI agreement which implements the 2017 BEPS Action Plan. A likely reason is a lack of administrative capacity: International Monetary Fund, 'International Corporate Tax Reform' (2023) IMF Policy Paper 2023/001, 18.

the IMF put it in 2014, low- or middle-income countries 'would be well-advised to sign treaties only with considerable caution'.[10] One is left wondering why those countries have signed so many treaties with high-income nations over the last decades.[11] We argue that the answer is twofold: it boils down to the external effects of third countries' tax treaties, and to existing inequality between treaty partners.

Like contracts, tax treaties have the potential to generate both internal and external (or: spill-over) effects. The internal effect of a treaty is the immediate impact on the treaty partners' tax revenues (through the channels of tax base allocation and withholding tax rate reduction) and on their investment stocks.[12] Following the abovementioned interpretation of tax treaties 'shifting the costs of relief to developing countries', the tax revenue effect may tend to be zero-sum – the gain to one treaty partner is a loss to the other. The internal effect on FDI must be distinguished from the substitution of FDI between alternative foreign states. For instance, when a country-A/B treaty leads to +100 investment from A to B, and -60 investment from A to the rest of the world, the internal effect of the treaty from A's perspective is +40, and the external or spill-over effect is -60.[13] This implies that A and B have created a benefit (to be distributed between them) at the expense of the rest of the world. That this spill-over effect should occur, follows from two plausible efficiency assumptions: the worldwide allocation of investments will equalise expected after-tax returns to capital; and a new A/B tax treaty will increase the expected after-tax return to capital for bilateral A/B investments. The effect becomes bigger when residents of third countries can get access to the treaty, for instance by locating a letterbox company in country A that notionally holds the interests of a third-country investor in country B.

Even though B's neighbouring (low- or middle-income) countries would be able to attract investments through unilateral tax policy, any loss in FDI from country-A investors that they experience as a result of the A/B treaty should make them more willing to conclude a treaty with A as well. Such external effects should be divergent in size across countries and might be small in many cases, for instance, when treaty partners have limited economic ties, or because non-tax factors overshadow taxation in affecting returns to investment. However, the effects should be large in at least some cases, for instance when a treaty partner has a particularly large outward FDI stock or performs a hub function in international tax planning.

If the demand for joining country A's treaty network is large enough, it may well be that countries must be prepared to pay an entrance fee in the form of unattractive treaty conditions. This is the negative side of the network effect of tax

---

[10] International Monetary Fund, 'Spillovers in International Corporate Taxation' (2014) IMF Policy Paper, 24.

[11] This growth is neatly documented by Leduc and Michielse (n 6) 133–38.

[12] Strictly speaking, this is an external effect. It is not the governments of both countries that adapt their investment choices, but their residents. Only the subsequent effect on both states' tax revenues is truly internal. We ignore this for simplicity.

[13] Again, this is a simplification, as FDI responses do not equal welfare effects.

treaties, as discussed by Dagan.[14] This spill-over might be especially burdensome for low- and middle-income countries with relatively small domestic tax bases. Corporate income tax revenues from FDI often comprise a relatively large share of their tax revenue,[15] which increases the need to participate in treaty networks, at least to stimulate development in the short run. Thus, external effects and existing inequality intersect here.

Those factors constrain not only the freedom of developing countries to conclude treaties, but also those countries' ability to decide upon treaty content. To begin with, participating in the treaty network only makes sense if a country first adopts the rules underlying income taxation in order to comply with common international tax principles. Hence, as Avi-Yonah notes, 'the process of integration into the world economy forces change'.[16] Moreover, as stressed by Brauner, the existing treaty network is dominated by 'the OECD, its Model, its negotiators' network, and the availability advantage of its work'.[17] Hearson observes the role of a specialised tax community of tax professionals and civil servants, that regards the OECD Model Treaty as a panacea, whatever the outcome for low- and middle-income countries and that aims to disseminate OECD standards. He notes that experts from lower-income countries who 'want to be part of this (…) community [have] little room (…) to challenge such a long-standing consensus, even where it exhibits a strong bias against them'.[18] In a recent survey of tax treaty negotiations, Brauner argues that '[t]his imbalance is completely unaccounted for by the current tax treaty interpretation canon', and he draws an analogy with the 'dilemma (…) which exists under contract law when it comes to interpretation of unbalanced contracts'.[19] We would add that the (partial) absence of voluntary consent and the constrained choices that developing countries face resemble the situation which the theory of contracts calls 'coercion'.[20]

What also plays a role is that low-income countries often have limited resources available for treaty negotiations and international tax policy. Tax treaties are formulated in tax-technical language and have complex economic consequences, such as changes in FDI and strategic tax planning behaviour. When treaty partners have unequal access to the expertise required to oversee the treaty's consequences, this can be regarded as a contracting failure caused by asymmetric information.

---

[14] T Dagan, 'Tax Treaties as a Network Product' (2015) 41 *Brooklyn Journal of International Law* 1081. Generally, network effects are positive externalities. The point here is that low- and middle-income countries participate in this network without apparently obtaining much of the positive effects.

[15] R de Mooij, T Matheson and R Schatan, 'International Corporate Tax Spillovers and Redistributive Policies in Developing Countries' in BJ Clements and others (eds), *Inequality and Fiscal Policy* (Washington DC, IMF, 2015).

[16] RS Avi-Yonah, 'Tax Competition, Tax Arbitrage and the International Tax Regime' (2007) 61 *Bulletin for International Taxation* 130.

[17] Y Brauner, 'Tax Treaty Negotiations: Myth and Reality' (2021) University of Florida Levin College of Law Legal Studies Research Paper Series No. 22-15, 59.

[18] Hearson (n 5) 6.

[19] Brauner (n 17) 59, although he rejects the contractual analogy in itself: Brauner (n 1).

[20] We discuss the precise definition of coercion in section III.

Of course, a country can hire outside expertise to partially alleviate information asymmetries, but as mentioned above, it will be dependent on experts who generally aim to disseminate OECD standards. Hence, the problem of information asymmetry intersects with the abovementioned problem of 'coerced' contracts.

A similar intersection occurs in the use of the OECD model convention as a standard-form contract. In contract theory, standard-form contracts are usually regarded as a subset of information asymmetry problems because they are drafted by a single party before negotiations start, implying a take-it-or-leave-it situation, and generally signal an imbalance in power, knowledge and expertise among the contracting parties. Brauner, while rejecting the contractual analogy in itself, compares these attributes to the current practice of tax treaty negotiations.[21] Arguably, the repeated use of the OECD model tax convention does make treaties easier to draft and negotiate, which actually alleviates problems of information asymmetry. However, the more parties rely on an OECD-based standard form, the less freedom they have to challenge the OECD consensus.

In sum, the fairness issues raised by bilateral tax treaties boil down to international analogues of market failures and contracting problems which relate to externalities, coercion, and asymmetric information – and intersections between them. We will examine the theory behind those respective problems in the next three sections.

II. Externalities

The costs imposed on, and benefits enjoyed by third parties are not usually taken into account by contracting parties, and are hence neither part of their reasons to conclude a contract nor of the mutual entitlements and obligations that follow from that contract. These externalities, therefore, constitute a 'social' cost or benefit – they may lead to both inefficient contracting and inefficient non-contracting, such that freedom of contract may not lead to net welfare improvements, let alone Pareto optimality.[22] Contract law is one of the government's instruments to reduce externalities.

Civil contract law does so by protecting good morals and public order (*boni mores*) through the doctrine of prohibited contracts.[23] As Smits notes, 'underlying (…) violation of (…) *boni mores* (…) lies not only the wider interest of society in general, but often also the wish to protect people who are not a party to the contract'.[24] Likewise, English common law takes into account the illegality of contracting contrary to public policy, a concept that is considered not very

---

[21] Brauner (n 17) 59.

[22] RH Coase, 'The Problem of Social Cost' (1960) 3 *Journal of Law and Economics* 1.

[23] eg, article 138 BGB, Germany; article 3:40 BW, Netherlands.

[24] JM Smits, 'The Expanding Circle of Contract Law' (2016) 27 *Stellenbosch Law Review* 227, 232.

far removed from its civil-law counterparts.[25] Yet, neither civil law nor common law currently observes a clear-cut concept of externalities, and both define the 'third party' narrowly.[26] One reason is that the concept of 'public policy' generally refers to the national realm only, such that third parties in foreign countries are rarely taken into account.[27] Contract theory that seeks to expand the regulation of external effects is more exploratory and normative than descriptive. Relevant theories depart from notions such as 'ethical consumerism' and 'corporate social responsibility'.[28] Most of those concepts are vague because the underlying reason for, and method of dealing with externalities depends greatly on one's philosophical justification of the freedom of contract. The liberal and welfare consequentialist perspectives that provide two common underpinnings of contract freedom[29] are conceptually incommensurable, and neither provides a clear standard to judge externalities in the first place.

From a liberal or libertarian perspective, one could view freedom of contract as a prerequisite for individual autonomy, which should be promoted as a good in itself. Consequently, externalities are problematic because they harm the autonomy of other individuals. As almost all human conduct affects others, the definition of justifiable versus inappropriate harms requires decisions about the right level of state intervention and the design of balancing tests for conflicting individual rights.[30] As illustrated elsewhere in this chapter, these decisions inevitably rely on assumptions, political choices, or moral values that go beyond the sole pursuit of 'autonomy'.

From a contrasting, consequentialist perspective, freedom of contract would be instrumental to some other goal. A much-explored goal is welfare maximisation, to which freedom of contract should contribute as parties enter into contracts for mutual benefit.[31] A classic example is a factory polluting a river and giving fisheries downstream compensation that outweighs their damages. All parties experience a Pareto welfare improvement, despite the fisheries losing some autonomy. When transaction costs prevent resource allocation via contracting, the initial distribution of property rights is crucial: can the factory use the river freely,

---

[25] V van den Brink, 'De rechtshandeling in strijd met de goede zeden' (PhD thesis, University of Amsterdam, 2002); C Mak, *Fundamental Rights in European Contract Law* (Alphen aan den Rijn, Wolters Kluwer, 2008) 32–33.

[26] Smits (n 24) 232.

[27] ibid 233.

[28] JM Smits, 'Enforcing Corporate Social Responsibility Codes Under Private Law: On the Disciplining Power of Legal Doctrine' (2017) 24 *Indiana Journal of Global Legal Studies* 99.

[29] See. eg. Nozick's idea of contract as just acquisition, based on libertarian freedom: R Nozick, *Anarchy, State and Utopia* (New York, Basic Books, 1974); Coase's analysis of the efficiency of contracts, rooted in welfare economics: Coase (n 22).

[30] MJ Trebilcock, *The Limits of Freedom of Contract*, 2nd edn (Cambridge MA, Harvard University Press, 1998) 61–64.

[31] For an exploration of the distinction between welfare economics, utilitarianism and other forms of welfare consequentialism, see ER Morey, 'What are the ethics of welfare economics? And, are welfare economists utilitarians?' (2018) 65 *International Review of Economics* 201.

or should it negotiate with the fisheries before polluting it? Negotiations with two hundred individual fisheries (or, in international taxation, countries) are perhaps too burdensome. In those cases, choices about the initial set of property rights will affect welfare. In making these choices, governments must make assumptions about transaction costs and economic outcomes. The chosen set of rights will curb at least one party's autonomy, based on no other moral standard than those assumptions.

Of course, under consequentialism, freedom of contract could be instrumental to any other goal, such as resource equality or justice – whatever their definition. But the further those goals deviate from the mutual benefit of the two contracting parties, the more complex the law of contracts will become. For instance, it would be infeasible to serve egalitarian purposes by judging externalities on a case-by-case basis depending on the respective resource endowments of contracting parties and third parties. Instead of burdening parties who contract with poor people, society as a whole takes on redistributive duties through the tax-and-transfer system.[32] We will revert to this issue later, but note here that case-by-case decisions generally will not make the rules that guide externalities any less arbitrary.

In sum, neither a deontological commitment to individual freedom, nor a consequentialist approach is able to provide a clear-cut solution to externalities without invoking external values or standards.[33] In the remainder of this section, we draw a parallel between these perspectives and existing theories of international tax justice. In international taxation, spill-overs stem from divergent tax rates, overlapping tax jurisdiction, dissimilar tax base definitions, special regimes to attract non-residents, and anti-abuse rules to deter residents from using attractive features of other tax systems. They may lead to cross-border relocation of taxpayers, FDI, and paper profits, which in turn induces competitive tax rate setting by governments.[34] Because this competition is mainly aimed at attracting mobile capital and rich individuals, countries' tax burdens shift from capital towards labour, and the progressivity of tax systems declines.[35] Thus, spill-overs reduce the range of policy options that states can realistically pursue, and hence undermine their fiscal self-determination or sovereignty,[36] which can be regarded as the international analogue of individual autonomy.[37] Additionally, spill-overs widen

---

[32] See Trebilcock (n 30) 98–101.

[33] There are also perspectives that are neither consequentialist nor deontologically committed to the promotion of autonomy, eg, virtue ethics. As those are virtually unexplored in theories of international tax justice, we do not consider them in this chapter.

[34] P Genschel and P Schwarz, 'Tax competition: a literature review' (2011) 9 *Socio-economic review* 339.

[35] eg, S Ganghof, *The Politics of Income Taxation* (Colchester, ECPR Press, 2006); B van Ganzen, 'Determinants of top personal income tax rates in 19 OECD countries, 1981–2018' [2023] *Journal of Public Policy*.

[36] P Dietsch and T Rixen, 'Tax Competition and Global Background Justice' (2014) 22 *The Journal of Political Philosophy* 150, 156.

[37] Dietsch (n 2).

the difference in fiscal autonomy between countries, as low-income nations face a particularly salient trade-off between attracting taxpayers and FDI on the one hand, and raising domestic revenues in a way that matches democratic preferences on the other. As noted by De Mooij et al., corporate income tax revenues from FDI comprise a relatively large share of those countries' tax mixes.[38] Furthermore, developing countries are particularly vulnerable to policy spill-overs caused by tax havens, because they have limited administrative capacity to tackle base erosion and profit shifting (BEPS) strategies.[39]

In the existing tax fairness literature, the normative implications of those spill-overs have given rise to concepts like 'sovereign duty' (Christians)[40] and 'fiscal policy constraint' (Dietsch and Rixen),[41] centred on the idea that states should not pursue unilateral tax policies that are aimed at damaging other states' taxing rights. Like the abovementioned perspectives on the freedom of contract, the underlying theories of international tax fairness differ in the normative weight they assign to autonomy (ie, national sovereignty) and in the extent to which they make taxation instrumental to some external goal. For instance, Risse and Meyer assert that '[a]ny state should design its fiscal policy to advance justice, both domestic and global'.[42] From their perspective, it is in principle irrelevant whether tax competition reduces countries' range of realistic tax policy options; what matters is whether it disables countries from meeting their basic duties of justice towards their citizens. Governments should refrain from implementing policies with such a detrimental effect on other countries, or they should compensate those countries via international redistribution.[43] By contrast, Dietsch and Rixen argue that unilateral tax policy should not be made instrumental to international redistribution by biasing the normative enquiry into tax policy spill-overs.[44] For that normative enquiry, they propose a fiscal policy constraint (FPC) that proscribes policies that are both strategically motivated and negatively affect the aggregate fiscal autonomy of states. The ban on strategic policies would allow countries to pursue non-strategic policies that match the preferences of their electorates, even if those preferences include low taxes that incidentally attract foreign tax bases. Those local preferences are key to realising justice, as national communities have different conceptions of what justice entails. Because part of today's injustice boils down

---

[38] de Mooij, Matheson and Schatan (n 15) 177.

[39] ibid.

[40] A Christians, 'Sovereignty, Taxation and Social Contract' (2009) 18 *Minnesota Journal of International Law* 99.

[41] Dietsch and Rixen (n 36).

[42] M Risse and M Meyer, 'Tax Competition and Interdependence' (2019) 27 *The Journal of Political Philosophy* 480, 492.

[43] Resultingly, a competitive tax policy that attracts tax base from poor countries may give rise to redistributive duties. Additionally, in extreme cases, poor countries would be allowed to become tax havens for paper profits of taxpayers from rich countries, insofar as those rich countries fail to meet international redistributive duties.

[44] Dietsch and Rixen (n 36) 166. See also P Dietsch and T Rixen, 'Debate: In Defence of Fiscal Autonomy: A Reply to Risse and Meyer' (2019) 27 *The Journal of Political Philosophy* 499.

to existing inequality between countries, with some nations lacking the resources to be fiscally autonomous in the first place, Dietsch and Rixen acknowledge that redistributive duties may co-exist beside the FPC – but those duties constitute a separate normative issue.[45] Risse and Meyer, however, find the approach too procedural and want to 'determine the range of permissible tax regimes first, by appealing to substantive principles of global justice' – only within that range can countries follow their democratic preferences.[46]

The arguments in this debate are conceptually incommensurable because they are based on different normative premises, namely a deontological attachment to autonomy versus a consequentialist view in which international tax law is instrumental to justice. This will turn out relevant in the remainder of this section, where we use those respective views to normatively assess the spill-overs of tax treaties (ie, increased bilateral investment at the expense of the rest of the world). We will pay particular attention to the autonomy-based position, exemplified by Dietsch and Rixen's stance on unilateral tax policy. This position appears the most intuitively appealing and the least controversial, because the scope of its normative enquiry (asking whether a tax policy harms other countries' autonomy) is narrower than a pursuit of 'global justice'.[47] Relatedly, its focus on autonomy seems most compatible with the freedom of contract, and hence to countries' existing freedom to conclude tax treaties.[48]

The starting question in this assessment is whether the spill-overs of bilateral tax treaties are normatively different from the situation in which two countries change their tax policies unilaterally. If not, no further analysis would be required. We see a key difference with respect to democratic decision-making. Unilaterally, the application of Dietsch and Rixen's FPC is feasible under the simplifying assumption that governments act in accordance with their citizens' preferences,[49] and provided that one is able to distinguish those preferences from strategic intentions. To identify those intentions, one should ask whether a country would still implement a policy if the resulting 'benefits (...) in terms of attracting tax base from abroad did not exist'.[50] If it would, the policy is motivated by local preferences; if it would not, the policy is strategically motivated, and thus illegitimate insofar as it reduces countries' aggregate fiscal autonomy. It is difficult to answer this question in a bilateral setting, which lacks a single decision-making authority.

---

[45] ibid. See also text to n 44.

[46] Risse and Meyer (n 42) 495.

[47] According to Dietsch and Rixen, this protection of national autonomy should be acceptable even to moral cosmopolitans. It indirectly serves the interests of all individuals worldwide because nation states are more democratic and better able to match policies to local preferences than a world government: Dietsch and Rixen (n 36) 172–75.

[48] As discussed above, freedom of contract can also be compatible with consequentialist views, but those tend to be welfare consequentialist and not, like Risse and Meyer's approach, 'justice' consequentialist.

[49] Dietsch and Rixen (n 36) 153.

[50] Dietsch and Rixen (n) 164.

Treaties are products of complex games of negotiation in which the respective treaty partners have strategic intentions vis-à-vis each other. Those individual intentions exist alongside any unified strategic intentions vis-à-vis third countries. And as illustrated by numerous treaty interpretation disputes, it is questionable whether both countries will ever speak with one voice regarding their intent behind the treaty. Thus, should one focus on the treaty partners' individual intentions; on some aggregation of their individual intentions; or only on their unified intentions vis-à-vis third countries, if observable? Another issue is that treaties are packages of multiple provisions, of which some may be strategically intended and some not. Should one look at those specific provisions or only at the total package? Without spelling out all possible combinations of these options, we will highlight some difficulties.

First, focussing on the treaty partners' individual intentions behind the treaty as a whole, one would have to separate the prospect of increased inward investment from other potential benefits (such as double tax relief for domestic residents investing abroad, or tax-technical assistance). If at least one of both countries would not have signed the treaty were it not for the prospect of more FDI, the treaty would not be legitimate under the FPC – at least, if the treaty reduces aggregate fiscal autonomy. Most developing countries close treaties to attract FDI, so they will be under particular scrutiny of the FPC – or any normative standard that judges externalities based on a distinction between democratic preferences and strategic intentions.

Matters are different when looking at countries' individual intentions behind specific treaty provisions. A typical developing country that expects inward investment would prefer high withholding taxes as an easy source of revenue, but would generally be forced to accept a low rate due to the 'market power' of developed countries. Can one still argue, then, that its intentions are strategic? Furthermore, as the FPC is centred on 'attracting tax base from abroad', it focusses on this developing country's intentions and disregards the preferences of capital-exporting (developed) countries. Those preferences probably include low withholding taxes, which exert large externalities. Thus, paradoxically, it would be relatively lenient towards 'harmful' treaties. The latter problem can be solved by expanding the FPC's notion of 'strategically attracting tax base' such that it also includes tax base attracted by the treaty partner. The underlying argument would be that capital-rich nations should reasonably know that stimulating capital export is inseparable from creating a capital import elsewhere.

However, this does not help when two capital-rich, developed nations agree on a 0 per cent withholding tax rate, neither as a competitive policy to attract tax base, nor to stimulate capital export, but simply because they believe that withholding taxes are unnecessary distortions to the allocation of investments. Indeed, the view that corporate income taxes would suffice to tax investments at source has long been prevalent in the OECD. In this case, as highlighted in the previous section, not levying withholding taxes on bilateral investment flows might exert substantial externalities on developing countries, but the FPC must allow it, because it clearly matches both developed countries' democratic preferences.[51] Similar situations could arise with other treaty provisions, such as particular distributions of taxing rights on active and passive income.

The only solution here would be to adopt an even broader conception of the FPC, under which we consider it strategic that tax treaties discriminate between countries by giving only taxpayers in the partner country access to certain benefits (such as lower withholding tax rates). Both treaty partners should reasonably know that their investment conditions resultingly improve at the expense of the rest of the world, and that could be regarded as 'strategically attracting tax base'. This implies that all treaties are strategic and that they should be banned insofar they reduce aggregate fiscal autonomy. Under the view that treaties reduce aggregate fiscal autonomy by nature, they should indeed be banned, and only a purely multilateral tax system would suffice. Under the view that they only do so when they include provisions that generate clear externalities, such as 0 per cent withholding tax rates, we would need world-wide minimum standards regarding those provisions. The downside would be a significant reduction in fiscal autonomy for countries that genuinely believe in low withholding taxes. An additional problem is that national autonomy encompasses more than fiscal autonomy alone. Countries may well conclude tax treaties to achieve non-fiscal ends, such as strengthening their international relationships. Under the expanded application of the FPC, this form of autonomy would be subordinated to fiscal autonomy. From a liberal point of view, it is debatable whether this approach would protect countries' aggregate autonomy.[52]

Alternatively, when not expanding the FPC's application, one would have to accept that this standard is unable to prevent the externalities of several treaties, mostly those between rich countries. To what extent is that problematic? From the liberal perspective that underpins the FPC, the answer depends on whether those externalities violate countries' autonomy, because that is where the freedom of contract between the two treaty partners ends. Again, the key issue is whether countries genuinely believe that withholding taxes are unnecessary in the presence of adequate source-country corporate taxation. In that view, the loss of autonomy boils down to the existence of corporate tax competition, the reliance of developing countries on corporate tax revenues from FDI, and the limited administrative capacity of those countries to tackle BEPS strategies.[53] The primary solution would be to curb corporate tax competition; the unilateral FPC would do that job, and no further action would be required.[54] We consider this solution problematic for

---

[51] Compare a unilateral 0% CIT rate: that would be prohibited under the FPC, because it is unlikely to be a non-strategic, democratically preferred policy.

[52] We thank a reviewer for the latter point.

[53] See de Mooij, Matheson and Schatan (n 15).

[54] Adhering to an affirmative conception of national autonomy, rich countries might also have to provide technical tax assistance and perhaps even financial transfers, but these things would be normatively separate from the enquiry into corporate tax spill-overs: see text to n 40 and n 48.

the very same reason why the FPC aims to protect national autonomy, namely the existence of value pluralism about the content of a just tax policy. This pluralism not only encompasses the issue of tax rate setting, but also the relative importance of goals like capital import neutrality, revenue-raising capacity, administrability, and simplicity. Withholding taxes are comparatively easy to administer and could be a rich revenue source for developing countries, but they conflict with the efficiency- and neutrality-based OECD vision.[55] The problem is that visions pro and contra withholding taxes cannot coexist because of the externalities caused by tax treaties. Even though developing countries might be happy to receive technical tax assistance, they must involuntarily set low withholding tax rates and introduce complex anti-avoidance legislation to prop up their corporate tax systems. Thus, freedom of contract under the FPC is unable to protect national autonomy by accommodating value pluralism.

This means that we are left with 'autonomy-defying' theories of tax justice if we want to curb the externalities of tax treaties. For instance, we could eliminate the distinction between strategic and non-strategic policies from the FPC and solely aim to prohibit treaties that reduce other countries' fiscal autonomy. We are then left with a consequentialist, global standard that rules out all negative externalities without attaching any weight to local preferences. That would cause a significant and arbitrary upward bias in tax rates. Of course, consequentialism can also make tax treaties instrumental to other goals, such as 'justice'. To make this goal feasible, justice could, for instance, be equated with 'ensuring that all countries can meet basic duties of justice towards their citizens'; we then arrive at Risse and Meyer's standpoint. With respect to contract theory, the main lesson from this analysis is that freedom of contract offers little guidance as to the protection of non-parties' interests.

III. Coercion

The problem thus remains that low- and middle-income countries are unfree in their choices about whether or not to conclude tax treaties, and unfree in deciding upon treaty content with developed countries. This may result in poor treaty conditions, and it negates a key assumption behind contract freedom, namely that parties enter into agreements voluntarily. Of course, even in an ideal-type free market, all contracts are based on constrained choices, because individuals' incomes are limited and most goods are scarce. To define 'coercion', the theory of contracts must identify the point at which parties' choices become so constrained that their consent to an agreement should be considered involuntary.[56]

---

[55] For an examination of the goals of efficiency and neutrality, see P Hongler, *Justice in International Tax Law* (Amsterdam, IBFD, 2019).

[56] Authors use different words to describe this situation. Stewart, for instance, argues that 'coercion' and 'duress' 'refer to situations where α threatens to violate β's rights; situations where there

Section II has covered only one cause of constrained choices in the context of bilateral tax treaties: the external effects of neighbouring countries' unfavourable treaties, making the country in question relatively unattractive for FDI unless it joins this network. These externalities must be distinguished from the situation in which a capital-poor nation needs to give up taxing rights anyway in order to become attractive. That problem is not specific to tax treaties, but it may affect treaty outcomes when countries are 'coerced' to accept unfavourable treaty conditions because they lack attractive alternatives. Although it is difficult in practice to distinguish coercion from externalities as the main cause of an unfavourable treaty outcome, it is important to analyse both issues separately, because the issue of unfreedom caused by unequal bargaining positions would remain even when some multilateral effort would deal with externalities.

As with externalities, the various perspectives underpinning the theory of contracts have different approaches to defining 'coercion'. A welfare consequentialist approach would infer parties' voluntary consent from the contract, increasing both parties' welfare. As Trebilcock notes, this approach begs the question, because contract theory assumes that transactions are welfare-improving for the reason that contractors close them voluntarily.[57] Even if one accepts the inverted line of reasoning, it seems morally problematic to look only at the welfare consequences of enforcing a contract, instead of the circumstances under which it was signed.[58] In the context of international tax law, such an approach would be unable to address the unfairness of poor treaty conditions due to countries' unequal bargaining positions, as long as developing countries receive minor benefits from their treaties.

More generally, Stewart argues that all consequentialist theories are unsuited to evaluate voluntary consent, because they would override parties' autonomy to voluntarily enter into contracts if those contracts conflict with some external goal.[59] Thus, whereas a consequentialist solution seemed more appropriate for the problem of externalities, it appears more convincing to solve the problem of coercion by invoking some conception of autonomy. To this end, liberal or libertarian theories would distinguish voluntarily signed contracts from coerced contracts by asking whether a contracting party's offer expands or restricts the other party's set of meaningful options – that is, whether it increases or decreases that party's autonomy, respectively. But then we are back at the difficulty of defining a 'harm' to someone's autonomy. As explained in the previous section, liberalism must inevitably compose a list of rights and wrongs.

A negative conception of autonomy (ie, 'freedom from …'), would only rule out explicit threats and obstacles, disregarding countries' unequal bargaining positions. By contrast, the notion of positive freedom is more appealing in the context

is no such threat but the proposal is nonetheless improper are normally cases of exploitation or unconscionability': H Stewart, 'A Formal Approach to Contractual Duress' (1997) 47 *The University of Toronto Law Journal* 175, 185. We use 'coercion' for both situations throughout this chapter.

[57] Trebilcock (n 30) 83–84.
[58] Stewart (n 56) 224, 226.
[59] ibid 182.

of coerced treaties, because it seems to capture the idea that states should be capable of freely choosing between different options – or treaty content – available to them.[60] A nation's autonomy in this sense would mean its ability to sovereignly implement policies according to the democratic preferences of its citizens. This aggregate autonomy includes but is not limited to fiscal autonomy, which concerns the democratic implementation of tax and redistributive policies.[61] Although a tax treaty restricts a country's set of tax policy options and may hence reduce fiscal autonomy, it is an exercise of, and ideally enhances 'aggregate' autonomy through increases in bilateral trade and tax base inflow and through the enhanced freedom of citizens to conduct cross-border activities. By contrast, if concluding a tax treaty is the only way for a capital-importing nation to attract enough FDI, and if this treaty's provisions are so unfavourable that they severely reduce fiscal autonomy, the treaty can be argued to reduce the country's set of meaningful options and thus be considered 'coerced'. Testing empirically whether a treaty increases or restricts a country's autonomy according to this definition closely resembles a welfare economic analysis. This analysis would still be unable to distinguish unfair treaties, because it remains unclear why a treaty partner would be obliged to give away more taxing rights once the treaty is marginally beneficial for the country in question.[62] In fact, maximising the capital-poor nation's taxing rights would harm the treaty partner's own autonomy according to the definition above.

For similar reasons, Trebilcock notes that autonomy-based approaches have no clear answer to cartelisation, whereby consumers face higher prices and a lower consumer surplus than under perfect market conditions, even though they face no explicit 'threat' from monopolistic producers. Arguably, the consumers who are priced out of the market face the largest decreases in autonomy, but theories of coercion focus on the voluntary consent of those who remain in the market. Autonomy-based approaches do not clarify why exactly it is problematic to overcharge those consumers. Introducing a right to be free of monopolistic conduct would be unhelpful. Illustratively, it seems unproblematic for a monopolistic seller of a rare stamp to extract the full consumer surplus of a collector who has an idiosyncratic preference for this particular stamp.[63] Incidentally, a welfare consequentialist approach would not be able to determine voluntary consent either, because overcharged consumers apparently find it beneficial to remain in the market.[64]

These insights can be applied analogously to the world of international tax, where the OECD is the dominant 'supplier' of treaty provisions and the

---

[60] See I Berlin, 'Two concepts of liberty' in I Berlin, *Four Essays On Liberty* (Oxford, OUP, 1969); A Sen, 'Equality of What?' in S McMurrin (ed), *Tanner Lectures on Human Values, Volume 1* (Cambridge, CUP, 1980).

[61] See Dietsch and Rixen (n 36) 51–52.

[62] Incidentally, this 'autonomy-based' approach again requires external normative standards, namely the variables that measure 'autonomy'. Hence, this test is not truly 'empirical': Stewart (n 56) 250–51.

[63] Trebilcock (n 30) 92.

[64] ibid 93.

self-proclaimed 'market leader in developing [tax] standards and guidelines'.[65] The OECD Model Convention is in fact so dominant that it also affects treaties between non-OECD countries, and its influence clearly trumps that of the alternative UN Model.[66] OECD countries together own 70 per cent of worldwide outward FDI stocks,[67] such that a capital-poor nation that aims to attract investments by joining a tax treaty network needs to conclude treaties with multiple OECD countries – by definition, because one treaty is not a network. Although the OECD itself is not a cartel, each OECD country will find itself in a monopoly or oligopoly position vis-à-vis this capital-poor nation.

Morally, an unfavourable treaty outcome that would result from the OECD's monopoly position seems more problematic than the abovementioned example of asking a high price for a rare stamp. Unfortunately, Trebilcock's own approach is unhelpful here, because it focusses on 'situational monopolies (…) where (…) transaction-specific market power is exploited opportunistically to extract commitments in return for quid pro quos that have a zero or negative social value, or for quid pro quos, which, while socially positive, cannot in the normal competitive environment surrounding the type of transaction in question justify anything like the commitment extracted for them'.[68] A semantic problem is that the OECD's position is more accurately described as a *structural* monopoly, which Trebilcock proposes to remit to antitrust laws – and those laws do not exist in international taxation. Nevertheless, when using his criterion for situational monopolies, the question would be whether the 'price' paid by developing countries in terms of treaty conditions is a competitive market price.[69] Barring the question of how to define market prices in a tax treaty context, this seems to imply that developing countries with less attractive investment opportunities should accept lower quid pro quos, ie, poorer treaty conditions. We find this problematic. It is questionable in the first place whether developed countries can fully abdicate responsibility and point at international redistributive duties to alleviate unequal bargaining positions. But even when accepting that argument, one would use treaty outcomes as a standard to determine developing countries' voluntary consent.[70] That seems to run into the same problem that welfare consequentialist theories face, namely that prices and voluntariness are simply two different things.

---

[65] OECD, 'The OECD's Current Tax Agenda' (2008) 74–75, as cited in A Christians, 'Taxation in a Time of Crisis: Policy Leadership from the OECD to the G20' (2010) 5 *Northwestern Journal of Law & Social Policy* 19. Illustrative is UNGA Res 77/244 (30 December 2022), '[n]oting also the work of the [OECD/G20] Inclusive Framework on [BEPS]' and '[recognizing] the timeliness and importance of strengthening international tax cooperation to make it fully inclusive (…)' – a call that seems directed at the OECD.

[66] P Pistone, 'General Report' in M Lang and others (eds), *The Impact of the OECD and UN Model Conventions on Bilateral Tax Treaties* (Cambridge, CUP, 2014).

[67] OECD, 'FDI stocks (indicator)' (2023). DOI: 10.1787/80eca1f9-en (accessed on 27 June 2023).

[68] Trebilcock (n 30) 101.

[69] This follows from the latter component of his criterion. We assume that treaties are socially positive as we exclude the issue of externalities from our analysis of coercion.

[70] See Stewart (n 56) 230.

We examine the issue of market prices in more detail using Gordley's approach, which aims to solve the problem of unequal bargaining positions by invoking the principle of equality in exchange.[71] According to Gordley, the value of performances exchanged in contracts should be equal, because self-interested parties should have no mutually redistributive intentions. Resultingly, when the value of performances exchanged is unequal, one can infer that one party is weaker than the other, and this should be a ground for contractual invalidation or revision.[72] We highlight this approach because it bears resemblance to Christians and Van Apeldoorn's Equal Benefit Principle for international tax law. That principle 'holds that having undertaken to cooperate with each other, states are entitled to equally share in the (net) benefits produced by such cooperation.'[73] These net gains discount the gains a country would have had, had its inputs been put to use in a solely domestic situation (ie, for opportunity costs).[74] The argument recalls the Musgraves' proposed criterion of national neutrality of FDI.[75] A national community is only better off by engaging in FDI rather than domestic investment if the return to FDI exceeds the domestic return foregone, that is: the sum of (1) all private benefits and (2) the tax revenue foregone by reduced domestic investment. 'Equal benefit' then applies to the excess return.

To see the consequences of both approaches, consider the following example. Developed country A concludes treaties with developing countries B and C, which both lack FDI. Profit margins on investments in B are high; those in C are low, for instance because C's natural resources are expensive to mine. In both countries, marginal returns on investments diminish with the aggregate amount of FDI. Barring tax revenues, each unit of investment would yield equal benefits for B and C in terms of positive domestic spill-overs from human and financial capital inflow, which both countries need. Investments in both countries would not be profitable without a tax treaty. As B and C have limited resources to tackle corporate tax BEPS strategies, both would prefer to levy withholding taxes on returns to investment income. Under the assumption that the worldwide allocation of investments equalises expected after-tax returns to capital, country-A investors will first invest in B, and once the marginal profitability of additional investments has declined to the level that C offers, they will invest equally in both countries. Hence, B trumps C in the amount of FDI; in the total investment income earned by A's investors; and in the tax revenues on this income raised by A's government.

Like Trebilcock's approach, Gordley's principle of equality in exchange would prescribe that the value of what B offers A (investment income and resident-country

---

[71] J Gordley, 'Equality in Exchange' (1981) 69 *California Law Review* 1587.
[72] ibid.
[73] A Christians and L van Apeldoorn, *Tax Cooperation in an Unjust World* (Oxford, OUP, 2021) ch 1.2.
[74] ibid ch 1.7.
[75] RA Musgrave and PB Musgrave, *Public Finance in Theory and Practice* (New York, McGraw Hill, 1973).

tax revenues on this income) should equal the value of what A offers B (giving up taxing rights). As B's offer is rather attractive, so should the treaty conditions offered by A. By contrast, A would be allowed to force an unfavourable treaty upon C, because C has little to offer.

Under Christians and Van Apeldoorn's Equal Benefit Principle, all countries would first have to account for the domestic opportunity costs of their inputs. As gross benefits are a function of capital and labour, and B and C are fully dependent on foreign capital, we assume for the sake of simplicity that their domestic opportunity costs equal zero, such that their treaties' gross benefits equal net benefits. By contrast, gross returns on country-C investments earned by country-A investors are only marginally higher than those investors' opportunity costs, such that net returns approach zero.[76] If A taxes domestic and foreign investment income equally, A's net tax-revenue benefit also approaches zero.[77] Because nearly all net benefits produced by cooperation between A and C accrue to C, C would have shared those benefits with A, for instance, by giving up taxing rights in a treaty, or even through compensatory payments. When the net gains of cooperation are shared multilaterally, some of A's relatively high net benefit earned by investing in B would be redistributed to country C. That seems fair, but the problem remains that C would need to give up a large portion of its own net gains from FDI, simply because its domestic opportunity costs equal zero.

All of those outcomes, especially the latter, seem highly unfair. Invoking a less procedural and more substantive conception of fairness, one might at least want to give B and C equal amounts of taxing rights, or even argue that C deserves more taxing rights than B. Recall that there will be fewer investors in C, such that positive spill-overs from human and financial capital will be lower. Hence, C will be unable to reap substantial benefits from its natural resources. Withholding tax revenues might compensate for this to some extent, while not necessarily reducing FDI or the income earned by country-A investors. This idea resembles the proposal of Infanti, who takes up the Musgraves' point that tax treaties could be used for tailor-made redistribution of taxing rights between rich and poor countries,[78] arguing that such treaties can be made instruments for development aid.[79] That proposal remains at a considerable distance from current tax treaty practice; it is highly consequentialist, overriding developed countries' voluntary consent to a treaty if that treaty runs counter to the goal of developing aid. However, this section has made clear that the procedural accounts of fairness

---

[76] Net returns will not be negative, because otherwise the investors would have stayed home.

[77] Incidentally, resident-country tax benefits do not affect this country's aggregate benefits anyway because they are paid by residents. Source-country taxation does make the source country better off at the expense of the resident country: Christians and van Apeldoorn (n 73) 31.

[78] RA Musgrave and PB Musgrave, 'Inter-nation equity' in RM Bird and JG Head (eds), *Modern Fiscal Issues: Essays in Honour of Carl S. Shoup* (Toronto, University of Toronto Press, 1972).

[79] A Infanti, 'Internation Equity and Human Development' in Y Brauner and M Stewart (eds), *Tax, Law and Development* (Cheltenham, Edward Elgar, 2013).

that can be derived from contract theory also provide unsatisfactory solutions to inequalities in bargaining positions.

IV. Asymmetric Information

The question of whether parties transact voluntarily is closely connected to the question of whether they are adequately informed about the content and conse- quences of the agreements they enter into. Besides voluntary consent, informed consent is a key assumption in the theory of contracts.[80] Information imperfec- tions may affect both parties (symmetric) or one party (asymmetric). As we have already noted, developing countries often have limited resources for tax treaty negotiations, they might lack the expertise to deal with the tax-technical issues of treaties, and they are confronted with a model treaty and its commentary drafted by foreign, OECD-based experts. Developed OECD countries generally do not face these problems. Therefore, this section will focus on asymmetric information imperfections.

Defining 'inadequate information' is perhaps even harder than defining 'coer- cion'. Unlike coercion, which can be regarded as simply befalling a contracting party, the adequacy or inadequacy of information is endogenous: it is a function of the (costly) effort that a party puts into acquiring additional information to better understand the content and consequences of the contracting options available.[81] Some nearly unanswerable questions arise: how much effort should a party reason- ably put into acquiring additional information; how to deal with parties who have limited resources for their search; and what role should the better-informed party play?

From a liberal perspective, and invoking a positive conception of autonomy, one could argue that contracting parties should have sufficient resources for gath- ering information so that they are capable of making informed choices regarding the options available to them.[82] However, as with the issues of externalities and coercion, invoking some conception of autonomy does not answer the overarching question as to when someone is autonomous – in this case: how much information does 'informed consent' require?

Welfare consequentialist approaches have no clear answer either, because they run into what Trebilcock calls the 'Paretian dilemma'.[83] On the one hand, if the relevant welfare-based criterion is that both parties feel better off when they sign a contract, there would be informed consent in nearly every case. On the other, if

---

[80] eg, BH Bix, 'Contracts' in F Miller and A Wertheimer (eds), *The Ethics of Consent: Theory and Practice* (Oxford, OUP, 2009).

[81] KL Scheppele, *Legal Secrets: Equality and Efficiency in the Common Law* (Chicago, University of Chicago Press, 1988) 25, as cited in Trebilcock (n 30) 102.

[82] See Berlin (n 60); Sen (n 60).

[83] Trebilcock (n 30) 103.

parties should experience ex-post at least the welfare improvement they expected ex-ante, every minor negative deviation from their expectations would negate informed consent, such that almost no contract would be upheld.

Recalling our previous observations on market prices, we would add that using treaty outcomes as a normative standard may be morally problematic and that even a marginal increase in either autonomy or welfare does not necessarily indicate that a contracting party has had access to adequate information. For these reasons, we find Gordley's principle of equality in exchange, examined in the previous section, equally unsuited to determining informed consent as it is to determining voluntary consent.[84]

In the remainder of this section, we do not aim to provide a comprehensive theory of voluntary consent, but will instead discuss two types of information asymmetries that bear particular resemblance to the world of international tax law: standard-form contracts, and inequalities in resources for acquiring information.

Standard form contracts have the reputation of expressing inequality: a large player selling the consumer a product on the basis of terms and conditions that take away all consumer rights. Consumers do not read standard form contracts, and if they do, they will not understand their implications. Moreover, renegotiating standard form contracts may be very time-consuming and often even impossible: their existence implies a take-it-or-leave-it context. Tax treaty negotiations tend to produce standard form treaties, based on the OECD Model Tax Convention and the Commentaries on this model.[85] Standard form treaties may serve the useful purpose of reducing transaction costs – for instance, it would make little sense to renegotiate concepts like 'permanent establishment' and 'principal purpose' in each and every new treaty without acknowledging that such concepts have a tradition. Arguably, the repeated use of certain OECD standards makes treaty negotiations easier and can hence partially alleviate problems of information asymmetry. Nevertheless, the risk of a take-it-or-leave-it situation is evident, especially because there exist imbalances in power, knowledge and expertise between OECD and developing countries, respectively.[86]

Trebilcock argues that the existence of take-it-or-leave-it contracts is not necessarily problematic, as long as there is 'a margin of informed, sophisticated, and aggressive consumers', who discipline the market by either renegotiating contract terms or switching to suppliers who offer more favourable contracts.[87] But as explained in the previous section, the 'market' for tax treaties does not work this way.[88] Joining a treaty network entails closing treaties with not one, but multiple countries, such that attractive, capital-rich treaty partners find themselves in a monopoly or oligopoly position vis-à-vis capital-importing nations. This position

---

[84] See text to n 71 to n 79.
[85] Brauner (n 1) 35–38; Pistone (n 66).
[86] Brauner (n) 59.
[87] Trebilcock (n 30) 120.
[88] See text to n 65 to n 78.

could enable them to dictate treaty content, as signalled by the dominance of the OECD Model Convention relative to the UN Model Convention.[89] The issue of asymmetric information thus intersects with the issue of coercion, which, as we have concluded, is difficult to solve by invoking contract theory.

In the current world of bilateral treaties, however, contract theory does offer one pragmatic solution, namely *contra proferendem* treaty interpretation – that is, interpretation of a standard form term against the party who supplied it.[90] This would prevent some of the adverse consequences of unclear treaty provisions for countries that are not acquainted with OECD interpretation traditions. An advantage of this approach is that it avoids the abovementioned discussions about voluntariness: one does not require the exact definition of 'informed consent' to observe that the party responsible for drafting a standard-form contract is in a relatively strong position. Still, as noted by Brauner, the OECD/non-OECD distinction does not always capture existing imbalances in power and expertise, even when a treaty is based on the OECD Model – think of a treaty between Slovenia and China.[91] Moreover, solutions in the phase of treaty interpretation only work when there is ex-post unclarity, and not when treaty provisions are clear but nevertheless unreasonable.

Insofar as those unreasonable provisions result from information asymmetries, we should more closely look at the preceding negotiation process. As mentioned, a relevant issue is resource inequalities, manifested in countries' divergent levels of tax-technical expertise and hence their capacity to acquire relevant information for treaty negotiations. When a country lacks such expertise, it may, for instance, not be capable of foreseeing whether a treaty will intensify the use of BEPS strategies by taxpayers – especially when the treaty partner is a tax planning hub. A more concrete example of how a lack of expertise may lead to adverse consequences – albeit in a multilateral setting – is the concessions obtained by developing countries in the negotiations on Pillar 2. One important gain was the recognition of a Qualifying Minimum Domestic Top-Up Tax (QMDTT). It allows source countries to tax the amount that would otherwise be due by the Ultimate Parent Entity under the Income Inclusion Rule (IIR). The QMDTT therefore reverses the precedence of the residence state as proposed in the original Pillar 2 design.[92] This is potentially a large success for developing countries. However, developing countries also obtained a second concession: a Substance-Based Income Exclusion (SBIE). Called 'carve-outs' in previous drafts of Pillar 2, the SBIE allows source states to have low or zero tax rates on profits from real investments (in the form of an imputed return to payroll and tangible assets that need not meet the 15 per cent test). On its own merits, the SBIE allows developing countries to attract real

---

[89] Pistone (n 66).
[90] eg, Principles of European Contract Law article 5:103.
[91] Brauner (n 17) 61.
[92] MP Devereux, J Vella and H Wardell-Burrus, 'Pillar 2: Rule order, incentives, and tax competition' (2022) Oxford University Centre for Business Taxation Policy Brief.

investment with favourable tax conditions. But in fact, it may only reduce the amount of QMDTT that they can collect (as it is easier for qualifying taxpayers to meet the 15 per cent test when a substantial part of their profits is not taken into account).[93] One wonders how this surprising result has come about.

Two problems arise when dealing with bilateral information asymmetries resulting from resource inequalities. Perhaps the easiest of the two is a problem of definition: what level of resources do we consider adequate to acquire information? This problem is related to the overarching question explored above: how much information does 'informed consent' require? The latter question is nearly unanswerable, but a pragmatic solution could be to use some index of development or economic power (for instance, GDP) as a proxy for a country's capability to acquire information. This avoids the need to draw a crude line to separate voluntary from involuntary decisions; instead, the differential between the two respective treaty partners in terms of the particular proxy variable would indicate the extent to which the stronger/richer partner should take into account the interests of the weaker/poorer partner.[94]

But then the second problem arises: how to do so? It is one thing to determine whether the poorer country knew which treaty provisions would have served its interests best, but once we conclude that it did not sufficiently know, it is quite another to determine what is in fact 'best'. To avoid undemocratic and imperialistic solutions, we could limit ourselves to relatively uncontroversial provisions, such as the right to levy withholding taxes – it is clearly best for low-income countries to retain that right, as the UN Model Convention expresses on behalf of those countries. However, more complex solutions involve more detailed political choices, and moreover, all treaty provisions that require considerable technical skill and specialised legal knowledge may be more problematic, especially for understaffed tax administrations – hence, we run into the very problem that we tried to solve.[95] For example, provisions against treaty shopping can in principle help developing countries tackle withholding tax avoidance through shell companies, but may require considerable specialised effort – and not always with much success. Principle Purpose Tests and Limitations on Benefits provisions are 'rich countries'' inventions, developed for tax administrations with adequate experience in international taxation. It is doubtful whether multilateral solutions would be able to alleviate the remaining information asymmetries. At least, they might avoid value imperialism when countries have an equal voice in their design. But again, the downside would be a significant reduction in countries' autonomy to conclude treaties which best fit their circumstances.

---

[93] MP Devereux, J Paraknewitz and M Simmler, 'Empirical evidence on the global minimum tax: what is a critical mass and how large is the substance-based income exclusion?' (2023) 44 *Fiscal Studies* 9.

[94] See also text to n 71 to n 78.

[95] See International Monetary Fund (n 9).

V. Conclusion

This chapter has examined discussions on fair tax base distribution in bilateral tax treaties through the lens of contract theory. Contract theory appears useful to categorise what currently makes the international tax system unfair: fairness issues boil down to contracting problems of externalities, coercion, and asymmetric information. However, contract theory does not provide a solution for these problems that can be applied in a bilateral setting.

One reason is that neither of the two main philosophical theories that underpin contract freedom – liberalism and welfare consequentialism – is able to provide clear standards to deal with the interests of third parties, and to determine whether a party's consent to an agreement is voluntary and informed. Another reason is that in a tax treaty context, all three examined problems intersect and, in the end, boil down to tax competition. For instance, one might try to solve information asymmetries by giving developing countries tax-technical assistance to better understand the content and consequences of a treaty, but then the problem remains that this country is coerced into signing a treaty based on OECD standards, as a result of the powerful bargaining position of OECD countries. In turn, one could adjust the treaty's provisions to make it more favourable for the developing country in question, but then the problem arises that its neighbouring countries might have signed less favourable treaties that better facilitate taxpayers' BEPS strategies, and hence attract more FDI.

These conclusions tentatively suggest that we should move toward a multilateral system based on global minimum standards for treaty content, or maybe even a true multilateral treaty. However, this solution would significantly reduce countries' autonomy (that is, contract freedom) to draft treaties that fit their particular circumstances. We have shown that theories of unilateral tax justice are unable to provide satisfactory normative criteria to guide the balancing act between national autonomy and foreign interests in a context of bilateral tax treaties. We hope that our analysis can serve as a starting point for further normative work on this issue.

3

Justice as Mutual Advantage in International Taxation

Theories of fairness in international taxation were not well-developed until recently, in part because equitable taxation might be thought to require an international consensus on the divisions of the right to tax income from cross-border transactions, and this appeared 'difficult, if not utopian' under the prevailing political and economic conditions.[2] The recent OECD/G20 BEPS agreement heralds a new era in international tax policy. This new era calls for new approaches to fairness in international taxation. The dominant twentieth-century approaches to normative analysis of international tax cooperation are not adequate for the new task. Tax neutrality principles such as capital-import neutrality, capital-export neutrality, national neutrality, and capital-ownership neutrality are not well suited to allocating taxing rights or evaluating agreements to limit tax competition. In principle, philosophical theories of distributive justice should come to our aid in providing principles that are not beset by the same ambiguities as tax neutrality principles. In practice, however, the leading theories of distributive justice in political philosophy, including both egalitarian theories and consequentialist theories, seem an awkward fit for the context of international tax agreements and have had limited influence on debates in international tax policy. Much of the best recent normative work in international tax theory takes a more bespoke approach to normative tax theory, drawing on some aspects of the global distributive justice literature but mostly defending tax-specific normative principles rather than applying principles from a larger distributive theory to the tax context.[3]

[1] I am grateful to Alex Houghton for research assistance and to Benita Mathew for editing this chapter.
[2] N Kaufman, 'Fairness and the Taxation of International Income' (1998) 29 *Law & Policy in International Business* 145, 203.
[3] eg, P Dietsch, *Catching Capital: The Ethics of Tax Competition* (New York, OUP, 2015); T Dagan, *International Tax Policy: Between Competition and Cooperation* (Cambridge, CUP 2018); A Christians & L van Apeldoorn, *Tax Cooperation in an Unjust World* (Oxford, OUP 2021).

The primary aim of this chapter is to introduce tax theorists to an alternative normative framework grounded in a long tradition of political philosophy, justice as mutual advantage, and argue for its usefulness in evaluating international tax policy. This approach is, in the terms introduced by Dietsch and Rixen in chapter one of this volume, associativist insofar as it is grounded in normative relations between states. It takes a hardline realist approach to normative theory both insofar as it provides analysis that takes the status quo as largely given and insofar as it aims to build theories that are apt given the motivations of the agents in question. The resulting theory is a somewhat extreme version of a realist-associativist theory. As will be argued at greater length, this has two advantages. First, the mode of analysis is apt for the context of international agreements between states, which have both normative and prudential reasons to favour the interests of their own citizens over those of foreigners. Second, the theory relies on an austere set of normative and empirical assumptions. This means that the theory is more permissive than theories that adopt more ambitious and controversial normative premises. But it also means that international tax agreements that are unjust according to justice as mutual advantage are likely to be found unjust under more demanding theories as well. Justice as mutual advantage may therefore help to identify outcomes that people with a wide range of moral views can agree are unjust even if many of them embrace theories of justice that make more stringent demands. This is an important advantage given well-grounded concern that international tax agreements often do not serve the interests of developing nations.[4] Justice as mutual advantage can thus serve as a minimal criterion of justice that identifies a relatively uncontroversial floor for just agreements. It can be embraced by its proponents as a complete theory of justice and could be recognised by others as providing necessary but not sufficient conditions for just agreements.

I will also make tentative attempts to trace out the normative implications of this framework. These conclusions are only tentative because they draw on contested empirical claims and because the application of justice as mutual advantage to tax policy will depend on which particular version of the theory is adopted. It is possible to embrace the normative approach explained and defended here while thinking that it has very different implications for international tax policy. In any case, I hope that others will be encouraged by this sketch to develop the implications for tax policy of justice as mutual advantage in greater detail.

The first part of this chapter will briefly sketch the deficiencies of the current leading approach to normative analysis of international tax policy. The second section will introduce justice as mutual advantage. The third section applies justice as mutual advantage to the problem of how to allocate taxation rights between nations. The fourth section will consider objections to and challenges for justice as

---

[4] M Hearson, *Imposing Standards: The North-South Dimension to Global Tax Politics* (Ithaca, Cornell University Press 2021) 5.

mutual advantage as a theory of international tax fairness. The final part provides concluding thoughts.

I. Justice in International Tax – The Need for New Approaches

Normative accounts of international taxation have traditionally focused on tax neutrality: capital-import neutrality, capital-export neutrality, national neutrality, capital-ownership neutrality, and so forth.[5] These principles were more apt for a world in which international tax policy was made through bilateral agreements with a normative focus on economic efficiency. By now, there is widespread dissatisfaction with this approach, although there is less consensus about the nature of the shortcomings.[6] For one thing, the various standards of neutrality are inconsistent with one another unless all nations adopt the same tax rates and the same rules for allocating taxation rights.[7] This means that one needs a further theory to determine which form of neutrality is the most important and why tax neutrality, rather than some other distributive principle, should control international tax policy.[8] Moreover, aside from the practical difficulties of implementation, neutrality principles are not sufficient to determine the proper allocation of tax revenue between nations, as different allocations of taxing rights could be consistent with any given neutrality principle. Neutrality principles therefore act as constraints on the parameters of any international tax agreement, but they do not fully determine the content of such agreements and may be agnostic between wildly different solutions.

A more ambitious approach to international tax policy involves the application of some theory of global distributive justice.[9] Some theorists believe that egalitarian theories of distributive justice apply at the global level and require policies that redistribute wealth across national boundaries from wealthy nations

---

[5] This line of analysis was introduced by P Musgrave in 1963. See P Richman, *Taxation of Foreign Investment Income, An Economic Analysis* (Baltimore, The Johns Hopkins Press 1963).

[6] M Graetz, 'Taxing International Income: Inadequate Principles, Outdated Concepts, and Unsatisfactory Policies' (2001) 26 *Brooklyn Journal of International Law* 1357.

[7] Dagan (n 3) 58.

[8] D Weisbach, 'The Use of Neutralities in International Tax Policy' (2015) 68 *National Tax Journal* 635.

[9] There is a long-standing debate between those who believe that egalitarian principles of distributive justice should apply at the international level, eg, T Pogge, 'An Egalitarian Law of Peoples' (1994) 23 *Philosophy & Public Affairs* 195, and those who believe that although egalitarian principles apply at the national level, a less redistributive approach is appropriate at the international level, eg, T Nagel, 'The Problem of Global Justice' (2005) 33 *Philosophy & Public Affairs* 113. The following discussion applies to global egalitarians and not to egalitarians who reject application of egalitarian distributive principles at the international level.

to the global poor.[10] These theorists are divided among themselves about which principles should be applied and what the 'currency' of distributive justice should be. With respect to the former, some theorists believe utilitarian principles should be applied, whereas others favour something closer to Rawls' difference principle.[11] With respect to the latter, some believe that distributive shares should be evaluated in terms of resources, whereas others are evaluated in terms of utility or in terms of capabilities.[12]

Despite these important differences, all of these approaches count as idealist in the scheme introduced in the first chapter of this volume by Dietsch and Rixen.[13] Although utilitarianism is often cast as a counterpoint to egalitarianism, the two approaches to international tax fairness have similar implications for the problems discussed in this chapter and face similar challenges. Global egalitarian theories suggest redistribution to the least well-off, who disproportionately live in the poorest countries. On the very plausible view that the marginal utility of income is much higher in poor countries than in rich countries, utilitarian analysis would likely also suggest reallocating large amounts of tax revenue to the developing world. There are, of course, important differences between these approaches. But because the global distributive justice approach to international tax policy suffers from similar weaknesses in both its egalitarian and its utilitarian guises, I will discuss both families of theories together here, at the risk of some imprecision.

There are two important obstacles to looking to egalitarian or utilitarian theories of distributive justice to find principles of fair international tax policy. First, international tax policy emerges from negotiations between states that purport to represent the interests of their own citizens. There is no institution changed with achieving distributively fair outcomes at the international level or with designing international economic policy so as to serve the welfare of people everywhere in the world. Even if some theoretically correct set of globally redistributive policies could be identified, there would be no institution with any semblance of the right institutional incentives to pursue them. If, as seems plausible on both utilitarian and egalitarian views, the proper course of action would be to divert substantial tax revenue from developed nations to undeveloped nations (or at least to the subset of them with the institutional capacity to use the revenue well), then pursuing justice would seem politically hazardous for any democratic government in

---

[10] eg. S Caney, *Justice Beyond Borders: A Global Political Theory* (Oxford, Oxford University Press, 2005); Pogge (n 9). I will pass over the important distinction between those such as Pogge who would believe that duties of global distributive justice are created by our institutional order and those such as Caney who believe that such duties arise independently of our institutional order and analyse both sorts of views under the heading of global egalitarianism.

[11] R Goodin, *Utilitarianism as a Public Philosophy* (Cambridge, Cambridge University Press, 1995); J Rawls, *A Theory of Justice* (Cambridge, Mass., Harvard University Press, 1971).

[12] eg, N Daniels, 'Equality of What: Welfare, Resources, or Capabilities?' (1990) 50 *Philosophy and Phenomenological Research* 273.

[13] See ch 1, in this volume.

the developed world that is brave enough to do so. The behaviour of democratic governments in wealthy states suggest that the electorates of such states care a bit about the global poor, but not nearly enough to support the kinds of policies that would be required under global egalitarianism or utilitarianism.[14] This misfit between the ambitions of idealist theorists and the design of our existing institutions suggests that idealist theories must be, at minimum, supplemented by realist theories that are better able to provide principles that could structure international cooperation.

Second, international tax policy, even in its most ambitious forms, divides taxation rights and tax revenue between states rather than conferring benefits on individuals directly. This means that in order to translate the international division of tax revenue into effects on individual people, national governments must spend money in ways that benefit their citizens, especially their poorest citizens.[15] The extent to which they do so effectively varies greatly across governments. The poorest states would stand to receive the largest amount of new tax revenue under an egalitarian distributive scheme. However, the very fact of continued wide-spread extreme poverty is prima facie evidence that a state will not, in fact, spend new revenue to the benefit of less advantaged citizens since extreme poverty for a long period of time calls into question the quality of governance.[16] Distributing tax revenue to the very poorest states will select for poorly governed recipients.[17]

Conditioning transfers of tax revenue on good governance might, in theory, address this problem, but this is probably a non-starter politically. As a practical matter, it is difficult to design metrics that measure governance effectively, especially if one is trying to differentiate between well-governed countries and poorly-governed countries. However, more importantly, it is unlikely that governments in less developed countries would consent to rules that explicitly call into question their own trustworthiness and constrain their ability to determine fiscal policy. Trying to bypass untrustworthy or corrupt governments by allowing outsiders to make spending decisions might be helpful in the worst-governed states but

---

[14] It might be thought that the significant foreign aid budgets of some developed nations should cast doubt on this conclusion. There are, however, important differences between the two situations. First, the amount of corporate tax revenue foregone would be likely to be large in comparison with even the most generous foreign aid budgets. Second, foreign aid in the form of goods and services purchased from domestic suppliers create a domestic constituency in favour of foreign aid. Third, unlike foregone tax revenue, the donor state can retain control of how foreign aid is spent. It thus does not necessarily rely on trust in the government of the recipient state to spend the money wisely. Fourth, spending on visible projects abroad may have reputational benefits that are not replicated by international agreements on the division of corporate tax revenue.

[15] J Stark 'Tax Justice Beyond National Borders – International or Interpersonal?' (2022) 42 *Oxford Journal of Legal Studies* 133.

[16] Obviously, some instances of extreme poverty are explained by wars or natural disaster devasting an economy in the recent past.

[17] eg, P Collier and D Dollar, 'Aid Allocation and Poverty Reduction' (2002) 46 *European Economic Review* 1475.

would raise difficult questions about national sovereignty and the extent to which governance quality is maintained when providing services to outsiders rather than one's own citizens. When developed nations do spend money directly for the purported benefit of foreigners in the form of foreign aid, the results are often far from encouraging.[18] The implicit loss of sovereignty might be worthwhile if it provided assurance of good results. But whatever advantages foreign governments have in general competence, they might give back in their lack of accountability to the citizens of recipient nations.

Distributing tax revenue on an international level based on egalitarian or utilitarian principles is therefore unlikely to be adopted given the structure of our institutions and probably beyond the ability of our current institutions to implement effectively, even if it was. I have not made any argument here to suggest that global egalitarianism or utilitarianism are mistaken as ideal theories of distributive justice. It may be that one of these theories shows that we should make radical changes in our institutional order so as to discharge our duties of distributive justice to the global poor. In any event, the current wave of international tax agreements will be negotiated under the current institutional order. We need normative theories fit for this purpose. Global egalitarianism and utilitarianism seem unpromising as guides to fairness in international taxation as designed and implemented by our current institutions. This is not to say that egalitarian and utilitarian theories might not be useful as a measuring stick to evaluate the effects of various international tax policies.[19] In other words, the correct ideal theory of global distributive justice might be useful in telling us if policies make changes for the better or for the worse. But even if so, we should not expect the policies to even roughly approximate the policies that would be suggested by the theories or that the theories will tell us anything illuminating about the principles embedded in the policies. For this, we will need a theory that is both realist and associativist in character.[20]

In response to the inadequacies of tax neutrality principles and the utopian character of leading theories of global distributive justice, a number of leading scholars have defended the view that nations ought to pursue the interests of their own citizens (hereinafter 'national interest') in setting international tax policy and negotiating international tax agreements.[21] This theory seems to align well with the current institutional design, in which governments are typically either elected by their citizens or justify their rule by reference to the benefits that they provide for their citizens. Unlike global egalitarian distributive theories, national interest

---

[18] eg, W Easterly, *The Tyranny of Experts: Economists, Dictators, and the Forgotten Rights of the Poor* (New York, Basic Books, 2015).

[19] As will be argued below, it is likely that adopting international tax agreements based on justice as mutual advantage will lead to outcomes that will rank as modest improvements over the status quo on both egalitarian and utilitarian standards.

[20] See ch 1 in this volume.

[21] Dagan (n 3) 59; Graetz (n 6) 137–77; D Shaviro, *Fixing International Taxation* (New York, OUP, 2014) 143.

seems compatible with the incentives of policymakers, at least if one sets aside the more general issue of whether democratic accountability does enough to resolve the principal-agent problem inherent in government representing the interests of citizens. Moreover, relatively competent governments should have the knowledge and institutional capacity to pursue this goal, even if sometimes imperfectly.

National interest therefore seems a plausible guide to international tax policy. However, it also faces some clear challenges. For one thing, direct pursuit of national interests may be self-defeating in the sense of causing outcomes that are inferior in terms of national interests.[22] This could be the case if every nation would be better off with a global tax policy agreement than in the absence of such an agreement, but given the existence of the agreement, most nations could do better by not joining the agreement. This is a real possibility since a policy of aggressive tax competition could be more attractive as more nations forego tax competition. In this case, direct pursuit of national self-interest will result in an outcome that is inferior to international cooperation, even when evaluated from the perspective of national self-interest. Pursuit of national self-interest tempered by norms of fair play is more promising, but this will require some account of fairness.

Another difficulty is that national interest might turn out to counsel very aggressive behaviour. For example, powerful developed nations might find it in their interest to make a less powerful nation an offer they cannot refuse in the form of an agreement to prohibit certain forms of tax competition useful for the less powerful nation on the pain of highly punitive tariffs or rules restricting cross-border transactions. This could undermine the policy autonomy and arguably even the sovereignty of countries that might otherwise find it in their interest to engage in tax competition. The upshot of national self-interest is that powerful nations will probably have the tools to deter highly coercive policies and continue to engage in tax competition if it is in their interest to do so, but less powerful nations might find themselves forced to capitulate in response to threats. Even if one is sceptical that powerful nations have positive duties to aid foreign nationals, this sort of predatory behaviour might be too bitter a pill to swallow.

A final concern is that national self-interest seems insufficiently ambitious as a normative theory. Even if it seems overly optimistic to expect governments to be deeply concerned with the welfare of foreign nationals, it is less clear that national governments cannot be expected to be constrained by some modest sense of fairness in dealing with foreigners. National interest as such is not a theory of fairness at all. If global egalitarian and utilitarian theories are too ambitious, national self-interest seems insufficiently so.

I do not wish to be dismissive of the 'national interest' perspective. The national interest proponents might have it right. This theory is better than nothing, such that if more ambitious theories fail, the national interest theory seems

---

[22] This is a problem for direct pursuit of self-interest in many contexts. See D Parfit, *Reasons and Persons* (Oxford, OUP, 1984) 3–7.

like a reasonable fall-back position. But before embracing this minimalist and somewhat gloomy approach to normative theory in international tax, we should try to do better. The rest of this paper will try to do so.

II. Justice as Mutual Advantage

Given the questionable prospects of idealist theories of distributive justice and deficiencies of the national self-interest theory, it is worth looking for a theory that could offer a middle path between ideal theory and bare national self-interest. Such a theory would need to describe multilateral relations rather than merely bilateral relations[23] between collective agents such as states that have partially overlapping and partially conflicting interests. One such approach to distributive justice is sometimes discussed under the heading of justice as mutual advantage. This family of theories sees fair norms as those that arise from co-operation between mostly self-interested agents and divide the benefits of co-operation in a way that serves the interests of all co-operators. The term, 'justice as mutual advantage' was introduced by political philosopher Brian Barry in *Theories of Justice* in 1989 and contrasted with his preferred alternative, 'justice as impartiality'.[24] It represents a venerable tradition of political thought stretching back at least to Thomas Hobbes[25] and David Hume[26] and arguably to theories discussed in Plato's *Republic*.[27] More recently, it has been developed by Robert Sugden, Ken Binmore, David Gauthier, James Buchanan, Brian Skyrms, and Peter Vanderschraaf among others.[28]

According to Barry, justice as mutual advantage regards justice as 'the name we give to the constraints on themselves that rational self-interested people would agree to as the minimum price that has to be paid in order to obtain the co-operation of others'.[29] He contrasts it with 'justice as impartiality' which regards justice as 'the content of an agreement that would be reached by rational people under conditions that do not allow for bargaining power to be translated into an advantage'.[30] Justice as mutual advantage appeals to agents' enlightened long-run self-interest and thus

---

[23] See ch 2 in this volume.

[24] B Barry, *A Treatise on Social Justice, Volume I: Theories of Justice* (Berkeley, University of California Press, 1989), 8.

[25] D Hume, *A Treatise of Human Nature* (edited by LA Selby-Bigge, Oxford, Clarendon Press, 1886).

[26] T Hobbes, *Leviathan* (1651) in E Curley (ed), *Leviathan, with selected variants from the Latin edition of 1668* (Indianapolis, Hackett, 1994).

[27] Barry (n 24) 6.

[28] K Binmore, *Natural Justice* (Oxford, OUP, 2005); J Buchanan, *The Limits of Liberty* (Chicago, The University of Chicago Press, 1975); D Gauthier, *Morals by Agreement* (Oxford, OUP, 1986); B Skyrms, *The Stag Hunt and the Evolution of Social Structure* (Cambridge, CUP, 2012); R Sugden, *The Economics of Rights, Cooperation, and Welfare*, 2nd edn (London, Palgrave MacMillan, 2004); P Vanderschraaf, *Strategic Justice: Convention and Problems of Balancing Divergent Interests* (Oxford, OUP, 2018).

[29] Barry (n 24) 6–7.

[30] Barry (n 24) 7.

allows initial differences in bargaining position to be translated into differences in outcome. Justice as impartiality appeals to some conceptions of equality and does not allow initial differences in bargaining position to translate into differences in outcome. Although presented as competing theories, Barry allows that most leading liberal theories of justice contain aspects of both approaches.[31] Moreover, it is entirely plausible to view the two approaches as being apt for different situations. For example, one might believe justice as impartiality to be apt for distributive questions on the national level because governments should treat their own citizens as moral equals, while another might believe that justice as mutual advantage is more appropriate for international distributive questions because national governments ought to seek international co-operation on terms that advance the interests of their own citizens.

Theories of justice as mutual advantage conceive of justice as adherence to rules that serve the long-term interests of all parties by restricting various kinds of negative-sum activities and encouraging co-operative actions.[32] Justice sometimes requires that agents sacrifice their short-run interests to achieve the long-term advantages of co-operation with others. As David Hume put the point in *A Treatise of Human Nature*: 'I learn to do a service to another, without bearing him any real kindness; because I foresee, that he will return my service, in expectation of another of the same kind, and in order to maintain the same correspondence of good offices with me or with others. And accordingly, after I have serv'd him, and he is in possession of the advantage arising from my action, he is induc'd to perform his part, as foreseeing the consequences of his refusal.'[33] Because justice as mutual advantage appeals to long-term self-interest, it does not require a high level of altruism or intrinsic moral concern for others. It is thus apt for contexts in which the sort of mutual moral concern that underpins close interpersonal relationships runs out.

According to justice as mutual advantage, just rules divide the gains from co-operation in a way that gives all co-operators reason to uphold the rules of the co-operative scheme. In contrast to most egalitarian theories of distributive justice, justice as mutual advantage uses initial entitlements as a normative baseline and does not attempt to reallocate them. It also does not aim for outcomes that are equal or utility maximising (although it may achieve such results in particular cases). Instead, justice as mutual advantage is aimed at dividing the surplus created through co-operation in a way that provides all co-operators with an outcome that is no worse than they could expect to achieve through renegotiating the terms of co-operation. Where the parties start from the same initial endowments, this typically requires an equal division of co-operative surplus because each party has equal bargaining power. Where the parties have different initial positions,

---

[31] Barry (n 24) 148–49, 152.
[32] Barry (n 24) 6–7.
[33] Hume (n 25) *A Treatise of Human Nature*, Book 3, Part 2, Section 5, para 8.

the division of co-operative surplus might be unequal in ways that reflect differences in bargaining positions because of differences in relative contribution to the co-operative scheme or differences in outcomes if no co-operative agreement is reached.

Under conditions of unequal initial endowments, a mutually advantageous co-operative scheme is likely to preserve certain inequalities. Nevertheless, the requirement that the division of surplus gives all parties an incentive to continue co-operation tends to nudge outcomes in an egalitarian direction.[34] This is because those who have less valuable initial entitlements have less reason to support the existing distribution of resources and, thus, can more credibly threaten to reject an allocation of a division of gains from co-operation that does not reduce inequalities. Those who have greater initial entitlements, by contrast, have some incentive to spread the benefits of co-operation to ensure the perpetuation of the current cooperative scheme and thus protect their entitlements. Therefore, although justice as mutual advantage does not treat material equality as a moral ideal, its method of allocating the gains from co-operation tends to push outcomes in the direction of greater equality.

Justice as mutual advantage is especially apt for contexts such as those that arguably obtain between states negotiating international tax agreements. Roughly speaking, these are situations characterised by scarcity, potential for gains from co-operation, selfishness, and a rough equality of power. Scarcity means that resources are limited and that no party has as much as it would like. The parties are able to gain by co-operating with one another, but because their interests are partially conflicting and partially overlapping, there are only a limited number of policies that result in mutual benefit. The parties are at least moderately selfish in that they care mostly about their own interests, such that concern for the welfare of others is not sufficient to motivate co-operation. Finally, the parties are sufficiently similar that no one party can impose its preferred terms on the others by force at little cost and can therefore only secure certain kinds of advantages through co-operation. Justice as mutual advantage is especially apt for circumstances in which there is no external enforcement mechanism. Each party's interest in maintaining the co-operative scheme gives them incentive to enforce the rules structuring co-operation even when doing so requires inflicting costly punishments on rule violators. Where the parties can only cooperate by enforcing the rules themselves, a fair division of the gains from cooperation is essential for maintaining co-operation.

In addition to these external circumstances, it is important for justice as mutual advantage that the parties have certain psychological characteristics as well. They must be the kind of agents that are willing to adopt and abide by mutually advantageous rules when they expect others to abide by these rules as well. This sometimes

---

[34] K Binmore, *Game Theory and the Social Contract, Vol I: Playing Fair* (Cambridge Mass., MIT Press, 1994) 41–49, 52–53.

requires foregoing short-term gains in order to secure the long-term advantages of co-operation. Justice as mutual advantage seems especially apt for conditional co-operators: agents who cooperate with those they expect to co-operate but do not co-operate with those who they expect not to co-operate.[35]

III. Implications for International Tax Policy

There is significant congruence between the situation facing governments nego-tiating international tax agreements and those that are especially apt for justice as mutual advantage. National governments are, (if one is to be optimistic and assume public-spirited motivations), mainly concerned with protecting their tax base and increasing the well-being of their citizens. They tend not to be strongly motivated by the welfare of foreigners, except in exceptional cases when this is especially salient to their citizens. They might be able to gain by agreeing with other nations on common rules for the division of tax revenue from cross-border transactions and restrictions on negative-sum tax competition. Although some states are much more powerful than others, even powerful nations are not usually able to impose their preferred tax rules by force because the costs of direct coercion (ie, military force) would make such threats non-credible. Convergence on tax policy typically requires co-operation for mutual benefit. National governments are often prepared to enter into mutually beneficial international agreements and sometimes create enforcement mechanisms to restrain the temptation to cheat on these agreements in the future. Although no state follows a strict policy of condi-tional co-operation, for the most part, states co-operate only with other states they trust to reciprocate and adopt an untrusting attitude towards states believed to be hostile or uncooperative.

Justice as mutual advantage therefore seems apt for the context in which inter-national tax agreements are negotiated. Crucially, one need not believe that justice as mutual advantage is all that there is to justice to find it illuminating for interna-tional tax policy. It may be that domestic questions of distributive justice should governed by egalitarian or utilitarian principles, even if justice as mutual advantage is more appropriate for international tax co-operation. And it may be that some thicker conception of justice is preferable to justice as mutual advantage, especially if we develop international institutions that trigger stronger norms of distributive justice or enable redistributive distributive schemes at the international level that are implausible today. Of course, some political philosophers believe that justice as mutual advantage is the best account of justice in most or all contexts.[36] But using the theory to analyse international tax fairness in the present context does not require such a commitment.

---

[35] See C Bicchieri, *The Grammar of Society* (New York, CUP, 2006) 140–41.
[36] eg, Binmore, *Natural Justice* (n 28).

What does justice as mutual advantage tell us about fairness in international tax policy? The implications are multi-layered and will depend in part on which interpretation of justice as mutual advantage is adopted. A few points should be relatively uncontroversial. A minimum standard of justice as mutual advantage in international taxation is that international tax agreements should be in the interest of all parties to the agreement. That is, all such agreements should be Pareto improvements.[37] They must not be coercively imposed by powerful nations, for example, by threatening the security of nations that do not agree to unfavourable terms. Less powerful nations should not come away from an agreement in a worse position than they would be if they exercised their rights as sovereign nations to set tax policy independently and autonomously.[38] A corollary to this result is that a mutually advantageous agreement might require nations that are harmed by tax competition to compensate nations that benefit from tax competition as the price of an agreement to restrict tax competition. Just as agreements cannot be coercively imposed, they cannot be insisted upon on grounds other than the interests of the contracting parties. This is an important corollary because restricting tax competition is not necessarily a win-win outcome. Some countries, especially less developed countries without notable natural resource wealth, may be made worse off by a multilateral international tax regime that reduces tax competition and imposes minimum tax rules.[39] This might be because a country is better off with a combination of greater in-bound investment and higher wages than with higher tax revenue. In such cases, justice as mutual advantage might require compensation of such a country for the losses it incurs in agreeing to limits on tax competition. If restricting tax competition provides sufficient global benefits, it should be possible for the winners to compensate the losers while still being better off than in a world with no restrictions on tax competition.

The minimum standard of justice as mutual advantage is relatively undemanding. A more complicated question is how to evaluate the fair division of surpluses from such agreements. These gains might be realised either in terms of greater tax revenue or in terms of higher economic growth, or in both respects at once.[40] Different nations may have different preferences for trade-offs between tax revenue and economic growth. For this reason, two nations may enjoy a surplus of equivalent value even if their gains are realised in different ways, with one raising more tax revenue without diminishing economic output and the other increasing economic output without giving up tax revenue. Unlike the minimum standard of

---

[37] At least for parties to the agreement. There is no requirement that international tax agreements make non-cooperative parties no worse off.

[38] This is congruent with Dagan's argument that international tax agreements are unjust unless they benefit (or at least do not harm) the least well off in all nations, although it puts fewer constraints than Dagan's does on how states distribute gains from international cooperation among their own citizens. Dagan (n 3) 208.

[39] ibid 140–41.

[40] R Musgrave & P Musgrave, 'Inter-nation equity' in R Bird and J Head (eds), *Modern Fiscal Issues: Essays in Honor of Carl S. Shoup* (Toronto, University of Toronto Press, 1972).

justice, a fully specified theory of fairness in international tax policy will be very sensitive to which specific theory of justice as mutual advantage is adopted. My goal here will be to sketch what I take to be a plausible analysis of the fair division of surplus using a somewhat generic version of justice of mutual advantage without describing how this follows from a fully specified theory of justice.

Determining what is implied by justice as mutual advantage in this context requires answering two questions: how to model the pre-agreement non-cooperative baseline and how to divide gains from co-operation above the non-cooperative baseline. The first of these questions is prior and, as will be suggested below, is possibly more difficult. Theories of justice as mutual advantage might adopt approaches to modelling the co-operative baseline that are more Lockean in nature or more Hobbesian in nature.[41] The former recognises rights that place normative constraints on the conduct of states in the absence of co-operative agreements, whereas the latter places relatively few constraints on the non-cooperative baseline. The question of how to model the non-cooperative baseline will be returned to below. An austere version of justice as mutual advantage (in other words, one with relatively few normative commitments) might model the non-cooperative baseline as one with no international cooperation on tax policy but few constraints on each nation's tax policy. In particular, it would not be committed to any strong notion of autonomy under which states would be obligated not to adopt policies that constrain their neighbours' policy options. States would only enjoy autonomy in the sense of being free from physical coercion by their neighbours. This interpretation of 'justice as mutual advantage' thus differs from Peter Dietsch's more 'Lockean' approach, which treats the ability of states to exercise 'fiscal self-determination' as an important normative constraint on the policies that other nations may pursue.[42] It also would not endorse what Adam Kern calls 'the capture principle', which specifies that each state should have the right to tax income from economic activities within its territory.[43] States might attempt to tax gains arising on foreign territory insofar as they are able to tax those who derive income from these gains. Of course, there are often practical limits on their ability to do so without aggressing against their neighbours since a state's ability to tax gains from economic activity abroad relies on either economic activity crossing jurisdictional boundaries or taxpayers themselves moving between jurisdictions. The non-cooperative baseline thus envisions a world in which states might engage either in fairly aggressive forms of tax competition or adopt policies that attempt to tax gains generated by economic activity in other nations. This has important implications for the division of cooperative surplus because it gives states that are able to benefit from tax competition or are able to raise more revenue without international cooperation greater bargaining power.

---

[41] Barry (n 24) 297.
[42] Dietsch (n 3) 31.
[43] A Kern, 'Illusions of Justice in International Taxation' (2020) 48 *Philosophy & Public Affairs* 151, 155.

As will be discussed later, the implications of justice as mutual advantage for international tax fairness will be sensitive to the types of non-cooperative measures, such as trade restrictions, tariffs, limitations on investment, or restrictions on other forms of international cooperation, that are considered legitimate. All specifications of the theory, however, will measure gains against a non-cooperative baseline and will allow parties to use any bargaining power derived from this non-cooperative baseline as leverage in negotiations over the terms of cooperation. Finally, justice as mutual advantage does not require that the resulting policies be 'incentive compatible' in the sense explored by Van Apeldoorn elsewhere in this volume.[44] It may turn out that fair cooperation requires rules that are only stable if enforced with sanctions against parties that violate them. This might be the case if, for example, an international agreement prohibiting certain forms of tax competition makes tax competition particularly attractive for a nation if it can defect from the agreement without punishment. Incentive compatibility is an attractive feature of a policy under justice as mutual advantage because it reduces enforcement costs and thus leaves more surplus to divide between co-operating nations. But it is not a requirement of the theory, and it conflicts with justice as mutual advantage when maximal gains can only be realised by limiting fiscal policy options.

As this discussion suggests, the implications of justice as mutual advantage for international tax policy depend greatly on the answers to difficult empirical questions about which countries benefit or are harmed by restricting international tax competition. The way in which co-operative surplus is divided may be complicated. Restriction of tax competition is not necessarily a win-win outcome. In particular, some countries, especially less developed countries without notable natural resource wealth, may be made worse off by a multilateral international tax regime that reduces tax competition and imposes minimum tax rules.[45] This might be because a country is better off with a combination of greater in-bound investment and higher wages than with higher tax revenue. In such cases, justice as mutual advantage might require compensation for such a country for the losses it incurs in agreeing to limits on tax competition. If restricting tax competition provides sufficient global benefits, it should be possible for the winners to compensate the losers while still being better off than in a world with no restrictions on tax competition. Imagine three possible worlds. In World A, international agreements on limiting tax competition benefit only a few countries and harm many more. The benefits to the winners are not enough to offset the harm to the losers, and thus the international agreement cannot be mutually advantageous even if the winners compensate the losers. Justice as mutual advantage rules out international tax co-operation in World A because there is no outcome that makes all parties to the agreement better off. In World B, limiting tax competition benefits

---

[44] See ch 5 in this volume.
[45] Dagan (n 3) 140–41.

most nations but harms a few nations very significantly. The winners from the agreement are able to compensate the losers while still being better off than they would be without the agreement. Compensation is fixed at a level that provides improvements over the status quo for the pro-tax competition jurisdictions and the anti-tax competition jurisdictions that are roughly equivalent. Here, justice as mutual advantage shows how such agreements can be just while putting some limits on the parameters of agreements by requiring that the winners provide significant compensation to the losers. In World C, there are many winners from agreements to restrict tax agreements and very few losers. The winners gain far more than the losers lose, and so compensation is insignificant relative to the benefits realised by restricting tax competition. In World C, justice as mutual advantage permits international tax agreements. However, because a wide range of possible agreements are mutually advantageous, the minimum standard of justice as mutual advantage does little to constrain possible agreements. In World C, a fully specified theory of justice as mutual advantage will be necessary to provide useful guidance as to which mutually advantageous tax agreements are fair. As suggested above, this might consist of a division of the gains from the agreement in rough proportion to economic output but, with the jurisdictions that stand to benefit from tax competition gaining a bit more than would be suggested by the size of their economies.

The upshot of this analysis is that the minimal standard of justice as mutual advantage is most interesting for international tax policy in scenarios like World B, where there is some scope for mutually advantageous agreements and where not all nations will gain from restricting tax competition. A fully specific theory is necessary for cases like World C, where limiting tax competition is a win-win arrangement for almost all nations and there are a huge range of possible agreements that would be Pareto improvements. Finally, if there is no potential agreement limiting tax competition that is a Pareto improvement, justice as mutually advantage sensibly suggests that limiting tax competition will be unjust.

The second issue is how to divide the gains from co-operation between co-operating nations. Justice as mutual advantage suggests that the division of gains from co-operation should be sensitive to the bargaining position of the parties so that the resulting agreement will be stable because all parties will have an incentive to uphold the rules. This means that no party will be justified in believing that undermining the co-operative scheme will result in a renegotiation of the rules on more favourable terms. The basic idea is that a just outcome is one that would be reached by rational, self-interest parties bargaining from the non-co-operative baseline.[46] Theories of justice as mutual advantage differ in how they determine a fair division of the gains from co-operation. In keeping with the austere approach adopted thus far, I will consider a version of

---

[46] Barry (n 24) 296.

'justice as mutual advantage' that treats fair division of the gains from cooperation as approximated by the results of bargaining between rational agents
with limited altruism and limited normative constraints. There are several
candidates for a solution to bargaining by rational agents over the gains from
cooperation. Some theorists such as Ken Binmore[47] prefer the Nash bargaining
solution.[48] This solution divides gains from cooperation by choosing the division that maximises the product of the gains above the status quo for each party
to the agreement. By contrast, David Gauthier defends the principle of minimax relative concession as a guide to fair cooperation,[49] which is closely related
to the Kalai-Smorodinsky bargaining solution.[50] Minimax relative concession
divides the gains from cooperation in such a way as to minimise the difference
between the agreement point and the maximum possible cooperative gain for
the party that gains the least as measured as a fraction of their possible gains
about the status quo. Maximum possible gains for each party are calculated by
considering the co-operative agreement that would give that party the greatest
advantage while still providing each party with some gain over the status quo.
In other words, a maximum point must be within the set of possible agreements
that make each party better off. In non-technical terms, the minimax relative
concession agreement point is one that gets the parties as close to their best-case
scenario outcome as possible when considering only those outcomes that leave
all parties better off.

   Although the Nash bargaining solution and the principle of 'minimax relative
concession' differ, 'they are seldom very far apart even in asymmetric bargaining problems.'[51] For our purposes, what the two solutions have in common is
more important than their differences. Both measure gains from cooperation from the pre-agreement status quo. Both require a model of the possible
points of agreement that represent a Pareto improvement above the status quo.
And both solutions will typically divide the gains from cooperation in a way
that spreads gains across co-operators but rarely leaves any party at their best
possible outcome. Neither solution is egalitarian in the sense of aiming at equal
outcomes or in the sense of splitting gains equally, although each may do so in
some instances, especially when the parties are symmetrically situated. In this,
they differ from the 'equal benefit principle' defended by Christians and van
Apeldoorn.[52] And neither approach splits gains from co-operation in a way that
necessarily maximises utility, although each may do so in certain instances. In
this, they differ from a purely utilitarian approach to co-operation.

---

[47] Binmore, *Natural Justice* (n 28) 26–27.

[48] J Nash, 'Two-Person Cooperative Games' (1953) 21 *Econometrica* 128.

[49] Gauthier (n 28) 145.

[50] E Kalai & M Smorodinsky, 'Other Solutions to Nash's Bargaining Problem' (1975) 43 *Econometrica* 513.

[51] Binmore, *Game Theory and the Social Contract, Volume I: Playing Fair* (n 34) 82.

[52] Christians & Van Apeldoorn (n 3) 12–14.

Translating either the Nash bargaining solution or minimax relative concession to the context of international tax requires estimates of the pre-agreement baseline and of the maximum possible gain from the agreement for each party. The former has already been discussed in the context of modelling the pre-agreement normative baseline. The latter issue requires a means to estimate the gains for each party from every possible mutually advantageous agreement. To simplify a bit, the division of gains will depend on the position that each party would be in without an agreement and on the possible gains of each party for mutually advantageous agreements.

What are the implications for the division of gains under international tax policy agreements? The size of a nation's economy is a good starting point, both because it roughly tracks a nation's ability to raise tax revenue without an international agreement and because it is a good proxy for the ability to raise revenue under multilateral agreements that restrict tax competition. Economic might is also a rough proxy for leverage in international tax negotiations. All else being equal, a nation with a larger economy is a more important partner in international tax co-operation because its cross-border transactions will tend to have more effect on other parties to the negotiation. Nations with larger economies are more likely to inflict larger losses on their partners by declining to co-operate on international tax policy. A nation's bargaining position, therefore, should roughly track the size of its economy. If this is correct, then a starting point for analysis might be that the gains from co-operation should be allocated roughly in proportion to each nation's economy. This metric is more appropriate than, for example, allocation in proportion to each nation's initial tax revenue because there is no reason to think that a nation adopting a high-tax policy gives it more leverage in negotiations than a nation with an otherwise identical economy that adopts a low-tax policy. If anything, preferring high-tax policies undermines a nation's bargaining position: low-tax economies are *ceteris paribus* better positioned to succeed in tax competition and thus more likely to fare well without an agreement. Moreover, low-tax states have the option of using international agreements to restrict tax competition to raise additional tax revenue and so may have a somewhat wider set of possible options for gains from co-operation.

Allocating the gains from co-operation in proportion to economic output is a plausible starting point. It gives each nation an incentive to co-operate that is roughly equal to a proportion of their total economy. Economic might is, however, not the only consideration relevant to bargaining power. Some nations may be better able to realise gains from tax competition than others. Being more able to benefit from tax competition makes a threat to walk away from international tax co-operation more credible and should increase a nation's leverage in negotiations. Although the dynamics of tax competition are complicated, it is probably the case in general that less developed nations are more likely to benefit from tax competition because the trade-off between in-bound investment and tax revenue is weighted towards the former.[53] It is also likely the case that for some less developed countries, the terms of debate that presuppose taxation of corporate profits, are structurally disadvantageous. Taxation of corporate profits requires considerable expertise on the part of tax authorities and is an obvious complement to taxation of individual income since it provides a backstop to the income tax that prevents wealthy taxpayers from deferring tax on their income indefinitely by realising it through the corporate form. Less developed nations are, ceteris paribus, less likely to have sophisticated revenue authorities and less likely to rely heavily on income taxation.[54] Failure of international cooperation on the taxation of multinationals might therefore be less harmful for less developed nations than a cursory analysis of tax revenue would suggest because it would enable them to adapt forms of taxation better suited to their situations. Smaller jurisdictions might also have some comparative advantage in tax competition because they are able to capture relatively greater in-bound investment for each incremental reduction in tax rates.[55] If this is the case, then justice as mutual advantage might imply that co-operative surplus will be shifted slightly towards less-developed and smaller countries and away from wealthier and larger countries. Poorer countries and smaller countries would gain a bit more than the size of their economies would imply, while wealthier countries and larger countries would gain a bit less.

IV. Challenges for Justice as Mutual Advantage

Although promising as an approach to international tax fairness, justice as mutual advantage is not without its own challenges in the context of international tax policy. Several of these are worth exploring in some detail. First, most work on justice as mutual advantage has focused on interactions between individuals.[56] This work shows that fairness norms can emerge through repeated interaction between mainly self-interested agents, especially when these agents have some choice as to their co-operative partners.[57] International tax policy, however, is concerned with agreements between states. States are not unitary agents. They

---

[53] eg, D Elkins, 'The Merits of Tax Competition in the Global Economy' (2016) 91 *Indiana Law Journal* 905, 950; Dagan (n 3) 132–37.

[54] T Besley & T Persson, 'Why Do Developing Countries Tax So Little?' (2014) 28 *Journal of Economic Perspectives* 99, 104, 113–17.

[55] eg, R Kanbur & M Keen, 'Jeux Sans Frontières: Tax Competition and Tax Coordination When Countries Differ in Size' (1993) 83 *The American Economic Review* 877, 890; S Bucovetsky, 'An Index of Capital Tax Competition' (2009) 16 *International Tax and Public Finance* 727, 728.

[56] eg, Binmore, *Game Theory and the Social Contract, Volume I: Playing Fair* (n 34); H Gintis, *The Bounds of Reason: Game Theory and the Unification of the Behavioral Sciences* (Princeton, Princeton University Press 2009); Sugden (n 28).

[57] eg, N Baumard, J-B Andre & D Sperber, 'A Mutualistic Approach to Morality: the Evolution of Fairness by Partner Choice' (2013) 36 *Behavioural and Brain Sciences* 59–78; Sugden (n 28).

are comprised of an ever-charging roster of personnel and represent citizens who often have conflicting interests. Both of these features are potentially problematic. The first feature provides reason to doubt whether states can maintain consistent policies over time or uphold norms of co-operation over the long run. Unlike individuals who may be sufficiently motivated by reactive attitudes to enforce a co-operative scheme, states are more likely to need to create legal mechanisms to ensure that agreements formed today are enforced tomorrow. This does not seem an insurmountable obstacle to international tax co-operation, but it does represent a disanalogy between the contexts typically considered in leading work on justice as mutual advantage and the context of international tax policymaking.

Because states represent citizens with conflicting interests, they may not take decisions that reflect the interests of their citizens as a whole at any given point in time. The vagaries of interest competition may cause government policy to come apart from national interests or the state may pursue its own interests at the expense of those of its citizens. As a result, states may not reach or adhere to agreements even when they are in the long-run national interest. That a state might pursue sub-optimal or inconsistent policies or purse policies that frustrate fair dealing and make it an undesirable co-operative partner is a very real concern. However, principle-agent problems of this kind are pervasive in public policy.[58] They are neither particular to international tax policy nor uniquely problematic for justice as mutual advantage.

Moreover, even if governments often fail to pursue their own national interests, justice as mutual advantage can show how a nation's international tax policy falls short of standards of fair dealing and how this may frustrate its own long-run interests. Justice as mutual advantage evaluates fairness in terms of the status quo and the division of gains that allows for a stable co-operative scheme. It does not look to the outcome likely to be reached in light of the bargaining skills of the actual parties or the fidelity of governments to the welfare of their citizens. This is a subtle yet important difference because there is reason to worry that many less developed nations do not achieve outcomes in international negotiations that reflect the objective strength of their bargaining positions.[59] Some less developed nations, especially smaller ones, may lack the technical sophistication to participate as full equals in the negotiation of highly technical provisions that require not only legal expertise but also economic analysis of how technical changes in accounting rules will impact public finances.

A second challenge for the analysis offered in this paper is that the gains from international tax agreements will be difficult to calculate. This is both because the effects of such agreements are difficult to predict and because the benefits of restricting tax competition might come in different forms for different parties.

---

[58] eg, J Buchanan & G Tullock, *The Calculus of Consent: Logical Foundations of Constitutional Democracy* (Ann Arbor, The University of Michigan Press, 1962).
[59] Hearson (n 4) 50–51.

This challenge is not unique to justice as mutual advantage. But it does mean that we should temper our expectations for the practical advice that any normative theory can offer in this area. Conclusions will necessarily be tentative and highly approximate.

A third challenge is that international tax policy does not exist in a vacuum but co-exists with other areas of international economic co-operation such as trade policy. This complicates attempts to model the gains and losses from international tax agreements since losses in international tax agreements might be offset by gains in other areas of international relations. It also raises difficult questions about the right unit of analysis for normative evaluation. A trade agreement or tax agreement might look unfair on its own. But disadvantages in one domain could, in theory, be offset by advantages elsewhere. Any fully specified theory of tax fairness must determine whether disadvantages in tax agreements might legitimately be offset by advantages in trade, investment, or security, and whether leveraging bargaining power in one domain to achieve advantages in another is a violation of the sovereignty of weaker states by more powerful states. A theory of tax fairness based on justice as mutual advantage must determine which entitlements are part of the status quo, and which items are up for negotiation. Some versions of 'justice as mutual advantage', such as Ken Binmore's,[60] tend to be permissive in allowing renegotiation of the status quo whereas others, such as David Gauthier's,[61] treat initial entitlements as having special normative significance. A theory, such as Peter Dietsch's,[62] that treats state sovereignty and policy autonomy as part of the status quo will provide greater protection for less powerful nations and prevent advantages in other domains from being used to exact concessions in tax policy. However, it might be vulnerable to criticism that it unreasonably prevents exchanges of favours in tax policy for advantages in other domains. Some nations might find it in their interest to condition tax co-operation on co-operation in trade agreements or international investment policy. Restricting the scope of negotiations over tax co-operation might seem to limit the sovereignty of states in other important respects. Resolving this tension will require both a more fully specific theory of justice as mutual advantage and a well-developed normative theory of state sovereignty.

Finally, some critics may object that justice as mutual advantage is insufficiently demanding in the context of international tax policy and insufficiently protective of the interests of the global poor. It must be conceded that justice as mutual advantage will not be as protective of the interests of the global poor as global egalitarianism or global utilitarianism. However, as argued above, there is no reasonable prospect that international tax agreements will be regulated by principles drawn from these theories. The bite of the criticism that justice as mutual

---

[60] Binmore, *Natural Justice* (n 28); Binmore, *Game Theory and the Social Contract, Volume I: Playing Fair* (n 35).

[61] Gauthier (n 28).

[62] Dietsch (n 3).

advantage is insufficiently demanding depends on one's larger views on the effects of tax competition and international tax policy agreements. If tax competition harms the global poor and agreements to restrict it are likely to help, then one might hope for international agreements that serve global egalitarian ends, even if they are not primarily intended to do so. If, on the other hand, tax competition is often a useful tool for the poorest countries and international agreements restricting tax competition benefit wealthy nations who wish to maintain their high-tax fiscal policies at the expense of the global poor, then justice as mutual advantage could have a useful role in showing how certain agreements can be seen as unfair to the global poor without presupposing an egalitarian theory of distributive justice. In this case, justice as mutual advantage and global egalitarian theories will often come to the same judgement about tax policy proposals even if they start from very different premises.

V. Conclusion

Despite these challenges, justice as mutual advantage is a promising framework for normative analysis of international tax policy. It draws on a rich literature in political philosophy that has seldom been applied to problems of international distributive justice. Justice as mutual advantage is especially apt for the current policy environment in which most nations believe that they can realise gains by adopting new rules to allocate international tax revenue but disagree on what allocation would be fair. It tempers self-interest without demanding a level of self-sacrifice that is implausible under the current institutional order. Justice as mutual advantage respects states as sovereignty agents entitled to pursue their own interests while providing a standard for evaluating the fairness of the division of gains that can be realised by international tax co-operation. If idealist theories such as global egalitarianism and global utilitarianism are too ambitious and national interests are too unambitious, justice as mutual advantage might be just right. Its normative standards are not as demanding as those of many of its competitors. If international tax agreements fail to meet them, this is strong evidence that they are unfair. Justice as mutual advantage thus may show how international tax policies treat some developing nations unfairly without relying on egalitarian premises or controversial theories that support redistribution across international boundaries.

Justice as mutual advantage is well suited to undergird theories of justice in international taxation that are realist and associativist.[63] It has points of commonality with some of the most sophisticated recent work on fairness in international taxation that combine the command of political theory and political philosophy

---

[63] See ch 1 in this volume.

with engagement with the details of international tax law.[64] The austere version of the theory outlined above can provide a framework for understanding how other realist-associativist theories deviate from the basic model by adopting more exacting normative standards. For example, Christians and van Apeldoorn's equal benefit principle constrains the influence of differential bargaining power on the division of gains from cooperation far more than the austere model,[65] and Dietsch treats freedom to set policy as having greater normative significance than the austere model would.[66] In this brief sketch, I have not been able to work out all of the details of how justice as mutual advantage might apply to international tax policy or which version of the theory is most appropriate for this context. I hope that other tax theorists will try to develop this approach even if, as is entirely possible, they reach conclusions about the implications of justice as mutual advantage for international tax policy that conflict with those defended here.

[64] eg Dagan (n 3), Dietsch (n 3).
[65] Christians & Van Apeldoorn (n 3), 12–14.
[66] Dietsch (n 3) 31.

PART II

Reforming Business Taxation

4

The Shifting Economic Allegiance of Capital Gains

AMANDA PARSONS[1]

In our modern, digitalised economy, the time has come to reform the dominant model for taxing capital gains income. Under the current international tax sourcing rules, capital gains income from the sale of a company's shares is taxed in the investor's residence country. The countries in which businesses operate and engage in value-creating activities – the source countries[2] – are not granted taxing rights over this income.

This chapter argues that this model is no longer in line with the underlying principles of international tax law. New technologies and digitalisation have transformed the global economy in ways that the designers of the international tax system could never have envisioned in the 1920s. In this transformed economy, source countries must be allowed to tax capital gains income[3] to maintain fairness within the international tax system.

The basic question that drives the design of the international tax system can be stated quite simply. If residents of Country A invest in a business that is resident of Country B and conduct business activities in Country C, which of Countries A, B, and C should tax income stemming from this investment and business activities?[4] Only one country can be granted taxing rights over an item of income if double taxation is to be avoided.[5]

---

[1] This chapter is drawn from a recent article in the *Florida Tax Review*. A Parsons 'The Shifting Economic Allegiance of Capital Gains' (2023) 26 *Florida Tax Review* 308.

[2] References to the source country in this essay point to an expanded concept of the source country as encompassing both the country of production and the market country. See n 27 and accompanying text (discussing this expanded concept of source).

[3] For purposes of this chapter, 'capital gains income' refers exclusively to capital gains income from the sale of shares of a company, not any other capital asset.

[4] In their seminal 1972 essay, 'Inter-Nation Equity', Peggy and Richard Musgrave described the central questions of international tax as follows: 'If residents of country A invest in a business incorporated in B and operating in C, who should be permitted to tax the income on such capital and at what rate?' R Musgrave & P Musgrave, 'Inter-Nation Equity' in R Bird & J Head (eds), *Modern Fiscal Issues: Essays in Honor of Carl S. Shoup* (Toronto, University of Toronto Press, 1972) 64.

[5] There is a near universal agreement within international tax law that double taxation is undesirable. See R Avi-Yonah, *International Tax as International Law* (New York, CUP, 2006) 1.

Benefits theory and the resulting concept of economic allegiance have been and remain essential guiding principles in answering this question.[6] In the context of international tax, benefits theory is the principle that a country is justified in taxing income from economic activities that occur within its borders because it provides the taxpayer with benefits that facilitate those activities.[7] Flowing from benefits theory is the concept of dividing taxing authority amongst countries based on which country has the closest economic allegiance to an item of income or asset.[8] The endurance of these principles can be seen in recent efforts to reform the tax system to ensure that companies are taxed in the country where value is created.[9]

Applying the principle of allocating taxing authority based on relative economic allegiance, the architects of international tax law devised in the 1920s a system in which the source country can generally tax active business income and the investor's residence country can generally tax passive investment income.[10] Accordingly, capital gains income from the sale of company shares are typically sourced to the investor's residence country in the same way as other forms of passive income, such as interest.[11] The international tax system has remained relatively unchanged since the 1920s.[12] In the intervening century, fundamental transformations in the global economy have rendered this tax regime obsolete, leading to outcomes that are often incoherent and inequitable.

This failure of the international tax system, particularly in the context of the digital economy,[13] has been broadly recognised.[14] Political outrage over

---

[6] For a detailed discussion of benefits theory, see Part II.B below.

[7] See Avi-Yonah (n 5) 12; M Kane, 'A Defense of Source Rules in International Taxation' (2015) 32 *Yale Journal of Regulation* 311, 315, fn 10.

[8] The concept of economic allegiance and its relation to the benefits principle is discussed further in nn 42 to 51 below and accompanying text.

[9] See nn 77–87 and accompanying text.

[10] See HD Rosenbloom & S Langbein, 'United States Tax Treaty Policy: An Overview' (1981) 19 *Columbia Journal of Transnational Law* 359, 366–67; R Avi-Yonah, 'All of a Piece Throughout: The Four Ages of U.S. International Taxation' (2005) 25 *Virginia Tax Review* 313, 322.

[11] Organization for Economic Co-operation & Development, Model Tax Convention on Income and on Capital (2017) Art 11, 13. An exception to this is sale of shares in businesses that derive more than 50% of their value from immoveable property, such as land. ibid Art 13, para 4.

[12] See M Graetz & M O'Hear, 'The "Original Intent" of U.S. International Taxation' (1997) 46 *Duke Law Journal* 1021, 1023.

[13] A uniform definition of the 'digital economy' has proven elusive. See International Monetary Fund, Measuring the Digital Economy (2018) 7, www.imf.org/en/Publications/Policy-Papers/Issues/2018/04 /03/022818-measuring-the-digital-economy; L Faulhaber 'Taxing Tech: The Future of Digital Taxation' (2019) 39 *Virginia Tax Review* 145, 150–51. The centrality of network effects, data collection, and user participation are the features of the digital economy most relevant to this essay's analysis. References to the 'digital economy' will generally be connected to these characteristics, which are linked to the rise of the data economy as well as platform-based business models, both of which are of increasing important within the global economy. See J Cohen, *Between Truth and Power* (New York, OUP, 2019) 63–72. See generally G Parker et al., *Platform Revolution* (New York, W. W. Norton & Company, 2016).

[14] See, eg, Kane (n 7) 311; R Avi-Yonah, 'International Taxation of Electronic Commerce' (1997) 58 *Tax Law Review* 507, 515–16; R Mason 'The Transformation of International Tax' (2020) 114 *American Journal International Law* 353, 364–66; E Kleinbard, 'Stateless Income' (2011) 11 *Florida Tax Review*

multinational companies and their investors not paying their 'fair share' of taxes is ubiquitous[15] and a rallying cry has arisen in recent years that taxation should occur 'where value is created'.[16] These conversations have led to significant reform proposals, including the OECD Inclusive Framework, which proposed allocating taxing rights over corporate income to countries in which companies' users and customers are located.[17]

These proposed reforms represent an important step towards creating a more coherent and equitable international tax system that allows the countries in which value is created to tax multinational companies. But these reforms, along with the current conversations in the international tax community more generally, possess a key flaw: they focus exclusively on how to divide taxing authority over company income. They fail to recognise that the value created by a company's business activities manifests itself in two ways. In addition to company income, business activities lead to growth in the overall market value of the company. This growth in market value then translates into capital gains income when the investor sells their shares. Determining which country should be allowed to tax income stemming from growth in company value is essential to designing an equitable international tax system that is in line with its underlying principles. By focusing only on company income, the current conversation is missing half the picture.

This chapter fills this gap. Applying the benefits principle and the concept of allocating taxing authority based on the relative economic allegiance of income, it re-evaluates whether the investor's residence country or the source country should be allowed to tax capital gains income in our current economic environment. It concludes that two economic realities not anticipated by the original designers of the international tax system point towards granting taxing authority to the source countries.

The first involves the nature of value creation within the digital economy. Value creation is driven by the growth of large networks of users and customers, which provide the company with access to their free production of data as well as content. Networks of users and customers and access to their free content production and data are resources that have a particularly strong economic allegiance to the source country. Furthermore, this method of value creation also

---

699, 703–05; M Devereux & J Vella, 'Are We Heading Towards a Corporate Tax System Fit for the 21st Century?' (2014) 35 *Fiscal Studies* 449, 461.

[15] See, eg, White House, Press Release, Fact Sheet: The American Jobs Plan (31 March 2021), www.whitehouse.gov/briefing-room/statements-releases/2021/03/31/fact-sheet-the-american-jobs-plan/; R Lough, 'Explainer: Macron's quest for an international tax on digital services' *Reuters* (22 Aug. 2019), www.reuters.com/article/us-g7-summit-digital-tax-explainer/explainer-macrons-quest-for-an-international-tax-on-digital-services-idUSKCN1VC0VH; J Eisinger et al., 'The Secret IRS Files: Trove of Never-Before-Seen Records Reveal How the Wealthiest Avoid Income Tax' (*ProPublica*, 8 June 2021), www.propublica.org/article/the-secret-irs-files-trove-of-never-before-seen-records-reveal-how-the-wealthiest-avoid-income-tax.

[16] For a detailed discussion for the push to tax where value is created, see nn 72 to 87 below and accompanying text.

[17] Notes 73 to 76 and accompanying text.

defies the assumption that an increase in company market value will, in most instances, be accompanied by contemporaneous company profits.[18] To grow networks, digital companies forego income in the short and medium-term, betting on better business outcomes in the long-term. The market rewards this approach, and company values often skyrocket before any income is seen. As a result, unless source countries are able to tax capital gains income, digital companies can conduct substantial value-creating business activities in a country, exploiting that country's benefits and resources without ever having to pay taxes. This result is in clear violation of the benefits principle.

The second economic reality that points towards granting taxing authority to source countries is the rise of highly diversified investor portfolios and the resulting broad shareholder bases of multinational companies. This broad share ownership has weakened the economic allegiance of capital gains income to the investor's residence country. Diffuse ownership prevents most individual investors from having substantial influence on the success or failure of the business, contrary to the assumptions of the original designers of the international tax system.[19]

The chapter concludes that, given the realities of the modern digitalised economy, taxing authority over capital gains income should be allocated to the source country under the normative principles of international tax law.

I. International Tax Law: Structure, Origins and Principles

A. Structure and Origins

The first attempt to answer the question of which country should be allowed to tax cross-border income occurred in the 1920s, as members of the League of Nations sought to establish a coordinated international tax system.[20] The result is often referred to as the '1920s Compromise.' The challenge faced by these initial designers was to devise a system whereby a taxpayer operating internationally would only be taxed by a single country.[21] The work towards the 1920s compromise

---

[18] See Finance Committee, *Report on Double Taxation*, League of Nations Doc. E.F.S.73.F.19 (1923) [hereinafter Four Economists' Report]. As is explained in more detail in Part I.C below, the League of Nations commissioned this during the original design of the international tax system in the 1920s. The report's recommendations remain the core of the international tax system.

[19] See ibid 36.

[20] For a detailed history of the negotiations leading to the 1920s Compromise, see S Jogarajan, *Double Taxation and the League of Nations* (Cambridge, CUP, 2018).

[21] There was general agreement at the time that double taxation was undesirable. See, eg, B Wells & C Lowell, 'Income Tax Treaty Policy in the 21st Century: Residence vs. Source' (2015) 5 *Columbia Journal of Tax Law 1*, 13–14; Four Economists' Report (n 8) 2.

began with a 1920 meeting of the International Chamber of Commerce (ICC) and culminated with the release of several model treaties in 1927 and 1928 by League of Nations technical expert committees.[22] During both the ICC and League of Nations negotiations, the United States, Britain, and other allied nations were the central players.[23] The United States was represented by TS Adams, now known as the leading architect of the US international tax system.[24]

The 1920s Compromise answered the question of which country should be allowed to tax an item of cross-border income by establishing a 'classification and assignment' system. Current international tax law is a direct relic of the classification and assignment model established by League of Nations members in the 1920s.[25] Under international tax law, two countries are considered to have a legitimate claim to tax an item of cross-border income: the residence country and the source country.[26] The residence country is the country of the taxpayer's residence. The source country is the country that is the locus of the economic activities giving rise to income.[27]

Rather than allocating taxing authority exclusively to the country of residence or the country of source, the international tax system balances the taxing claims of the residence and source countries. It places items of income into different classes (such as royalties or business profits) and then assigns taxing authority over each

---

[22] Graetz & O'Hear (n 12) 1066; Jogarajan (n 20) 3–4.

[23] See generally Graetz & O'Hear (n 12) 1066–1089.

[24] ibid 1080–81.

[25] Rosenbloom & Langbein (n 10) 365–66.

[26] See H Ault & B Arnold, *Comparative Income Taxation*, 3rd edn (Alphen aan den Rijn, Wolters Kluwer, 2010) 429, 431; Mason (n 14) 355.

[27] The international tax system currently does not recognise the market country, the country in which companies have users and customers, as a locus of economic activities giving rise to income. The market country is, therefore, not considered to have a legitimate claim to tax income as the source country. A Parsons, 'Tax's Digital Labor Dilemma' (2022) 71 *Duke Law Journal* 1781, 1791–93. The concept of source is based on production, see, eg, I.R.C. § 861(a)(3); I.R.C. § 863(b); OECD (n 11) Art 7; see also Avi-Yonah (n 10) 320, and the international tax system currently does not recognise the production role that users and customers often play for companies. Therefore, a company having users or customers present in a country is alone not enough to make it the source country. This author has advocated in other work for the international tax system to recognise this production role of users and customers and grant their home countries taxing authority over income stemming directly from their work as the source jurisdiction. See Parsons (n 27). The recent Pillar One Blueprint reform proposed reallocating taxing authority over a portion of a company's profits to countries 'where there is an active and sustained participation of a business in the economy of that jurisdiction through activities in, or remotely directed at, that jurisdiction', OECD/G20 Base Erosion & Profit Shifting Project, Tax Challenges Arising from digitalisation – Report on Pillar One Blueprint: Inclusive Framework on BEPS 11 (Oct. 2020), www.oecd-ilibrary.org/docserver/beba0634-en.pdf?expires=1641849624&id=id &accname=ocid177456&checksum=E37EBF09CF8A96BF934C49842D8784EF. This reallocation can be viewed as expanding the concept of the 'source' of the economic activities giving rise to income to encompass market countries in addition to the countries of traditional production. When advocating for re-allocating taxing authority over capital gains income to the 'source' country, this chapter refers to the expanded concept of source as encompassing both the country of traditional production and the market country in which value-creating data and content production is being accomplished by company's users and customers.

class to either the residence country or the source country.[28] Generally, the source country is granted taxing authority over active business income, and the residence country of the taxpayer is granted taxing authority over passive investment income.[29] Capital gains income from the sale of shares of businesses is, therefore, taxed in the country of the investor's residence, not the country in which the business operates.[30]

B. Benefits Theory

This design of this system of classification and assignment was influenced by benefits theory and the resulting concept of assigning taxing authority over an item of income based on its economic allegiance to a country. Benefits theory espouses the principle that the source country is justified in taxing business activities occurring within such a country because it provides the benefits and resources necessary for those business activities to occur.[31] The benefits principle has remained a central normative feature of international tax law despite criticisms.[32]

Many of the criticisms of the benefits principle stem from scholars viewing of the principle as justifying tax as a form of direct compensation for government benefits. These scholars have argued that the benefits principle is theoretically incoherent because it is not possible to accurately measure the benefits received by each taxpayer, and the relative level and value of benefits received by a taxpayer does not necessarily align with their income.[33]

However, this criticism implies a very narrow view of benefits theory that treats taxes as individualised payments for specific benefits and services. In contrast, a modified benefits theory reflects a broader view that the benefits and resources provided by a country establishes the necessary nexus to justify taxation. This broader view of benefits theory has been present since the nineteenth century and

---

[28] Rosenbloom & Langbein (n 10) 365–66; S Dean, 'A Constitutional Moment in Cross-Border Taxation' (2021) 1 *Journal of Financial Development* 1, 1–3.

[29] See n 10 and accompanying text.

[30] OECD (n 11) Art 13.

[31] See n 7 and accompanying text.

[32] See J Slemrod & J Bakija, *Taxing Ourselves*, 4th edn (Cambridge, MIT Press, 2008) 61; K Vogel, 'Worldwide vs. Source Taxation of Income – A Review of the Arguments (Part III)' (1988) 16 *Intertax* 393, 398. This chapter does not argue that benefits theory or any other principle or factor has alone informed the evolution of international tax law. Notably, in addition to the benefits principles, the ability-to-pay principle has played an important role in the development of both domestic and international tax law. Slemrod & Bakija (n 32) 64. Furthermore, theoretical principles have often given way to realities of politics and administrability.

[33] See, eg, R Musgrave & P Musgrave, *Public Finance in Theory and Practice*, 5th edn (New York, McGraw Hill, 1989) 221; R Green, 'The Future of Source-Based Taxation of the Income of Multinational Enterprises' (1993) 79 *Cornell Law Review* 18, 29; N Kaufman, 'Fairness and the Taxation of International Income' (1998) 29 *Law & Policy in International Business* 145, 183–84. See also Kane (n 7) 314–318.

continued into the twentieth century.[34] As Klaus Vogel wrote in 1988: 'Turning to benefit theory arguments, I want to emphasize first that in a modern theoretical setting arguments of this type cannot and do not imply that taxes are prices for individual state services. Such an assumption would be far from reality.'[35]

It is this broader application of the benefits principle that animated the original development of the international tax system in the 1920s. TS Adams supported source-based taxation, specifically with respect to businesses, first under the benefits principle. He explained that the source country had a 'prior claim ... upon profits which public expenditures or the business environment maintained by the state have in part produced.'[36] He viewed the benefits principle as justifying source-based taxation both morally and politically.[37] The benefits principle was at the core of the US approach to international taxation during the 1920s negotiations and beyond.[38] Other countries' negotiators also expounded on the importance of the benefits theory in the 1920s Compromise negotiations. The benefits theory of taxation guided many of the recommendations made by the panel of experts gathered in 1925 by the League of Nations, often accompanied by appeals to a general sense of 'fairness'.[39]

The importance of the benefits principle in international tax law has continued over the intervening century. Reuven Avi-Yonah has identified the benefits principle as one of two norms (the other being avoiding double taxation) that together have led to a coherent and unified international tax system.[40] The benefits principle has continued to serve as a guide for international tax law's current sourcing rules.[41]

C. Economic Allegiance and Allocating Taxing Rights

This broader, modified benefits principle animated the development of the approach of allocating taxing authority based on the relative economic allegiance of an item of income. Georg van Schanz first introduced the concept of economic allegiance to international taxation. In his 1892 article 'Zur Frage der Steuerpflicht' (Regarding Tax Liability), Schanz bases the concept of economic allegiance on the benefits provided by both the countries in which income is earned and consumed.[42]

---

[34] See Vogel (n 32) 395–96.
[35] ibid 396.
[36] Graetz & O'Hear (n 12) 1036–37 (quoting TS Adams).
[37] See ibid 1036–38.
[38] See Avi-Yonah (n 10) 318.
[39] Jogarajan (n 20) 82.
[40] Avi-Yonah (n 5) 2, 11–12.
[41] See L Lokken, 'What Is This Thing Called Source?' [May-June 2011] *International Tax Journal* 25, 26; F Brown, 'An Equity-Based Multilateral Approach for Sourcing Income Among Nation' (2011) 11 *Florida Tax Review* 565, 574.
[42] See K Vogel, 'Worldwide vs. Source Taxation of Income – A Review of the Arguments (Part I)' (1988) 16 *Intertax* 216, 219.

He writes: 'I want to emphasize that indeed there is no tax for which no benefit relation relates.'[43] He argues that the benefits principle can be used to establish a tax base, or nexus, but eschews the idea of tax as a means of direct compensation for government benefits received.[44]

The benefits principle also underlies the concept of 'economic allegiance' as it is presented and applied during the 1920s negotiations. An important moment in the lead up to the 1920s Compromise was the release of the 'Four Economists' Report' in 1923.[45] The League of Nations commissioned a report on possible designs of an international tax system that prevented double taxation of cross-border income. The report put forward a classification and assignment system that was adopted in subsequent model treaties and that, as explained above, remains the basis of the international tax system to this day.[46] The organising principle of this classification and assignment system was 'economic allegiance'. Whether an item of income was assigned to the source country or the residence country was based on its relative economic allegiance to each.[47]

As Reuven Avi-Yonah has noted, the Four Economists' Report's articulation of economic allegiance has at its core the benefits principle.[48] He observes that '[the four economists'] definition of "economic allegiance" is clearly based on a benefits theory of taxation' and that they use this theory to justify both source-based and residence-based taxation.[49] The authors of the Four Economists' Report were critical of the quid pro quo approach to benefits theory.[50] However, their account of economic allegiance flows from the modified view of the benefits principle rather than the quid pro quo approach of which they were critical.

The authors describe economic allegiance as a problem of 'duties or obligations' of the taxpayer rather than benefits. But they then go on to describe those very duties as connected with benefits received.[51] They highlight the role that legal frameworks of governments play in allowing income from economic activities to come into the hands of the taxpayer[52] and speak of the fact that the overall economic life of a community makes possible the production of income.[53] The

---

[43] G von Schanz, 'Zur Frage der Steuerpflicht' (1892) 9 II *Finanzarchiv* 1, 4, translated and quoted in Vogel (n 42) 219.

[44] See ibid 219.

[45] Academics have disagreed on whether too much importance has been placed on the 1923 report in tax scholarship. Compare Graetz & O'Hear (n 12) 1027 with Avi-Yonah (n 10) 321–22.

[46] Four Economists' Report (n 18) 42. See also H Ault, 'Corporate Integration, Tax Treaties, and the Division of the International Tax Base: Principles and Practices' (1992) 47 *Tax Law Review* 565, 567–68.

[47] Four Economists' Report (n 18) 20.

[48] Avi-Yonah (n 10) 320.

[49] ibid 320.

[50] Four Economists' Report (n 18) 18. See Part I.A.

[51] The authors explain, '[i]t is undeniable that the individual owes some duty to the place where he lives. He receives benefits from, and confers benefits upon, that community. He receives benefits in that he enjoys not only the protection of the laws but the various conveniences that are afforded by the community where he chooses to live.' ibid 29.

[52] ibid 23.

[53] ibid 23.

relative extent and importance of benefits provided by a country were, thus, a key consideration in determining the economic allegiance of different categories of income for the report's authors.

In the report, the authors assessed the relative economic allegiance of different categories of income and recommended assigning taxing authority over each category to either the source or residence country. Their suggested framework reflected the general divide between active business income being allocated to the source country and passive investment income being allocated to the residence country.[54] In the report, the authors presented a detailed articulation of the concept of economic allegiance. This articulation helps both to elucidate the nature of the concept of economic allegiance and explain the historical context and assumptions that shaped the design of the international sourcing rules that persist to this day.

In assessing economic allegiance, the authors focused on the importance of the location itself, including land and other resources, to wealth production.[55] They weighed this importance against the contribution of the personality of the taxpayer and, in the case of businesses, the manager.[56]

Whether the taxpayer had a choice and ability to move the location of wealth production was another important factor in their considerations. If it was difficult to move the location of the wealth producing activities, economic allegiance to the source country was strengthened.[57]

The location where labour occurred was also viewed as important to economic allegiance – a taxpayer being able to contribute to wealth producing activities from their home country would reduce economic allegiance to the country of origin.[58] The authors viewed effective remote contributions and management as uncommon occurrences, however.[59]

The authors applied these considerations to various categories of income, further illustrating how they conceived of economic allegiance. In the case of agriculture, the relative contribution of the land itself versus the personality of the taxpayer was of central importance in their view. They explained: '[i]n most cases ... the yield of land depends to an overwhelming extent upon the land itself.'[60]

To determine the economic allegiance of business income, the authors separately considered three categories of businesses – mining, oil, and other extractive businesses; industrial businesses; and commercial businesses.[61] The authors found the economic allegiance to the source country to be strongest in

---

[54] Avi-Yonah (n 10) 322–23.
[55] Four Economists' Report (n 18) 27–31.
[56] ibid 27–31.
[57] ibid 31.
[58] ibid 30–31.
[59] ibid 30.
[60] ibid 28.
[61] ibid 29.

the case of mines and wells, likening it to almost as close of a connection as to agriculture, because yield from this type of business 'will in the main depend after all on the richness of the mine or the quality or quantity of oil'.[62] They also emphasised that the owner was not able to choose the location of the resources because mines and wells were immovable.[63] For industrial and commercial businesses, the authors found the connection with the source country to be somewhat weaker due to the ability to choose the location of the business activities, a greater influence of management on business success, and the possibility that management might be conducted from the taxpayer's residence country.[64] Despite this, they still concluded that the economic allegiance of these business profits laid with the source countries.

The Four Economists' Report considers separately from business income the economic allegiance of wealth in the form of corporate shares and associated income. They ultimately conclude that the economic allegiance of this capital gains income was closer to the shareholder's residence country than the source country.[65] Their assessment stems from two fundamental assumptions about the functioning of companies and business models, neither of which hold in our modern economic environment.

First, the authors assumed that a company whose value was increasing would also be earning income in the country in which they were operating. They explained that: '[c]orporate shares would, indeed, be worth nothing if the company had no earnings ….'[66] Therefore, while they acknowledged that increases in the value of a company's shares were 'in part bound up with the economic prosperity' of the country in which the business activities occur,[67] the countries that were providing the benefits necessary for these businesses to operate and grow in value would be compensated through tax revenues on company earnings. Under this assumption, allowing source countries to tax capital gains income was not necessary to align the international tax system with the benefits principle.

Second, the authors assumed that the owners of businesses would have a substantial impact on their success or failure and, therefore, a substantial impact on whether capital gains income was realised.[68] The importance of the owner to achieving capital gains strengthened the economic allegiance of that income to the owner's residence country, the location from which they were presumably contributing to business decisions while enjoying the benefits and resources provided by the country.

As explained in Part III below, neither of these assumptions holds in the modern economy. The imaginations of the four economists and other participants

---

[62] ibid 30.
[63] ibid 30.
[64] ibid 30–31.
[65] ibid 36–37.
[66] Four Economists' Report (n 18) 36.
[67] ibid 36.
[68] ibid 36.

in the 1920s Compromise could not predict the rapid technological advances of past decades and the ways in which they have transformed the global economy. As a result, the international tax system produces results that are out of line with the normative principles of benefits theory and economic allegiance. This misalignment and the perceived failings of the international tax system have sparked significant, albeit incomplete, debates and efforts at reform.

II. Taxing the Modern Economy: The State and Limitations of the Debate

The sentiment that the international tax system is broken and unfair has been pervasive in scholarly and political discourse.[69] The international tax system that was created in the 1920s has been largely unchanged since.[70] And it has proven inadequate in the modern economy. Countless features of the modern economy are beyond what could have been conceived of by economists and lawmakers in the 1920s. These business trends have challenged the international tax system in recent years and, in many instances, allowed multinational companies, particularly digital companies, to avoid paying taxes in the countries in which they are conducting business.[71] The ability to conduct business in a country without paying taxes there implicates the benefits principle and the accompanying concept of allocating taxing rights based on economic allegiance.

A broad political sentiment has emerged that, under the existing principles of international tax law, companies should be taxed 'where value is created.'[72] Taxing where value is created has accordingly been the political mantra of the past decade's efforts to reform international tax law. Most notably, the OECD/G20's Base Erosion and Profit Shifting (BEPS) Project has focused on the goal of reforming international tax law to ensure that profits are taxed in the location where

---

[69] See nn 12–16 and accompanying text.

[70] See Graetz & O'Hear (n 12) 1023.

[71] See C Dunahoo, 'Source Country Taxation of Foreign Corporations: Evolving Permanent Establishment Concepts' (2008) 86 *Tax Magazine* 37; A Christians, 'Digital Services Taxes and Internation Equity: A Tribute to Peggy Musgrave' (12 Aug. 2019) 95 *Tax Notes International* 589, 589.

[72] eg, the European Commission explained in a 2018 report that although '[i]t is an internationally agreed principle that profits should be taxed where value is created,' features of the digital economy have led to 'a disconnect between where the value is created, and where taxes are paid'. European Commission, Time to Establish a Modern, Fair and Efficient Taxation Standard for the Digital.

Economy (2018) 4, eur-lex.europa.eu/resource.html?uri=cellar:2bafa0d9-2dde-11e8-b5fe-01aa75ed71a1.0017.02/DOC_1&format=PDF. The UK government likewise explained in a 2017 position paper that '[t]he overall principle underpinning [the international tax system's] framework is to tax a multinational group's profits in the countries in which it undertakes its value-generating activities' and analysed a variety of potential reforms to ensure that this principle was upheld in the face of digitalization. Her Majesty's Treasury, Corporate Tax and the Digital Economy: Policy Paper (2017) 4, assets.publishing.service.gov.uk/government/uploads/system/uploads/attachment_data/file/689240/corporate_tax_and_the_digital_economy_update_web.pdf.

value is created.[73] In 2022, the OECD/G20 Inclusive Framework, which comprises 141 member countries, put forward a two-pillar solution to address the challenges of taxing the digital economy.[74]

Pillar One of this framework addressed the goal of realigning taxation with value creation. It built upon prior proposals by the European Commission and the United Kingdom to take user-generated value into account when allocating taxing authority over company income.[75] The framework proposed reallocating taxing authority based on active and sustained participation, which would allow countries in which companies have users and customers, but no substantial company-level operations, to tax companies.[76]

The benefits principle and concept of economic allegiance have underpinned these, as well as other proposals for the reform of the international tax system.[77] The influence of these principles is particularly clear in calls to realign the place of taxation and the place of value creation. Some scholars have questioned the validity of the political assertion that value creation is a common underlying principle that has guided the international tax system, arguing that it is a newly devised concept without a theoretical basis.[78] The political discourse surrounding taxing companies where value is created indicates, however, that allocating taxing authority based on value creation is not a new principle but an extension of the benefits principle and economic allegiance.[79]

---

[73] See Organization for Economic Co-operation & Development, Action Plan on Base Erosion and Profits Shifting (2013) 10, www.oecd.org/ctp/BEPSActionPlan.pdf.

[74] See OECD/G20 Base Erosion & Profit Shifting Project, Tax Challenges Arising from digitalisation – Report on Pillar Two Blueprint: Inclusive Framework on BEPS (Oct. 2020) 11, www.oecd-ilibrary.org/docserver/beba0634-en.pdf?expires=1641849624&id=id&accname=ocid177456&checksum=E37EBF 09CF8A96BF934C49842D8784EF [hereinafter OECD Pillar One Blueprint]; OECD/G20 Base Erosion & Profit Shifting Project, Tax Challenges Arising from digitalisation – Report on Pillar Two Blueprint: Inclusive Framework on BEPS (Oct. 2020), available at www.oecd-ilibrary.org/sites/abb4c3d1-en/index.html?itemId=/content/publication/abb4c3d1-en [hereinafter OECD Pillar Two Blueprint].

[75] Parsons (n 27) 1799–1801.

[76] OECD Pillar One Blueprint (n 74) 11.

[77] See, eg, R Avi-Yonah, 'The New International Tax Regime' (U of Michigan Public Law, Working Paper No. 21-031, 2022) 1–2; Brown (n 41) 568–69; European Commission, A Fair and Efficient System in the European Union for the Digital Single Market (2017), 2 eur-lex.europa.eu/legal-content/EN/TXT/PDF/?uri=CELEX:52017DC0547&from=en. See also S Shay, JC Fleming, Jr. & R Peroni, 'What's Source Got to Do With It? Sources Rules and U.S. International Taxation' (2003) 56 *Tax Law Review* 81, 91.

[78] See, eg, M Devereux & J Vella, 'Value Creation as the Fundamental Principle of the International Corporate Tax System' (European Tax Policy Forum Policy Paper, 2018) 3–5; W Schön, Ten Questions about Why and How to Tax the Digitalized Economy (Max Planck Institute for Tax Law and Public Finance Working Paper 2017–11) 4–5; A Christians, 'Taxing According to Value Creation' (2018) 90 *Tax Notes International* 1379, 1379. For a brief overview of scholarly critiques of the concept of value creation in the context of the OECD/BEPS reforms, see W Haslehner, 'Value Creation and Income Taxation: A Coherent Framework for Reform?' in Werner Haslehner & Marie Lamensch (eds), *Taxation and Value Creation* (Amsterdam, IBFD, 2021) 39, 40–41.

[79] See S Langbein & M Fuss, 'The OECD/G20-BEPS-Project and the Value Creation Paradigm: Economic Reality Disembouging into the Interpretation of the 'Arm's Length' Standard' (2018) 51 *International Lawyer* 259, 262; J Li et al., 'Value Creation: A Constant Principle in a Changing World' (2019) 67 *Canadian Tax Journal* 1107, 1112–14. See also Avi-Yonah (n 77) 1–2.

For example, the EU Commission asserted that '[c]ompanies engaged in digital activities, like all other companies, must share the tax burden needed to finance the public services on which they rely.'[80] It highlighted in particular the market infrastructure, judicial system, and high level of connectivity provided by the EU Member States, from which digital companies benefit.[81] The OECD/ BEPS initiative has repeatedly emphasised the need to grant a taxing right to countries when companies engage in the 'economic life'[82] of those countries. This same language of participation in a country's 'economic life' was used in the Four Economists' Report to explain when a country would be considered the 'origin of wealth,' thereby establishing an economic allegiance to that country.[83]

Recent discourse has gone even further in considering what benefits provided by countries should create a right to tax. Rather than just looking at government-provided benefits, policymakers have identified the benefits and resources provided by citizens themselves. The UK government argued in a 2017 position paper that taxing authority should be granted to countries based on the engagement and participation of users and customers on digital platforms.[84] The UK cited the value that this engagement and participation creates through data and content production, as well as the building of network effects and market power.[85] It ultimately concluded that not taking into account this value creation when allocating taxing authority led to a result that was 'inconsistent with the objectives' of international tax law.[86] The OECD/G20 BEPS Project and the European Commission have similarly discussed the potential need to grant taxing authority to users' and customers' countries based on the data, content, and network effects they provide.[87]

The debates of the past decade demonstrate that the benefits principle and the accompanying concept of economic allegiance are alive and well in the efforts of international tax policymakers to reform the international tax system. And these debates and reform proposals are significant steps in the work to realign the taxation of multinational companies with international tax law's normative goals. But

---

[80] European Commission (n 72) 4.

[81] ibid.

[82] See, eg, OECD/G20 Base Erosion & Profit Shifting Project (n 13) 178; OECD/G20 Base Erosion & Profit Shifting Project, Addressing the Tax Challenges of the Digitalisation of the Economy (Feb. 2019) 16, available at www.copenhageneconomics.com/dyn/resources/Filelibrary/file/7/187/1552035347/public-consultation-document-addressing-the-tax-challenges-of-the-digitalisation-of-the-economy.pdf.

[83] Four Economists' Report (n 18) 23.

[84] Her Majesty's Treasury (n 72) 8.

[85] ibid.

[86] Her Majesty's Treasury, Corporate tax and the digital economy: position paper update 6 (2018), available at assets.publishing.service.gov.uk/government/uploads/system/uploads/attachment_data/file/689240/corporate_tax_and_the_digital_economy_update_web.pdf.

[87] OECD/G20 Base Erosion & Profit Shifting Project (n 13) 170–71; European Commission, Proposal for a Council Directive on the Common System of a Digital Services Tax on Revenues Resulting from the Provision of Certain Digital Services (2018) 1–2, 9, data.consilium.europa.eu/doc/document/ST-7419-2018-INIT/en/pdf.

they do not fully address this task because they focus exclusively on how taxing authority over *company income* should be allocated. The current conversation leaves open the important question of how the existence of value-creating business activities in a country should affect that country's right to tax income stemming from growth in a business's value. Should an investor's capital gains income be taxed in the source country or residence country? The following part answers this question.

III. The Shifting Economic Allegiance of Capital Gains

A. The Nature of Value Creation in the Digital Economy

i. From Networks to Data

The digitalisation of the global economy has radically shifted the ways in which companies create value for their investors. This form of value creation looks very different from the businesses whose economic allegiance the four economists considered.[88]

In the digital economy, value creation begins with a company's network of users and customers. They create economic value from these networks by leveraging users and customers to produce content and, importantly, data. Content creation fuels the further growth of the network. The data that these companies collect is a valuable and forward-looking asset. It enables companies to improve products and services as well as predict and modify behaviour. The market has recognised the value of these networks and data and rewards companies that build user and customer bases, even when that comes at the expense of profits. Empirical studies have shown that an increase in the size of a company's network is tied to an increase in the market value of the company. For example, empirical evidence suggests that user traffic on e-commerce platforms is a more important indicator of stock price than the platforms' earnings.[89]

Users' participation and content creation are central to the business model of digital platform businesses in particular. In platform business models, the company creates, maintains, and polices the platform, but it is the interaction between participants that creates value. Networks of users and customers are particularly valuable in the case of certain platform business models, such as social

---

[88] See Four Economists' Report (n 18) 29–31.

[89] S Rajgopal, M Venkatachalam, & S Kotha, 'The Value Relevance of Network Advantages: The Case of E-Commerce Firms' (2003) 41 *Journal of Accounting Research* 135. See also S Rajgopal, M Venkatachalam, & S Kotha, 'Managerial Actions, Stock Returns and Earnings: The Case of Business-to-Business Internet Firms' (2000) 40 *Journal of Accounting Research* 529; NfX, '70 Percent of Value in Tech is Driven by Network Effects', www.nfx.com/post/70-percent-value-network-effects/#:~:text=The%20short%20 answer%3A%20over%20the,more%20than%20a%20%241%20billion.

media, where the content provided by users is the essence of the digital platform's good or service. The entertainment content that the platform offers is produced almost entirely by users, allowing these companies to expand using a fraction of the workforce that a traditional media platform would use. Take the example of Instagram. Facebook purchased the platform for $1 billion in 2012. At the time of its sale, Instagram had 27 million users on iOS alone.[90] It had 13 employees.[91]

The scale of content created by users' free content production is tremendous and rapidly growing. In an average minute in 2021, Facebook Live received 44 million views, 5.7 Snapchat users sent 2 million messages, and 575,000 tweets were sent on Twitter.[92] In that same minute, 1.4 million 'swipes' were made on the dating platform Tinder, 167 million videos were viewed on TikTok, 5.7 million searches were performed on Google, and 6 million people shopped online.[93]

Free content production is a key driver of value creation in the digital economy. But free data production is arguably even more important to value creation, and its influence extends beyond platform businesses and the tech industry.[94] Data has been described as the most important resource for companies in the modern economy.[95] Data produced by users and customers has created enormous amounts of wealth for digital companies and their investors – wealth that is directly tied to the actions, behaviours, and relations of people.

Data is a unique and controversial asset[96] that has become central to the global economy. These unique elements are important when considering whether the value created by data should be taxed. Data is non-fungible – each piece of data is unique.[97] It is a product of our behaviour and our relationships and interactions with one another.[98] The benefits and harms of data collection and use exist on the population level.[99]

---

[90] 'Facebook Buys Instagram for $ 1 Billion, Turns Budding Rival Into Its Standalone Photo App' (*TechCrunch*, April 9, 2012) techcrunch.com/2012/04/09/facebook-to-acquire-instagram-for-1-billion/.

[91] R Kumar, 'Understanding the basics of Network Effects – the Power of the Platform' (*Medium*, 28 July 2018) medium.com/world-of-iot/understanding-the-basics-of-network-effects-the-power-of-the-platform-2cfef215fe4a.

[92] A Ali, 'From Amazon to Zoom: What Happens in an Internet Minute in 2021?' (*Visual Capitalist*, 10 Nov. 2021) www.visualcapitalist.com/from-amazon-to-zoom-what-happens-in-an-internet-minute-in-2021/.

[93] Ali (n 92).

[94] See nn 122 to 123 and accompanying text.

[95] See, eg, 'The world's most valuable resource is no longer oil, but data' (*The Economist*, 6 May 2017).

[96] Whether data should even be an 'asset' that is commodified is a contentious question that has sparked much debate. See S Viljoen, 'Data as Property?' (*Phenomenal World*, 16 Oct. 2020), www.phenomenalworld.org/analysis/data-as-property/. It is beyond the scope of this chapter to question whether data should be commodified and, if so, who should legally own and economically benefit from that commodity. The current reality is that data is being commodified and appropriated by digital companies through a combination of contractual arrangements and trade secrecy laws. Cohen (n 13) 63. The market considers data to be the property of these companies when assessing their value, see nn 112 to 123 and accompanying text. It is this current reality which guides this essay's analysis.

[97] 'Data is giving rise to a new economy: briefing' (*The Economist*, 6 May 2017).

[98] See S Zuboff, *The Age of Surveillance Capitalism* (New York, Public Affairs, 2019), 100; J Sadowski, 'When data is capital: Datafication, accumulation, and extraction' (2019) 6 *Big Data & Society* 1, 26.

[99] See S Viljoen, 'Democratic Data: A Relational Theory for Data Governance' (2021) 131 *Yale Law Journal* 573, 603–617; Cohen (n 13) 67.

As a product of our actions and social relations, users and customers create data that companies are able to collect in a myriad of ways. People create data both when they actively input content and information onto a platform or interact with others' content.[100] Likewise, people create data when they navigate an online platform (scrolling and pausing on sites, clicking through links, or movements and hovering a cursor over a link),[101] when they navigate physical spaces, and when they interact with physical objects and one another.[102]

The level of data creation is massive and exponentially growing. As of 2020, it is estimated that 1.145 trillion megabytes of data is created every day, with the average person creating 2.5 quintillion bytes daily.[103] Data production is expected to reach 0.463 zetabytes per day by 2025.[104]

Data collection has become a central component of companies' business activities in the modern economy.[105] The possession of data has led to enormous gains in wealth for companies and their investors, who realise this wealth through capital gains income. How does users' and customers' data creation translate to wealth for companies? There are various ways in which companies currently monetise data, such as the direct sale or licence of data[106] and targeted advertising.[107] But, while many companies monetise their data currently, data is largely a forward-looking asset.[108] It is considered valuable because of what it signals about a company's potential revenues, not current revenues.

Companies can seize on the predictive value of data to optimise and expand their businesses. As Erik Brynjolfsson and Andrew Mcafee explain, '[t]he data revolution has turned customers into unwitting business consults.'[109] Digital

---

[100] See World Economic Forum, Personal Data: The Emergence of a New Asset Class (2011), www.weforum.org/reports/personal-data-emergence-new-asset-class.

[101] See C Crum, 'Google Eyes Mouse Movement as Possible Search Relevancy Signal' (*WebProNews*, 13 July 2010) www.webpronews.com/google-eyes-mouse-movement-as-possible-search-relevancy-signal. See also Q Guo & E Agichtein, 'Towards Predicting web searcher gaze position from mouse movements' (Conference Paper, Proceedings of the 28th International Conference on Human Factors in Computing Systems, Chicago, 20–15 April 2010).

[102] See Sadowski (n 98) 6–7. See generally Zuboff (n 98).

[103] J Bulao, 'How Much Data is Created Every Day in 2021?' (*Techjury*, 4 January 2022) techjury.net/blog/how-much-data-is-created-every-day/#gref.

[104] J Deshardins, 'How much data is generated each day?' (*World Economic Forum*, 17 April 2019) www.weforum.org/agenda/2019/04/how-much-data-is-generated-each-day-cf4bddf29f/.

[105] See Sadowski (n 98); 'The world's most valuable resource is no longer oil, but data' (*The Economist*, May 6, 2017); 'Data is giving rise to a new economy: briefing' (*The Economist*, 6 May 2017); Viljoen (n 99) 586.

[106] eg, the market for data on people's phone locations alone is estimated at $12 billion. J Keegan & A Ng, 'There's a Multibillion-Dollar Market for Your Phone's Location Data' (*The Markup*, 30 September 2021) themarkup.org/privacy/2021/09/30/theres-a-multibillion-dollar-market-for-your-phones-location-data. As of 2020, the size of the overall data brokerage industry was estimated at $200 billion. C Tucker & N Neumann, 'Buying Consumer Data? Tread Carefully' (*Harvard Business Review*, 1 May 2020) hbr.org/2020/05/buying-consumer-data-tread-carefully.

[107] H Beales, 'The Value of Behavioral Targeting' (*Network Advertising Initiative*, 2010), 8. See also Zuboff (n 98) 74–82.

[108] Sadowski (n 98) 5–6.

[109] E Brynjolfsson & A Mcafee, 'The Big Data Boom Is the Innovation Story of Our Time' (*The Atlantic*, 21 November 2011) www.theatlantic.com/business/archive/2011/11/the-big-data-

platforms have been most notable for using user data to innovate and improve their products, creating added value for their companies.[110] Data has allowed digital companies to enter new lines of business and develop new products. For example, Alphabet launched a new business under their life sciences unit, Verily, that uses data from the company's mobile devices to provide health insurance services.[111] Data increases company value because it can improve and add to a company's operations, products, and services and, therefore, increase the company's revenues and income at some future point.

Because of its potential to drive income creation, a company's data is central to its market valuation. This is demonstrated by the disconnect between the book value of companies and their market value – a phenomenon sometimes referred to as the 'data gap'. As an intangible asset, data does not appear on a company's balance sheet – the more valuable a company's data is, the greater the disconnect between the assets on their balance sheet and their market capitalisation.[112] Meta, for example, had a market capitalisation of $950 billion[113] at the end of 2021. It only held hard assets of $166 billion,[114] but it had a user base producing an average of 4 petabytes (4 million gigabytes) of data each day.[115] As Washington Post reporter Elizabeth Dwoskin has explained: 'Facebook's greatest asset is the data it has on billions of people.'[116]

The 'data gap' can also be seen in the growing disconnect between a company's earnings and market capitalisation.[117] The Microsoft acquisition of LinkedIn

---

boom-is-the-innovation-story-of-our-time/248215/. See also MIT Techonology Review Custom & Oracle, 'The Rise of Data Capital' (2016) 2, available at files.technologyreview.com/whitepapers/ MIT_Oracle+Report-The_Rise_of_Data_Capital.pdf?_ga=2.232341599.150145066.1698268211- 116203996.1698268211.

[110] M Schrage, 'Rethinking Networks: Exploring Strategies for Making Users More Valuable' (MIT Initiative on the Digital Economy, Research Brief Vol 1, 2016).

[111] K Brown, 'Alphabet's Verily Plan to Use Big Data for Health Insurance' (*Bloomberg*, 25 Aug. 2020, www.bloomberg.com/news/articles/2020-08-25/alphabet-s-verily-plans-to-use-big-data-as-health-insurance-tool.

[112] Experts in the field have attributed the frequent gap between the market capitalisation of digital companies and traditional market valuation to the value of data. H Baldwin, 'Drilling into the Value of Data' (*Forbes*, 23 March 2015), www.forbes.com/sites/howardbaldwin/2015/03/23/drilling-into-th e-value-of-data/?sh=5092b86565fa. It is difficult to find precise estimates measures of the value of data although progress has been made by both academics and policymakers. See, eg, Kean Birch et al., 'Date as asset? The measurement, governance, and valuation of personal data by Big Tech' [Jan.-June 2021] Big Data & Society 1, 7–9; OECD (n 13) 52–56. While the increased importance of data to the value of companies is undoubtedly a key factor in the disconnect between companies' market values and book values, the importance of intangibles other than data has also contributed to this disconnect. See B Lev & F Gu, *The End of Accounting and the Path Forward for Investors and Finance* (Chichester, Wiley, 2016).

[113] Meta Platforms Market Cap 2009-2022, Macrotrends, www.macrotrends.net/stocks/charts/FB/ meta-platforms/market-cap.

[114] Meta Platforms, Inc., Form 10-K 79 (3 Feb. 2022).

[115] Bulao (n 103).

[116] E Dwoskin, 'Regulators want to break up Facebook. That's a technical nightmare, insiders say' (*The Washington Post*, 11 December 2020) www.washingtonpost.com/technology/2020/12/11/ facebook-breakup-antitrust/.

[117] V Govindarajan, S Rajgopal & A Srivastava, 'Why Financial Statements Don't Work for Digital Companies' *Harvard Business Review* (26 February 2018); Lev & Gu (n 112) 34.

displays this disconnect, as do many other transactions.[118] In 2016, Microsoft acquired LinkedIn for $26.2 billion,[119] despite the company posting losses in the two previous years.[120] In pitching the acquisition to its shareholders, Microsoft focused on the size of LinkedIn's user base and user engagement, not revenues.[121] This process of focusing on and presenting users and user engagements to investors as key company assets is a common strategy seen amongst digital companies.[122] Through their engagement, these users produce a steady stream of data that increases the value of the company. While the data economy is most often thought about in the context of tech companies, data is an increasingly important asset for businesses across all industries. Big box retailers and financial services firms, for example, both gather large quantities of data. As Andrew W. Lo of the MIT Laboratory for Financial Engineering explained: '[f]or most companies, their data is their single biggest asset.'[123]

The market is rewarding companies, both tech companies and others, for building networks of users and customers, leveraging their network participation, content creation, and data production, even in the absence of income.

ii. Growth without Income

The nature of value creation within the digitalised economy has led companies to eschew income for lengthy periods to build a large network of users and customers whose participation, content, and data creation will fuel further growth of the company. Positive network effects fuel this growth. The importance of network effects can be seen most clearly in the context of platform business models.[124] For example, the more reviews users leave on an e-commerce website, the more useful that site is for other potential users, increasing website traffic and reviews. As website traffic increases, so does the motivation for third-party vendors to

---

[118] eg, following its 2013 IPO, Twitter had a market capitalization of $24 billion. J Pepitone, '#WOW! Twitter soars 73% in IPO' (*CNN Business*, 7 November 2013), money.cnn.com/2013/11/07/technology/social/twitter-ipo-stock/. In the years leading up to its IPO, Twitter was a loss company and had assets of less than $1 billion. Twitter, Inc., Form S-1, pp. 11–12 (3 October 2013).

[119] I Lunden, 'Microsoft officially closes its $26.2B acquisition of LinkedIn' (*TechCrunch*, 8 December 2016) techcrunch.com/2016/12/08/microsoft-officially-closes-its-26-2b-acquisition-of-linkedin/.

[120] K Flynn, 'LinkedIn earnings are just fine ahead of Microsoft merger' (*Mashable*, 4 August 2016) mashable.com/article/linkedin-earnings-ahead-of-microsoft-merger.

[121] Press Release, 'Microsoft, Inc., Microsoft to acquire LinkedIn' (13 June 2016), news.microsoft.com/2016/06/13/microsoft-to-acquire-linkedin/. See also D Laney, 'Your Company's Data May Be Worth More Than Your Company' (*Forbes*, 22 July 2020) www.forbes.com/sites/douglaslaney/2020/07/22/your-companys-data-may-be-worth-more-than-your-company/?sh=35104653634c; S McBride, 'Microsoft to buy LinkedIn for $26.2 billion in its largest deal' (*Reuters*, 13 June 2016) www.reuters.com/article/us-linkedin-m-a-microsoft/microsoft-to-buy-linkedin-for-26-2-billion-in-its-largest-deal-idUSKCN0YZ1FP.

[122] See generally K Birch et al., 'Data as asset? The measurement, governance, and valuation of digital personal data by Big Tech' (2021) 8 *Big Data & Society* 1.

[123] A Lo, quoted in MIT Tech. Review Custom (n 109) 3.

[124] See generally C Shapiro & H Varian, *Information Rules: A Strategic Guide to the Network Economy* (Boston, Massachusetts, Harvard Business Review Press, 1999).

join the platform and sell products because the pool of potential consumers has increased.

When a platform is first introduced, there are few incentives for users to join the network because there are few others with whom to have value-creating interactions. Positive network effects only kick in when a critical mass of users is reached. The critical mass point occurs when the value a user obtains from a good or service equals or exceeds the price.[125] Because of this necessity of reaching a critical mass to achieve the network effects that drive growth, digital platforms often turn to a business model of providing services for free or at a loss in order to attract users.[126] Revenues and profits only come later – after achieving a large network and dominant market position.[127]

This growth-orientated approach is not limited to platform businesses. The data economy also relies on a phenomenon known as 'data network effects'.[128] The predictive value of data allows companies to improve their products and services, launch into new industries, and optimise their operations. The control of large amounts of data also brings with it significant economic power.[129] The desire to achieve these 'data network effects' and the accompanying competitive advantage and power they bring can push companies towards eschewing current profits in favour of greater volumes of data collection from their growing network of users and customers.

For this reason, any attempts to achieve fairness in international taxation that focus only on how to tax company income will be incomplete. Companies often conduct substantial business activities in countries and create substantial amounts of wealth for their shareholders through increases in their market value before they ever create income. These companies' investors can cash in on this new method of value creation by selling their appreciated shares at any time they choose. As a result, the investors' residence countries can tax this value creation in real time. But the countries in which these companies are operating do not receive tax revenues. This trend results in source countries providing the resources to support value-creating economic activities without being able to tax any of that value creation. This is a clear violation of the benefits principle, and one that can only be resolved by income tax law if the allocation of taxing authority over capital gains income is revisited.

---

[125] See J Rohls, *Bandwagon Effects in High-Technology Industries* (Cambridge, MIT Press, 2003) 20–28.

[126] See P Collin & N Colin, *Taxation of the Digital Economy* (Report to the French Minister for the Economy and Finance, the Minister for Industrial Recovery, the Minister Delegate for the Budget, and the Minister Delegate for Small and Medium-Sized Enterprises, Innovation, and the Digital Economy, Jan. 2013) 28–29.

[127] ibid. See also Govindarajan et al. (n 117).

[128] See 'Data is giving rise to a new economy: briefing' (*The Economist*, 6 May 2017); RW Gregory et al., 'The Role of Artificial Intelligence and Data Network Effects for Creating User Value' (2021) 46 *Academy of Management Review* 1, 1; A Hagiu & J Wright, 'When Data Creates Competitive Advantage' (*Harvard Business Review Magazine*, Jan-Feb 2020).

[129] K Pistor, 'Rule by data: The end of markets?' (2020) 83 *Law & Contemporary Problems* 101, 105.

B. Diversified Portfolios and Broad Shareholder Bases

While the nature of value creation in the digital economy has strengthened the economic allegiance of capital gains income to the source country, diversification of investors' portfolios and the resulting broad shareholder bases of multinational companies have weakened the economic allegiance of capital gains income to the residence country. In an environment of diversified portfolios, index investing, fractional share ownership, and the resulting broad shareholder bases of multinational companies, the 1920s Compromise drafters' assumption that investors have a significant influence over the success or failure of a company no longer holds true. Technological advances beyond the imagination of the original designers of the international tax system and the digitalisation of global finance have enabled this new economic environment.

Broad shareholder bases have been driven, at least in part, by the emergence of mutual funds and ETFs. The first mutual fund in the United States was opened to investors in 1928, but by the mid-1950s there were only approximately 100 mutual funds.[130] In the following decades, mutual funds grew (with ebbs and flows) and by 1990 mutual fund assets were over $1 trillion.[131] Three years later, in 1993, the first ETF was introduced.[132]

As of 2020, approximately a third of the US stock market was held by mutual funds, or ETFs.[133] In 2019, passive index funds overtook funds that are actively managed.[134] This accompanies the general trend of institutional investment on behalf of underlying owners – about 70–80 per cent of US equities are owned through asset management companies.[135] These ownership patterns allow individual shareholders to hold very small stakes in thousands of companies and remain disconnected from their governance and management.

Advances in information and communications technology were necessary for the proliferation of these financial products, diversified investing, and broad share ownership of multinational companies. Access to the internet, electronic trading, computerised systems of settlement, and countless other advances allowed for the broad proliferation of financial products like ETFs that allow investors to easily diversify their portfolios and own these small stakes in thousands of companies.[136] This new economic reality calls for a re-evaluation of the

---

[130] Bianco Research, 'A Brief History of Equity Mutual Funds' (Aug. 20, 2018) www.biancoresearch.com/a-brief-history-of-equity-mutual-funds-2/.

[131] ICI, 2021 Investment Company Facebook (2021), 306.

[132] ibid.

[133] ibid 49–50.

[134] D Lim, 'Index Funds Are the New Kings of Wall Street' (*Wall Street Journal*, 18 September 2019), www.wsj.com/articles/index-funds-are-the-new-kings-of-wall-street-11568799004.

[135] J Azar et al., 'Anticompetitive Effects of Common Ownership' (Michigan Ross School of Business Working Paper 1235, 2015) 3.

[136] See A Marszk et al., 'Information and Communication Technologies for Financial Innovations' in Marszk et al. (eds), *The Emergence of ETFs in Asia-Pacific* (Cham, Springer, 2019) 53; K Kolchin, 'Electronic Trading Market Structure Primer' (Oct. 2019), www.sifma.org/wp-content/uploads/2019/10/SIFMA-Insights-Electronic-Trading-Market-Structure-Primer.pdf.

appropriate allocation of taxing authority over the capital gains income stemming from these diversified portfolios.

C. Re-evaluating the Economic Allegiance of Capital Gains

Which country should be allowed to tax items of cross-border origin has been driven by the relative economic allegiance of that income.[137] And the concept of relative economic allegiance has flowed from the benefits principle. Capital gains income stems from an increase in company market value. In determining which country should be allowed to tax this income, the crucial question is: what is the economic allegiance of the value creation that manifests as growth in company value? In the 1920s, it was determined that the economic allegiance of capital gains income was closest to the investor's residence country. The residence country has, therefore, been allocated taxing authority over capital gains income under our current international sourcing rules. A notable exception to this is capital gains income from the sale of a company that derives more than 50 per cent of its value from immoveable property, such as land.[138] In this case, the source country, the country where the property is located, is allowed to tax this capital gains income.

The economic transformations of the past decades warrant re-evaluating the appropriate allocation of taxing authority over capital gains income. The nature of value creation in the digitalised economy has a particularly close link to the source country, in the same way as value creation stems from property like land, indicating that the allocation of taxing authority over capital gains income to the source country should be expanded to become the dominant model, rather than the exception.

The nature of value creation in the digital economy involves networks of users and customers that drive company growth through their participation in the networks, free production of content, and, crucially, free data production. The economic allegiance of this means of value creation tips in favour of source countries.

These networks are made up of members of a country's population, and this population can be viewed as a type of resource of the country, in the same way as resources like land and oil. In the Four Economists' Report, income that came from agricultural as well as mining and oil extraction was considered to have a particularly close economic allegiance to the source country because the business's economic success relied on the resources of that country.[139] These users and customers also provide free labour to the company through their participation in networks and their creation of data and content. Reliance on local labour was also

---

[137] See Part I.C.
[138] OECD (n 11) Art 13, para 4.
[139] Four Economists' Report (n 18) 28–31.

considered a strong factor in favour of economic allegiance because income is tied to the source country in the Four Economists' Report.[140]

Data collection is also a key driver of value creation within the digital economy. To which existing economic activity data collection is most comparable has been a topic of intense debate. However, each comparison points towards a strong economic allegiance to the source countries.

Many consider data to share characteristics with agricultural yields or with natural resources. Julie Cohen likens the process of 'harvesting' personal data to harvesting within industrial agriculture.[141] Shoshana Zuboff describes informational capitalism as reducing people to 'human natural resources',[142] and the language of 'extraction' has been used when describing data collection.[143] This characterisation of data as akin to a natural resource that companies extract and collect – a 'new oil' – is pervasive in political, popular, and academic discussions of the digital economy.[144] Income stemming from agriculture and natural resource extraction was considered to have a closer economic connection to the source country than the residence country. If data is most comparable to these economic activities, the source country has a strong claim to value creation stemming from it.

This view of data as similar to a natural resource has been rejected by many scholars as inaccurate and ignoring the active role of people in creating data. As Jathan Sadowski explains, 'Data mining is a misleading name; a more apt term would be data manufacturing.'[145] Some of these scholars have suggested that data should instead be viewed as a form of capital.[146] One group of scholars, including Jaron Lanier, Eric Posner, and Glen Weyl, has gone further in recognising the role of humans in producing data, arguing that data should be viewed primarily as a product of the data subject's labour.[147]

Viewing data and data production in this way also results in a close economic allegiance between capital gains income and source countries. The Four Economists' Report found income from industrial businesses to have a strong economic connection to the source country.[148] One reason for this was the reliance on local labour to create income from industrial activities.[149] When the

---

[140] Four Economists' Report (n 18) 28–31.

[141] Cohen (n 13) 66.

[142] Zuboff (n 98) 100.

[143] See Sadowski (n 98) 1–2.

[144] See A Kapczynski, 'The Law of Informational Capitalism' (2020) 129 *Yale Law Journal* 1460, 1498; Sadowski (n 98) 2; see, eg, 'The world's most valuable resource is no longer oil, but data' (*The Economist*, 6 May 2017); 'Data is giving rise to a new economy' (*The Economist*, 6 May 2017).

[145] Sadowski (n 98) 2 (citation omitted). See also Kapczynski (n 144) 1498–99.

[146] See, eg, Sadowski (n 98) 7; MIT Tech. Review Custom (n 109) 2; Kapczynski (n 144) 1499.

[147] E Posner & EG Weyl, 'Data as Labor' in *Radical Markets: Uprooting Capitalism and Democracy for a Just Society* (Princeton, NJ, Princeton University Press, 2018); IA Ibarra et al., 'Should We Treat Data as Labor?' (2017) 108 *American Economics Association Papers & Proceedings* 38; J Lanier, *Who Owns the Future?* (New York, Simon & Schuster, 2014).

[148] Four Economists' Report (n 18) 30–31.

[149] ibid 30–21.

human role in creating data is acknowledged, and the process of data production and collection is viewed as a process similar to manufacturing, the importance of local production comes to the forefront. And this is even stronger when data is viewed as a product of the data subject's labour. The non-fungible nature of data also strengthens the importance of local production in this value creation. Personal data of users and customers can only be created by the unique activities and characteristics of those specific users and customers themselves – the company cannot create the data itself, nor could the same data be created by people in other locations.

Embedded within economic allegiance is the benefits principle. Digital business models go beyond simply relying on government benefits to facilitate their business activities. The population of the country is also providing benefits by virtue of participating in the network, engaging in value-creating interactions, and producing for free valuable data and content. This free provision by citizens of benefits, in a dynamic that many have argued is exploitative,[150] makes allowing their home countries (ie the source countries) to tax the capital gains income linked to this value creation even more important. Granting taxing authority to source countries directly compensates the government for benefits and can indirectly compensate citizens through lower tax rates or increased government services. This reallocation realigns taxation of capital gains with the goals of the benefits principle while also alleviating some of the exploitative outcomes seen in the digital economy.

Furthermore, the phenomenon in the digital economy of companies foregoing short- and medium-term income in favour of company growth also makes allocating taxing authority over capital gains income to source countries essential to satisfy the benefits principle and maintain fairness within international taxation. Source countries are typically able to tax a company's business income. The original designers of the international tax system assumed that a company growing in value would also have current income, so the benefits principle would be satisfied even if the source country was unable to tax capital gains income.[151] This assumption no longer holds, and, as a result, the only way that source countries will be compensated for the benefits provided by the government and the people themselves is if they are able to tax capital gains income.

IV. Conclusion and Paths Forward

The current model for taxing capital gains income must be revised to maintain a coherent and equitable international tax system in line with its driving norms.

---

[150] See generally E Posner & EG Weyl, 'Data as Labor' in *Radical Markets: Uprooting Capitalism and Democracy for a Just Society* (Princeton, NJ, Princeton University Press, 2018); N Couldry & U A. Mejias, *The Costs of Connection* (Stanford, California, Stanford University Press, 2019); Zuboff (n 18).

[151] See nn 66–67 and accompanying text.

Our modern economic environment departs greatly from that envisioned by the original designers of the international tax system. The nature of value creation in the digital economy relies extensively on benefits provided by source countries and their populations and often results in significant growth in company value within accompanying company income. This has shifted the economic allegiance of capital gains towards source countries. Diversified portfolios and broad shareholder bases of multinational companies have limited the influence of investors on company success, shifting the economic allegiance of capital gains income away from residence countries. In this environment, the current allocation of taxing authority over capital gains income exclusively to the residence country is no longer congruent with the benefits principle and accompanying concept of allocating taxing authority based on economic allegiance. The time has come for the international tax system to recognise the shift in the economic allegiance of capital gains and grant taxing authority over this income to source countries.

The aim of this chapter is to put forward a normative case for reallocating taxing authority to source countries, not to prescribe specific policies. However, there are feasible approaches to implementing this reallocation. One approach is a centralised global pooling of capital gains tax revenues from investors and subsequent redistribution based on a formula that serves as a proxy for relative corporate value creation in each country. Those proxies could include gross domestic product (GDP), consumer market size, or the volume of data extracted from each country.[152] The pooling and redistribution could be handled by a newly-created international administrative agency, which could be housed within an existing intergovernmental organisation, such as the United Nations.[153]

A second approach is an annual mark-to-market tax paid by the company on any increase in a company's market value, with taxing authority distributed amongst source countries based on a formula. The formula could be based on a company's relative revenues, the number of users or customers, or the amount of data extracted from each country. All publicly-traded companies, regardless of industry,[154] would pay the MTM tax to source countries. The rate of the MTM tax could be low, such as two to four per cent, to avoid overly heavy tax obligations for companies.[155] The tax could be non-refundable, but the company could be able to

---

[152] Alternately, the formula could be based solely on population, which would have significant redistributive implications. However, this approach raises important normative questions that are beyond the scope of this chapter.

[153] The need for an international tax agency in the face of the digital economy has been identified by other scholars. See, eg, CO Lucas-Mas & RF Junquera-Varela, *Tax Theory Applied to the Digital Economy* (Washington DC, World Bank Group Publications, 2021) 85–89; H Ordower, 'Uniform International Tax Collection and Distribution for Global Development, a Utopian BEPS Alternative' (2021) 12 *Columbia Journal of Tax Law* 126.

[154] For rationales for applying the tax to all companies, rather than 'ring-fencing' the digital economy, see nn 117–123 and accompanying text.

[155] The example provided below demonstrates the approximate increase in overall company tax liability that would occur as a result of the tax. Similar to the global minimum tax put forward by the OECD Pillar Two Blueprint, see OECD Pillar Two Blueprint (n 74), multilateral consensus on the rate of the MTM tax would be desirable.

carry forward losses for years in which its market capitalisation declined and offset taxes in subsequent years on a country-by-country basis.

The tax would not replace domestic taxation of capital gains income on the investor level. Because paying the MTM tax would reduce company assets and, in turn, market value, the MTM tax would function as a surrogate tax, indirectly taxing investors by decreasing the ultimate capital gains income they receive. The tax, therefore, partially reallocates taxing authority over income from corporate growth from residence countries to source countries.

These approaches are just two of many that could be employed to reallocate taxing authority over capital gains income to source countries. Further research will be essential to effectively implement this reallocation and realign international tax law with its underlying principles.

5

Destination-based Taxation, Incentive Compatibility and International Justice

LAURENS VAN APELDOORN

Several destination-based tax proposals have garnered attention in recent years. Companies are currently taxed predominantly in 'origin' countries, countries where mobile economic factors such as management, production, and intellectual property are located. This incentivises businesses to relocate economic factors for tax reasons, and, in turn, gives rise to tax competition between countries, which may be 'harmful'.[1] Since the corrosive effects of tax competition appear hard to tackle, even as several significant global initiatives – including the OECD's Pillar I and II of the BEPS project – are gaining momentum, the alternative of taxing in 'destination' countries, countries where the generally immobile consumer is located, is therefore increasingly seen as a promising reform strategy. In this chapter I specifically focus on *Taxing Profit in a Global Economy* (2021) by Devereux et al. as the most thorough defence of this approach available today. Not only do the authors present detailed outlines of two such proposals – 'Residual Profit Allocation by Income' (RPAI) and 'Destination-Based Cash Flow Tax' (DBCFT) – but they also support these proposals with arguments that seek to start from 'first principles', thus making them ideal interlocutors when considering questions of justice in relation to international taxation in general, and in relation to destination-based taxation in particular.

My aim in this chapter is twofold. By way of critical discussion of the arguments by Devereux et al. for destination-based taxation, I first wish to clarify how one ought to assess international tax reform proposals, in particular towards destination-based taxation, from the perspective of justice. I will argue for what I call the 'instrumentalist approach', exemplified in the work of Liam Murphy and

---

[1] OECD, *Harmful Tax Competition: an Emerging Global Issue* (Paris, OECD, 1998).

Thomas Nagel and going back to John Rawls, which treats taxes and tax systems as fundamentally instrumental to the realisation of justice. A tax or tax system may have many desirable characteristics but its all-things-considered defensibleness, as judged in the context of other socio-economic institutions, is dependent on it securing justice. I will demonstrate the implications of this approach by focussing specifically on Devereux et al.'s use of 'incentive compatibility' as a novel criterion to assess the attractiveness of international tax reform proposals. As the criterion is already being taken up elsewhere in the literature,[2] a significant part of this chapter will be devoted to clarifying the precise nature of that criterion. Second, I will argue that, on the one hand, Devereux et al. can develop a more powerful defence of destination-based taxation by explicating their tacit commitment to fiscal self-determination, a commitment that is compatible with a Rawlsian conception of international justice, while on the other hand, Devereux et al.'s emphasis on securing incentive compatibility risks ignoring distributive issues related to international cooperation that also have an important role in the Rawlsian conception.

In section I, I start by outlining the instrumentalist approach in opposition to Adam Smith's analysis in *The Wealth of Nations* (1776) which formed the inspiration for Devereux et al.'s selection of first principles. The instrumentalist approach takes justice as the only all-things-considered criterium for a good tax or tax system, rather than as one of possibly many 'canons' or 'maxims' of taxation. In section I, I give a brief outline of Rawls's theory of international justice, with the aim of fixing the analysis of destination-based tax proposals that follows. Rawls famously argued that justice requires that international institutions should protect the political autonomy of states, which in the present context can be further specified in terms of fiscal self-determination, and should equitably distribute the benefits of economic cooperation between states. This is what international tax reform should (help) accomplish with the instrumentalist approach to tax justice. In section II, I discuss Devereux et al.'s diagnosis of the problem at the heart of the international tax system today. The authors suggest that reform is necessary, in large part, because the current international tax system is incentive incompatible. I clarify the nature of the international tax system, suggesting that the authors are mistaken to suggest that (acts of) tax competition 'undermine' it, and proposing that incentive compatibility can be better understood in terms of a mismatch between individual incentives and the collectively optimal outcome that cooperative institutions seek to achieve. In sections III and IV I discuss Devereux et al.'s proposals for a universal move to destination-based taxation, focussing specifically on the role that incentive compatibility plays in those proposals. I argue that the criterion of incentive compatibility can at least partly be reduced to the criterion of justice, since by ensuring incentive compatibility, one secures the ends for which the international

---

[2] eg, EW Bond and T Gresik, 'On the incentive compatibility of universal adoption of destination-based cash flow taxation' (2023) 30 *International Tax and Public Finance* 1572.

tax system was established, which importantly includes the protection of fiscal self-determination. I therefore conclude that incentive compatibility can only play a role as a feasibility constraint on what justice requires, in so far as it rules out as infeasible certain institutional arrangements that would otherwise be preferable over feasible alternatives. Apart from that, it either is reducible to the criterion of justice or it is irrelevant to the instrumentalist approach that takes justice as the only all-things-considered criterium for a good tax or tax system.

I. Justice Among the 'Canons of Taxation'

Taking their lead from Adam Smith, Devereux et al. identify five criteria for a good tax.[3] Four of these – economic efficiency, fairness, robustness to avoidance, and ease of administration – are well-known, while the fifth – incentive compatibility – is novel but, the authors emphasise, nevertheless 'critical in an international context'.[4] Smith is certainly a natural place to start when considering the criteria for a good tax. In *The Wealth of Nations* Smith accepted the necessity and importance of taxation and introduced four 'canons of taxation'[5] that have become classic topoi in the study of taxes and tax systems. He argued against the Lockean worry that taxation, especially if it is without consent, is an infringement of citizens' property and turns them from free citizens into bondsmen or slaves. In fact, Smith observed, since revenue is a prerequisite for the government's ability to protect individual property and liberty, being taxed is an indication, 'not of slavery but of liberty', as it shows that 'as he has some property, he cannot himself be the property of a master'.[6] While Smith was hence convinced of the importance and necessity of taxation, he did worry about badly designed taxes. To evaluate different forms of taxation, he introduced four widely accepted 'maxims' or principles.[7] First, he argued, citizens should contribute to the financing of government in a manner that is proportionate to 'the revenue which they respectively enjoy under the protection of the state'.[8] Often described as a principle of equity or fairness, it reveals a commitment to non-discrimination and, proportional taxation.[9] Second, the tax must be 'certain, and not arbitrary':[10]

---

[3] MP Devereux, AJ Auerbach, M Keen, P Oosterhuis, W Schön and J Vella, *Taxing Profit in a Global Economy* (Oxford, OUP, 2021) 4, 33.

[4] ibid 15, 33.

[5] S Weston, *Principles of Justice in taxation* (New York, Columbia University Press, 1903) 178.

[6] A Smith, *An inquiry into the nature and causes of the Wealth of Nations* (Oxford, Clarendon Press, 1979) 857. See S Fleischacker, *On Adam Smith's Wealth of Nations* (Princeton, Princeton University Press, 2004) 195.

[7] ibid 827.

[8] ibid 825.

[9] I McLean, 'The Politics of Land Value Taxation' in M O'Neill and S Orr (eds), *Taxation: Philosophical Perspectives* (Oxford, OUP, 2018) 187, argues that Smith is committed to progressive taxation.

[10] Smith (n 6) 825.

it must be predictable and transparent to taxpayers as well as third parties about how the tax is levied and what the required contribution will be. Third, taxes must be levied in a manner that is most convenient to the taxpayer.[11] And finally, taxes must be efficient, that is to say, they must be designed to maximise revenue relative to the financial and other burdens they place on citizens. Not only was Smith concerned with the public costs of revenue collection and the compliance costs for individuals and companies, he was also mindful of harmful incentives that could lead to declining productivity and the detrimental economic effects of fines imposed for tax evasion.[12] Smith used these principles – fairness, certainty, convenience, and efficiency, in short – to evaluate and recommend, among others, taxes on land and inheritances.[13]

One question that comes to mind when following Smith today in employing a catalogue of canons or maxims to assess taxes, is how they should fit together to form a coherent whole, in particular in relation to justice. As Samuel Fleischacker observes, Smith did not invoke any general principles of justice but 'argued against policies and institutions primarily by showing their "inconvenience" or by invoking moral notions that he knew to be already widely accepted among his readers'.[14] The concept of distributive justice as it is understood today was unfamiliar to Smith.[15] And Smith did not clearly distinguish between convenience and justice. While his first maxim is unlikely to amount to a full account of what justice requires in taxation, he praises all four principles (and not only the first) for their 'evident justice and utility'.[16]

Today, it is widely, though not universally, held that justice is, in the words of John Rawls in *A theory of justice* (1971), the 'first virtue' of social institutions.[17] In the design of social institutions, justice must take priority over all other concerns one might have. Laws and institutions may have many commendable features, but 'no matter how efficient or well-arranged' they are, they 'must be reformed or abolished if they are unjust'.[18] This general point – which Rawls himself admitted was 'expressed too strongly'[19] – was not so much intended to say anything substantive about what justice requires but rather to help establish what justice is about.

---

[11] ibid 826.

[12] ibid 826.

[13] D Boucoyannis, 'The Equalizing Hand: Why Adam Smith Thought the Market Should Produce Wealth without Steep Inequality' (2013) 4 *Perspectives on politics* 1051, 1061.

[14] Fleischacker (n 6) 173.

[15] S Fleischacker, *A Short History of Distributive Justice* (Cambridge, Harvard University Press, 2004) 27–28.

[16] Smith (n 6) 827.

[17] J Rawls, *A Theory of Justice* (revised edition) (Cambridge, Harvard University Press, 1999) 3. See for debate, eg, GA Cohen, *Rescuing Justice and Equality* (Cambridge, Harvard University Press, 2008) 302–315; R Goodin, 'Why Social Justice is Not All that Matters: Justice as the First Virtue' (2007) 3 *Ethics* 413.

[18] Rawls (n 17) 3.

[19] ibid 4.

It focused attention on justice as a property of institutions (rather than as a property of individual action or individual moral character) and it expressed a view about the relationship between justice and other (normative) properties of institutions. It suggested that a judgement about the justice of an institution is an all-things-considered judgement about the rules that regulate the institution, a judgement about the acceptability of its continued existence that integrates all relevant moral as well as practical considerations.

What the relevant moral and practical considerations are is, of course, dependent on what justice requires. In the domestic context, Rawls was concerned with how social primary goods such as wealth, opportunities, and fundamental rights are distributed among individuals by the major political and social institutions in society. He thought that socio-economic inequalities can be just, but only if they are attached to positions that individuals have a fair and equal opportunity to occupy, and these inequalities are to the greatest benefit of the least-advantaged members of society. By identifying this as a principle of justice, Rawls was suggesting that this principle expressed an all things considered judgement about the values at play in the distribution of socio-economic goods (such as the importance of preventing arbitrary facts about individuals – their race or social class – from determining their ability to occupy advantageous and/or meaningful positions in society, or the value of pareto improvements that make everybody better off even if this leads to socio-economic inequalities) as well as about the feasibility of its actual implementation (for instance, on the basis of factual judgements about the operation and effects of labour markets). If the principle did not integrate all these relevant moral and practical considerations, the all-things-considered conclusion might be that there is reason to reform the institution even though it is fully just (for instance, because one's conception of justice has not fully accounted for an important moral value), or that there is no reason for such reform even though justice has not been fully realised (for instance, because it requires something that is in fact impossible to achieve). One may disagree with Rawls on the substance of his conception of justice – one may disagree about the selection of social primary goods as the metric of justice and reject his principles – while nevertheless accepting that justice is the first virtue of social institutions and, hence, that a theory of justice gives us an all-things-considered account of rules that should govern the major political and social institutions in society.

In *The Myth of Ownership* (2002), Liam Murphy and Thomas Nagel trace the implications of this approach to justice for the assessment of taxes and tax systems. Their work is best known, unsurprisingly given the title, for its emphasis on the conventional nature of individual property. They argue, in a manner reminiscent of Adam Smith's observations about taxation as a sign of civil freedom, that individual property is the result of a set of institutions that necessarily includes taxation. It is therefore logically incoherent to object to taxation solely for the reason that it violates individual property rights. One cannot have an absolute entitlement to pre-tax property holdings, because without taxation there would be no property in the first place.[20] It also means, according to Murphy and Nagel, that the justice of taxation cannot be assessed against a baseline of pre-tax allocations of property, since these pre-tax allocations are ultimately morally arbitrary. Rather, we must 'evaluate the legitimacy of after-tax income by reference to the legitimacy of the political and economic system that generates it, including the taxes which are an essential part of that system'.[21] On this point they part company with Smith. Smith indicated in his first maxim that the fairness of a tax is, at least in part, determined by the proportionality of the tax in relation to the person's (pre-tax) property or income. Murphy and Nagel, in contrast, think that such assessments, which reference a morally arbitrary base-line, can never give an adequate picture of what justice requires in matters of taxation.

Underlying these arguments is the Rawlsian approach to justice as the first virtue of social institutions. What matters ultimately is that the major political and social institutions secure justice. This means, on the one hand, that other criteria one might think relevant for the design of a good tax system, such as ease of administration, or convenience to the taxpayer, are secondary to the realisation of justice. As Murphy and Nagel put it, '[a]nyone who advocates the tax policy that is, simply, "best for economic growth" or "most efficient" must provide not only an explanation of why the favored policy has those virtues, but also an argument of political morality that justifies the pursuit of growth or efficiency regardless of other social values.'[22] A full account of what outcomes should be pursued by the tax system, given the various social values at play, is an account of distributive justice.[23] On the other hand, the tax system forms a part, and possibly a relatively small part, of the institutional structure that gives rise to a particular distribution of the benefits and burdens in society. A particular tax must therefore be assessed in terms of how it contributes to a just distribution. Often debated features of taxes – such as the choice of tax base, the progressivity of the tax rate, or the incidence of the tax burden – according to Murphy and Nagel only have 'instrumental significance'.[24] What matters is 'whether a given change in the tax law will increase or reduce inequality, the level of welfare of the worst off, equality of opportunity, and so on', since those effects help determine whether distributive justice is realised. Any particular characteristic of the tax is 'important only insofar as it helps us advance that aim'.[25] That being said, distributive outcomes are characteristically under-determined by individual taxes and even by the tax system as a whole. Distributive outcomes are, for instance, often as dependent on

---

[20] L Murphy and T Nagel, *The Myth of Ownership* (Oxford, OUP, 2002) 32.

[21] ibid 33.

[22] ibid 12.

[23] ibid 38, 131: 'The real issue of political morality is the extent to which social outcomes are just.'

[24] ibid 98.

[25] ibid 131.

decisions concerning government spending as they are on the taxes that make such spending possible. This means that 'what counts as justice in taxation' cannot be determined 'without considering how government allocates its resources'.[26] I will from now on call this the 'instrumentalist' approach to justice in taxation, this in contradistinction, for instance, to Smith's 'canons of taxation'. The upshot of the instrumentalist approach is that justice is both the most important normative standard in the evaluation of taxes, having precedence over all criteria, and it will often deliver results of limited practical significance, especially if a tax is considered in isolation of other major socio-economic institutions, since justice ultimately concerns the overall distribution of benefits in society.

II. International Justice

It is noteworthy that Devereux et al. say many things about justice in the domestic context that cohere with the instrumentalist approach. They note that fairness in the domestic context likely requires 'the overall tax and benefit system' to be progressive in some form.[27] This is a substantive point about what justice requires, but it also appears to express Murphy and Nagel's suggestion that a particular tax should be assessed in light of the overall distribution of benefits it helps establish in a society. When assessing the fairness of business taxation, Devereux et al. argue that we should focus on the effective incidence of the tax on individuals. Rather than demanding that a business pay its 'fair share' of taxes, for instance, we should consider the contribution of business taxation to a fair distribution of the benefits in society.[28] It also means that the unfairness, if any, of large multinationals having a competitive advantage over local businesses when having access to advanced tax planning techniques to reduce their tax burden, must 'really depend on a comparison of the individuals who are made worse off by the taxes'.[29] And it means that it is of little use to assess the incidence of taxes in isolation of government spending, or to object on fairness grounds that a particular tax has a regressive incidence, since what matters is that the 'overall fiscal system', and not 'each individual tax within the system' is progressive.[30] These are all points consistent with the instrumentalist approach.

In the international context, however, Devereux et al. are less clearly wedded to this approach. They suggest that fairness concerning business taxation in that context amounts to the question 'which country should have rights to the revenue

---

[26] ibid 14.
[27] Devereux et al. (n 3) 35–36, with progressivity here meaning roughly that the wealthier the individual, the higher the tax burden on that individual.
[28] Devereux et al. (n 3) 35–36.
[29] ibid 40.
[30] ibid 37.

from taxing the profit of a multi-national business',[31] suggesting that what ultimately matters, in relations between states, in this respect is the distribution of tax rights between countries. However, as I will elaborate in sections IV and V below, this only concerns one aspect of the global institutional structure of which justice may be a property. If one takes an instrumentalist approach to international tax justice, one must be concerned with how the common framework that regulates national tax systems among other international institutions, contributes to justice. What justice requires at the international level may, of course, be different from what justice requires at the domestic level. To many authors, including Rawls, justice as a property of international institutions is not primarily concerned with how these institutions affect the distribution of basic goods between individuals, but rather with how they affect states. In *The Law of Peoples* (1999), Rawls argued that justice at the international level applies to (or requires)[32] an institutional framework – primarily consisting of public international law – that protects and enhances states' independence and territorial integrity. His primary concern was with the 'political autonomy' of states, by which he meant the ability to independently develop and maintain (minimally) just domestic institutions, plausibly requiring both being protected from interference by other states and being afforded a certain amount of effective control in securing national policy objectives. One may think of the establishment of an effective legal system necessary for the realisation of individual rights and of certain arrangements in the realm of health care, social security, and the domestic (re)distribution of wealth. Additionally, he accepted that when states engage in international cooperation, by facilitating international trade, for instance, the benefits should be fairly distributed between them. While he did not further develop this part of his theory, he admitted that a full theory of international justice must include an account of 'standards of fairness for trade and other cooperative institutions'.[33] The impact of international institutions on individuals as members of those states is a derivate and incidental concern, in part because the effect of global institutions on particular individuals, is mediated by, and to a large extent determined by, domestic policy and law. Hence, while Rawls thought that justice in the domestic context concerns the distribution of social primary goods such as wealth and opportunities between individuals, he denied that this also holds internationally. Global inequalities of wealth or opportunities between individuals may be unjust, but only because they are the result of global institutions that fail to adequately protect the political autonomy of states, or of international institutions that regulate international cooperation in a way that does not fairly distribute the benefits of cooperation between states.

---

[31] ibid 38.

[32] See for a discussion of this equivocation, A Abizadeh, 'Cooperation, Pervasive Impact, and Coercion: On the Scope (not Site) of Distributive Justice' (2007) 4 *Philosophy & Public Affairs* 35, 318–358.

[33] J Rawls, *The Law of Peoples* (Cambridge MA: Harvard University Press, 1999) 38, also 42–3, 115.

Rawls's treatment of international justice has been subject to intense scrutiny and critique.[34] My reasons for nevertheless taking it as my point of departure in the proceeding discussion are threefold. First, the current international tax system displays features that cohere with the Rawlsian conception of international justice, the full implementation of which therefore appears feasible, or at least more feasible than some other more radical approaches. Second, Devereux et al. appear to implicitly accept features of the Rawlsian conception – in particular the emphasis on the importance of political autonomy – but they do not, or so I will argue, fully develop the implications in their criteria for the assessment of the international tax system. Their analysis can therefore profitably be elucidated in light of that approach. Finally, my objective in this chapter is not primarily to establish what justice requires in international taxation, but to gain clarity on how to approach this question in the first place, in particular when it comes to the incorporation of additional normative standards such as incentive compatibility. In that respect, the instrumentalist approach to justice in international taxation asks: to what extend do the international institutions that regulate taxation contribute to the realisation of justice, that is to say, a world where states are politically autonomous and the benefits of their cooperation are equitably shared? While other considerations – such as incentive compatibility – may be relevant in fleshing out an answer to that question, they must ultimately be instrumental to the realisation of justice. What this instrumentalist approach means for Devereux et al.'s defence of destination-based taxation is the topic of rest of the chapter.

III. The International Tax System and Tax Competition

One significant concern expressed throughout Devereux et al.'s work, fundamentally motivating the policy reforms they propose, is the concern that tax competition 'undermines' the international tax regime. In this section, I will argue that, based on a plausible understanding of the relevant terms, this concern is misguided. Certainly, tax competition may well lead to the disintegration of the international tax system as we know it today, but individual acts of tax competition must be understood as generally permitted by, and in conformity with the international tax system, rather than undermining it. The authors fail to clearly register this because they fail to note the extent to which the international tax regime today is designed (even if unsuccessfully) to protect it, and they do not explicate their latent concern for the political autonomy of states as a concern of international justice.

---

[34] For an early critique see Allen Buchanan, 'Rawls's Law of Peoples: Rules for a Vanished Westphalian World' (2000) 4 *Ethics* 110, 697–721.

I start by clarifying what Devereux et al. mean by the international tax system or international tax regime.[35] Two possible definitions are indicated in the text. First, the authors suggest that the international tax system consists of the combined national tax systems, to the extent that these national systems are concerned with the taxation of individuals and companies in an international setting. A complete description of the international tax system would then include the tax codes of all countries as well as all applicable bilateral and multilateral treaties. They write, for instance, that the international tax regime 'is made up of individual countries' domestic laws and an extensive network of DTCs [bilateral double tax conventions]',[36] noting that 'underlying the existing regime' (not coinciding with it), are certain shared concepts, principles and practices, that one might describe as a 'common framework'.[37] This framework concerns general features that all or most national tax systems share, such as a commitment to separate accounting, whereby the subsidiaries within a multinational corporation are treated as if they are separate entities, and the practice of taxing active income (income generated through participation in business activity) primarily in the country of 'source' and passive income (income generated without participation in business activity) primarily in the country of 'residence'.[38]

The difficulty with this first definition of the term 'international tax system' is that it appears impossible for countries to ever 'undermine' it in any meaningful way. A central concern of the authors is that incentive incompatibility threatens to 'undermine the international tax system'.[39] However, since the international tax system in this first definition includes all relevant national law, whatever it may be, any changes in the tax law of individual countries imply a change in the international tax regime but not a subversion or a breakdown of it, since by definition it consists of the combined national legal systems in force at any one time.[40]

Hence, when the authors speak of incentive incompatibility as a threat to the international tax system, it is likely that they mean to refer to the common framework of concepts, rules, and principles (perhaps together with shared or common goals or purposes), that underlies, or is embedded in the national tax systems and applicable treaties. The idea must be that an international tax system exists because the combined national tax laws of countries express a certain degree of coherence and are aligned with certain rules or principles – such as

---

[35] The authors use these terms interchangeably and I will follow them in doing so.

[36] Devereux et al. (n 3) 87.

[37] ibid 87, 89, 92.

[38] ibid 92. 'Source' and 'residence' are concepts in national law, where the source country is the country where the income is deemed to have arisen and the residence country is the country where the income earner is deemed to be resident for tax purposes.

[39] Devereux et al. (n 3) 125, 130, also speak of a threat to the 'viability of the existing system'.

[40] It is true that any changes may have detrimental effects – the authors note the importance of legal stability for promoting international investment – but that concern would be better captured by speaking of undermining international investment, rather than speaking of undermining the international tax system.

those just mentioned – because there is some level of international consensus on (national) policy objectives that can be achieved through international coordination or cooperation. This is how the term is often used elsewhere in the literature. Avi-Yonah, for instance, observes a 'remarkable degree of convergence' in domestic tax law and the tax treaty network and establishes on that basis the existence of an international tax regime in the form of 'generally accepted principles of international taxation'.[41] He also argues for the further, possibly more controversial claim that these principles are part of customary international law.[42] But one can accept the existence of a 'system' consisting of common agreed principles without accepting that these principles rise to the level of customary international law.

This second definition of the term 'international tax system' as a common framework of shared concepts, principles, and practices is implied when the authors speak of certain changes in the national tax system as having the tendency to undermine the 'international consensus'.[43] Incentive incompatibility threatens the international tax system if and when countries are led to implement tax laws that deviate from the common framework consisting of established common concepts, principles, and practices that underly the various national tax systems.[44] The authors appear to express this thought in different ways: incentive incompatibility concerns situations where countries have incentives to undermine an 'international consensus', to fail to 'cooperate', or to undermine or diverge from a 'common system' or from 'the norms established by a group of agents'.[45] These different phrases can be thought to express the same general idea, namely, that incentive incompatibility concerns a situation where individual countries have incentives to deviate from common, agreed upon principles, rules, or standards. In the context of international taxation, the authors' concern is that incentive incompatibility plagues the international tax system, consisting of a framework of such common principles, rules, or standards, because the strategic environment this common framework fosters simultaneously incentivises countries to diverge from it. Such unilateral policies are unappealing because they may lead to uncertainty and distortions in the efficient worldwide allocation of capital. As they put it elsewhere, 'competition continues to put downward pressure on effective tax rates, thus threatening the system's viability in the long run'.[46] The long-term viability

---

[41] RS Avi-Yonah *International Tax as International Law* (Cambridge, CUP, 2007) 1, 4.

[42] ibid 5ff.

[43] Devereux et al. (n 3) 15.

[44] Of course, Devereux et al. may reject this understanding of the term. But it appears to me that they would then have to rephrase their concerns about the threat that incentive incompatibility poses in terms of the possibility that national tax policy changes undermine, not the international tax regime itself, but the common framework underlying it. This choice appears terminological, so I will proceed, in line with other authors, by taking the term 'international tax system' to refer to generally accepted principles and practices of international taxation.

[45] Devereux et al. (n 3) 15, 55, 56, 33, 83.

[46] ibid 130, also 124.

of the international tax system is at stake when countries are unable to effectively raise revenue by adhering to the rules and principles of that system.

While this concern appears warranted, it is hard to square with the authors' treatment of tax competition as a paradigmatic case of incentive incompatibility. Tax competition takes many forms as countries strategically adjust tax policies in order to attract or retain individuals, businesses, and investments. Competition over statutory tax rates is a clear and often mentioned example. The authors note in several passages that securing incentive compatibility would preclude countries from engaging in tax competition by reducing statutory tax rates. They write, in a passage that introduces the criterion of incentive compatibility and is therefore quoting at length:

> In broad terms, the idea of incentive compatibility is that each individual economic agent can achieve her best possible outcome while following the norms established by a group of agents. This implies that there can be no gain to failing to cooperate with other agents. In the context of business-level taxes on profit, tax competition illustrates the absence of incentive compatibility. Suppose two countries, A and B, both have identical tax systems with tax rates of 25% on profit from activities taking place in each country. If A then reduces its tax rate, it will create an incentive for businesses to move their real activity to A, and also to shift profit to A. Both of these impose a cost on B – known a 'negative spillover' in economists' jargon. A likely response from B is to reduce its tax rate as well. ... Such competition can take many forms – a reduction in the statutory tax rate, but also more generous provisions, for example, for deductions for interest. There are two key points here. First, that each individual country has an incentive to undercut the other. But, second, the ultimate result of doing so is to potentially make both countries worse off – since they end up with tax rates below those they would prefer.[47]

Two countries with identical tax systems that tax income on a source basis have an incentive to lower tax rates below the initial 25 per cent in order to attract or retain income-generating business activities within their borders. This can be expected to lead to a so-called 'race to the bottom'. Although engaging in tax competition is individually rational for a country looking to attract capital and increase its tax base, it leads to collectively sub-optimal outcomes, the authors note, since countries end up with tax rates below those they would prefer. This is an example of incentive incompatibility.

However, this outcome, though unappealing, is not a situation where the international tax system, understood as a framework of common principles or rules, is 'undermined'. Can countries engaging in statutory tax rate competition that end up with tax rates below those they would prefer, be understood as diverging from any international consensus or common framework? It appears not. In the stylised example provided by the authors, one might identify a framework of principles in the agreement or common practice by both countries to tax on a

---

[47] ibid 55.

source basis, and – fleshing out the example a bit more – to operate with uniform definitions of the taxable base ('income') and of 'source', in such a way that income is always deemed to have arisen in one and only one of the two countries. This coordination ensures that double taxation (and double non-taxation) is avoided, which reduces or eliminates tax distortions in the worldwide allocation of capital investments. However, there is no common rule or 'norm' that restricts the countries' freedom to determine the rate at which they tax the income that is deemed to have arisen in their territory. First, even if both countries can agree that the outcome is suboptimal, because they both would have preferred to tax at higher rates, this does not imply that they can agree upon a single rate at which both would prefer to tax, such that the reductions of the statutory rates, induced by tax competition, can be identified as diverging from that norm. Their shared policy objective to tax income at their preferred, or otherwise reasonable, level, appears impossible to operationalise as an action-guiding norm. Second, it appears that the current international tax system, as commonly understood, purposefully lacks such action-guiding norms concerning, among other things, tax rates. One of its features is that it is in significant respects 'sovereignty preserving':[48] it leaves significant freedom for countries to shape their own tax systems, including by setting desired tax rates and thereby levels of revenue generation. This is by design, because states are reluctant to cede what they consider to be a core component of their sovereignty.[49]

Devereux et al. do not clearly distinguish between incentives to engage in tax competition and incentives to diverge from a common framework of rules or principles, because they do not theorise the protection of political autonomy or fiscal self-determination as a constitutive commitment of the international tax system. They give the impression that tax competition is at odds with established norms, while it is in fact the foreseeable, albeit non-intended, effect of adherence to the very rules and principles forming a common framework within which international taxation takes place. Certainly, tax competition is corrosive to the commitment of countries to established norms, but this is because established norms are in effect unsuccessful in securing the policy objectives – including the mutual protection of fiscal self-determination – that countries set out to secure though coordination and cooperation.

The problem at the heart of the international tax system, in other words, is not 'defection' from common rules, but being unable to achieve the goals for which these common rules were established. Acts of tax competition are individually rational, but they lead to collectively sub-optimal outcomes. The

---

[48] T Rixen, *The Political Economy of International Tax Governance* (Basingstoke, Palgrave Macmillan, 2008) 63.

[49] They aim to coordinate their respective tax systems in such a way that they can retain their capacity to tax while simultaneously ensuring that taxation does not (significantly) distort international capital flows.

situation fails the criterion of incentive compatibility, which requires that 'the best policy from a national perspective coincides with the best policy from a global perspective.'[50] However, engaging in tax competition as the best policy from a national perspective can be called 'defection' only in a figurative sense, because there is no norm or rule that prohibits it. And it would therefore also be false to say in this context, as Devereux et al. sometimes do, that when engaging in tax competition, countries are 'undermining any international consensus,'[51] or are diverging from a 'common system.'[52] 'Cooperation' (the policy that would secure the collectively optimal outcome if followed universally) and 'defection' (the individually rational policy that is collectively suboptimal) take place within the same cooperative framework.

In what follows, I will first show how the arguments for their proposal can be strengthened by making explicit how the authors' emphasis on incentive compatibility responds to the normative pull of fiscal self-determination, after which I will note a possible drawback of their proposal to move to destination-based taxation, as seen from the same conception of international justice that also includes requirements for the fair distribution of the benefits of international cooperation.

IV. Incentive Compatibility and Fiscal Self-Determination

Devereux et al. introduce two different business tax reform proposals, 'Residual Profit Allocation by Income' (RPAI), and 'Destination-Based Cash Flow Tax' (DBCFT), the former more modest in its scope than the latter. In brief, the RPAI treats routine profit, the profit a third party would expect to earn for the relevant functions or activities, in accordance with existing rules of separate entity accounting using familiar transfer pricing methods, and hence in conformity with current origin-based tax rules. It allocates the residual profit to destination countries according to the 'residual gross income' of the multinational in that country, which is the sales to third parties less the costs attributable to those sales (hence accounting for the costs of goods and services sold). The RPAI, hence, concerns a partial shift to destination-based taxation, while conforming to many aspects of the current system, including treating business income as a tax base. The DBCFT entails a more fundamental departure from established principles as business cash flow (rather than business income) is treated as a tax base, which is then allocated to destination countries by means of a 'border adjustment' according to which exports are not taxed but imports are.

---

[50] Devereux et al. (n 3) 83.
[51] ibid 15.
[52] ibid 33.

Devereux et al. note many attractive features of these two types of taxes but emphasise, in particular, the role of incentive compatibility. To the extent that these taxes are levied in the location of the relatively immobile factor – the consumer – there are few incentives for companies to redirect investment or profits or for countries to lower tax rates, which would secure the long-term stability of the international tax system.

This concern for incentive compatibility, I will now argue, can at least partly be understood as a concern of justice. Incentive compatibility is then not an independent criterium but the further explication of what international justice requires in matters of taxation.

If one subscribes to a Rawlsian account of international justice, the protection of the autonomy of states in matters of taxation must form a crucial criterion for the design of the international tax system. In *Catching Capital: The Ethics of Tax Competition* (2015), the most detailed and carefully developed version of this position, Peter Dietsch argues that international tax reform should focus on securing and enhancing states' fiscal self-determination.[53] He distinguishes between formal, or de jure, and effective, or de facto, self-determination, the former consisting of the right to write and enforce law and the latter having the capacity to achieve set policy goals. While the international tax system has traditionally protected the former, through the allocation of tax rights to avoid double-taxation, this has come at the cost of the latter, with tax competition constraining states' effective tax capacity, including by setting tax rates at desired levels. Since effective tax capacity is essential for political autonomy (it is instrumental to reaching redistributive and other policy objectives), Dietsch concludes that international tax reform should be focused on multilateral enforcement mechanisms that shore up effective fiscal self-determination.

From this perspective, the problem at the core of the international tax system today is that it protects sovereignty in a way that is self-defeating: by protecting their capacity to compete on tax rates, states collectively limit their capacity to raise revenue, undermining the sovereignty they set out to protect. Devereux et al.'s own example of the corrosive effects of tax competition in the passage cited above can be used to show this in more detail.

The simple two player game suggested in the model's tax competition results from origin-based taxation and can be further fleshed out as follows. It allows the two players – countries A and B with identical tax systems – two basic choices: to keep tax rates at 25 per cent on profits from activities taking place in their country or to lower them to, let's say, five per cent. The resulting game is a prisoner's dilemma where the dominant strategy of the players gives rise to an outcome that is preferred by none of the players. The collectively optimal outcome is secured when both countries tax at 25 per cent. This outcome allows for an efficient worldwide allocation of capital because the investment decisions of individuals or

---

[53] P Dietsch, *Catching Capital* (Oxford, OUP, 2015).

companies are not affected by tax considerations while the respective tax rates are at the level preferred by both countries. However, both countries have an interest to 'defect' from this outcome by lowering their tax rate to five per cent. If the other country keeps the tax rate at 25 per cent, the defector will attract additional foreign capital, leading to positive spillovers and increased tax revenue. While the allocation of capital will not be efficient, leading to a reduction in national welfare – some of the country's own investors will decide to invest at home rather than abroad, even though the returns of investment abroad would have been greater, absent the tax), this negative effect can be outweighed by the positive spillovers that are the result of additional capital inflows. Tax revenue may even increase because the additional capital inflows lead to an increased tax base. This country that still taxes at a rate of 25 per cent will not only be confronted with an inefficient worldwide allocation of capital that reduces the national welfare (some investors invest abroad even though welfare returns would have been greater had they not taken into account the tax differentials) it also suffers capital outflows that reduce its tax base. Hence, the expected outcome of this game is that both tax at five per cent. While this outcome, too, secures an efficient worldwide allocation of capital (bracketing the negative welfare effects of a potential under provision of public goods), this outcome is unattractive because, as the authors put it, 'both countries end up with lower tax rates than they would have preferred'. From the perspective of a Rawlsian conception of international justice, this may not just be a case of frustrated policy preferences but one of injustice: an international tax system that severely restricts the capacity of states to tax at desired rates, is unjust because it insufficiently robustly protects their political autonomy.

Authors have long worried that tax competition, which appears to be the inevitable result of capital mobility, leads to collectively suboptimal outcomes and may have the structure of an (asymmetric) prisoner's dilemma.[54] The conventional conclusion has therefore been that it is necessary to introduce multilateral enforcement structures.[55] Countries must develop mechanisms to secure 'cooperation', which is to say, devise enforceable rules to lock countries in outcomes that are collectively optimal. This requires more hierarchical modes of governance that change the payoff structure of the game outlined above so that the individually rational course of action aligns with the collectively optimal outcome. Dietsch, for instance, argues for a multilateral agreement that includes the establishment of an International Tax Organisation with a dispute-settlement mechanism, to enforce rules limiting the right of states to engage in tax competition, in order to protect the capacity of states to set tax rates at desired levels, while ensuring that they

---

[54] eg, VH Dehejia, and P Genschel, 'Tax competition in the European Union' (1999) 3 *Politics & Society* 27, 403–30; S Bucovetsky 'Asymmetric tax competition' (1991) 2 *Journal of Urban Economics* 30, 167–81. K Clausing 'The nature and practice of capital tax competition' in P Dietsch and T Rixen (eds) *Global Tax Governance: What is wrong with it and how to fix it* (Colchester, ECPR Press, 2016).

[55] Rixen (n 48) 49; T Rixen, 'Institutional reform of global tax governance: a proposal' in P Dietsch and T Rixen (eds), *Global Tax Governance* (Colchester, ECPR Press, 2016).

do not 'misuse' this capacity with an eye on attracting mobile economic factors.[56] In the simple example just outlined, one could think of a bilateral treaty that binds both countries to tax income at 25 per cent and attaches penalties to violations of that agreement.

Seen from this perspective, the central insight by Devereux et al. is de jure and de facto fiscal self-determination can be secured together, and that multilateral enforcement may not be necessary. This is attractive from the perspective of a conception of international justice that requires the protection of the political autonomy of states. An international tax system centred around destination-based taxation does not give rise to a prisoner's dilemma. It would be 'self-enforcing' in the sense that it would lead countries that pursue their own national interests to secure the collectively optimal outcome. Taxing at the location of the relatively immobile economic factor reduces incentives for companies to change investment and accounting decisions in light of tax rate differentials, hence reducing the incentive for countries to engage in tax competition. And since taxes do not significantly affect investment decisions differential tax rates do not lead to inefficiencies in the worldwide allocation of investments. Hence, destination-based taxation, conversely, protects states' de facto fiscal self-determination (by reducing the pressures of tax competition) while simultaneously safeguarding their de jure fiscal self-determination (by avoiding the constraints of significant multilateral coordination and enforcement). From the perspective of political autonomy, this outcome should be preferred over institutional schemes, such as those proposed by Dietsch, where de facto self-determination is protected only at the cost of constraining de jure self-determination.

This perspective suggests a (partially) reductive account of incentive compatibility as a criterion for a good international tax system. In this context, it is not an independent criterion but a further specification of what justice requires on a Rawlsian account of international justice, that identifies political autonomy as a central commitment in the design of international institutions. There is a disconnect between the policy objectives of countries coordinating their tax systems and the common framework of rules and principles they have devised to reach those objectives. States wish to coordinate their tax systems in order to minimise the distortionary effects of taxes from a worldwide perspective while simultaneously protecting their capacity to tax. However, because the common framework allows for tax competition, which tends in the long run to undermine the tax capacity of states, it frustrates at least one of the goals for which it was established. If international justice requires that states are politically autonomous, which includes the capacity to effectively develop and maintain (minimally) just domestic institutions, then the international tax system that secures incentive compatibility, where the exercise of de jure fiscal self-determination aligns with the protection of de facto self-determination, rather than undermining it, is an obviously desirable ideal.

---

[56] Dietsch (n 53) ch 2.

V. Incentive Compatibility and Distributing the Benefits of Cooperation

The Rawlsian account of international justice, however, is not limited to the protection of political autonomy; it also demands an equitable distribution of the benefits of international cooperation. The international tax system plausibly forms part of a cooperative scheme. By avoiding double (non-)taxation (the likely consequence of an absence of international cooperation) mutually beneficial national welfare gains are possible as the result of a more efficient international allocation of capital. One of the primary objectives of the authors of the 1923 League of Nations report on double taxation famously was to resolve the 'interference with economic intercourse and with the free flow of capital',[57] and this has been the primary objective of international tax coordination and cooperation ever since. From the Rawlsian perspective, the resulting benefits, secured through mutual adjustments of national tax systems, must be equitably shared. Further questions, going beyond the scope of this chapter, are how we should demarcate the cooperative practice that permits the quantification of these benefits, and what counts as an equitable distribution. Regardless of how one answers them, the implication is that the international tax system should ensure that the national tax systems it regulates contribute to a just international distribution of the benefits of cooperation. If one is concerned with the cross-country distributions of (business) income, one must consider not just how the (right to) tax revenue is allocated between countries but what is the international incidence of the revenue so collected: when considering the distributions of the benefits of international cooperation, a tax is irrelevant if its incidence falls on one's own population while it is crucial if its incidence falls on foreigners.[58] This is one of the lessons of the instrumentalist approach to justice, that Devereux et al. heed in the domestic context, when they, for instance, emphasise the need to consider the incidence on individuals of business taxes, and it is important to also keep this in mind in the international context. Devereux et al. may not fully appreciate this when they approach the question of justice in international taxation as being fundamentally about 'which country should have rights to the revenue from taxing the profit of a multi-national business'. The distribution of tax rights or tax revenue is not a reliable indicator of the distribution of the benefits of cooperation

---

[57] GWJ Bruins, L Einaudi, RA Seligman and J Stamp, *Report on Double Taxation* (Geneva, League of Nations, 1923) 5.

[58] This is a different way of putting Musgrave and Musgrave's point, that what matters in the determination of what inter-nation equity requires, is not the allocation of tax revenues between countries per se, but how that allocation contributes to a fair distribution of the benefits of international investment. See R Musgrave and P Musgrave 'Inter-nation equity' in R Bird and J Head (eds), *Modern Fiscal Issues: Essays in Honour of Carl S. Shoup* (Toronto, University of Toronto Press, 1972) 70.

because it does not necessarily reflect the incidence of the taxes concerned. The international tax system, which concerns the common framework of rules and principles governing national tax systems in relation to mobile economic factors, helps shape the equitable distribution of the benefits of cooperation (however we further specify this), because it determines to what extent countries are able to impose taxes with incidences on foreigners and hence have cross-borders distributive effects.[59]

From the perspective of a Rawlsian conception of international justice, the general move to destination-based taxation, as proposed by Devereux et al. must be assessed in terms of how it affects the distribution of benefits of cooperation, in particular in comparison to current and conceivable alternative schemes of origin-based taxation. A prima facie concern in this respect is that it would likely benefit richer countries with large consumer markets. Devereux et al. note in particular that resource-rich net (goods) exporting countries stand to lose from the universal introduction of destination-based taxation (in particular DBCFT), compared to current arrangements.[60] They would receive no tax revenue from companies exploiting and exporting natural resources, since related income or resource specific rents would be taxed in the country of the consumer.[61] Whether this shift is unjust depends on the overall effects of the taxes on the distribution of the benefits of cooperation.

The question I wish to consider here is what role the criterion of incentive compatibility can play in recommending a move to destination-based taxation if these effects appear to be unjust. Take the choice between an international tax system based broadly on origin-based taxation with significant multilateral enforcement to ward off the corrosive effects of tax competition, or on destination-based taxation that is 'self-enforcing', and assume for the moment that the latter option contributes to what appears to be an unfair distribution of the benefits of international cooperation. Is the fact that the latter, but not the former, option satisfies the criterion of incentive compatibility a reason to support it?

The answer is affirmative only insofar as the criterion acts as a feasibility constraint, and effective multilateral enforcement to tackle tax competition in a broadly origin-based international tax system is practically impossible. According to the instrumentalist approach to tax justice, no institution that is impossible to achieve can be required by justice. If destination based taxation is the (only) feasible option, then it cannot be judged as generating an unfair distribution. This is how Devereux et al appear to treat incentive compatibility. They appear to judge reforms of the international tax regime that do not satisfy

---

[59] More indirectly it may also affect cross-border investment decisions. The instrumentalist approach seeks to judge institutional design in terms of a holistic assessment of these distributive consequences.

[60] Devereux et al. (n 3) 278.

[61] ibid 288, therefore recommend that these countries make up for that loss by levying a separate tax on natural resources.

it unstable and hence impracticable, regardless of how 'fair' they might otherwise appear. They are sceptical of the effectiveness of multilateral enforcement
in a context where countries have an incentive to unliterally defect from cooperative arrangements, as exemplified in the simple prisoner's dilemma discussed
above. In the context of the OECD's Pillar II, the authors emphasise the difficulties involved in enforcing source-based taxation – it requires 'robust and highly
coordinated rules (including on a tax rate)'.[62] Yet this is not only a question of
feasibility but also of justice. Since highly detailed rules constrain the de jure
self-determination of states, which is a disadvantage from the perspective of
international justice, even if it promotes greater de facto fiscal self-determination.

They admit that 'arms can be twisted politically' and that 'other consideration could be offered in return for a cooperation' but submit that little should
be expected from such external pressure to enter into cooperative schemes
with enforcement mechanisms.[63] This assessment may be too pessimistic, and
perhaps some evidence for this can be found in recent progress made on Pillar II,
although – as the authors emphasise – the devil, as always, is in the details.[64]
What should be emphasised, though, is that in the context of prisoners' dilemmas, the players have an interest in securing the collectively optimal outcome.[65]
Indeed, in section III, I have argued that the criterion of incentive compatibility is best understood as requiring that individual incentives within a common
framework of rules align with the goals for which the common framework was
established. The current international tax system, designed to minimise the
distortionary effects of taxes while protecting the tax capacity of states, facilitates
tax competition that potentially undermines both. In this context, states have an
incentive to create multilateral enforcement structures that align the individually
rational course of action with the collectively optimal outcome. It is therefore
false to suggest in general that countries have no incentive to establish multilateral enforcement of 'cooperative' behaviour. Certainly, once such enforcement is
established, countries then have an incentive to unilaterally 'defect', since the individually most attractive outcome of a prisoner's dilemma is the situation where
one is the (only) freerider. However, this observation merely highlights that
enforcement must be effective. If the design of such enforcement mechanisms is
feasible, then the fact that an international tax system based on origin-based taxation is incentive incompatible without such mechanisms, cannot hold weight in
the assessment of the all-things-considered requirements of its implementation.
After all, according to the instrumentalist approach to tax justice, justice is the
first virtue of institutions.

---

[62] Devereux et al. (n 3) 129.

[63] ibid 129–130.

[64] ibid 128–129.

[65] Complications arise if the prisoner's dilemmas are asymmetric and some players lack the incentive to reach a 'cooperative' outcome. In that case enforcement, for instance through 'side payments', is
necessary to establish cooperation. See Rixen (n 48) 44–46.

VI. Conclusion

By means of a discussion of *Taxing Profit in a Global Economy* by Devereux et al., I have aimed to clarify how international tax reform, in particular towards destination-based taxation, should be assessed on the instrumentalist approach to tax justice, which considers justice as the primary criterion for evaluating a good tax or tax system. That approach only allows other criteria, such as incentive compatibility, to play a role in international tax reform in so far as they do not detract from the realisation of justice. I have clarified the nature of incentive incompatibility, as Devereux et al. understand it, suggesting that it characterises a situation where the exercise of fiscal self-determination, taking place within a common framework of principles, gives rise to tax competition that undermines states' fiscal self-determination. So understood, the criterion of incentive compatibility is partly reducible to the criterion of fairness, on a Rawlsian account of international justice that prioritises the protection of states political autonomy. The criterion of incentive compatibility can play an independent role only as a feasibility constraint on justice. If it is true, as Devereux et al. appear to think, that effective prevention of tax competition through multilateral enforcement is impossible, then it is appropriate to seek institutional schemes that are incentive compatible and can secure collectively optimal outcomes without enforcement structures. However, if such multilateral enforcement is feasible, and justice requires origin-based taxation in order to fairly distribute the benefits of international cooperation, then the criterion of incentive compatibility has no weight.

PART III

Procedures: Public Institutions and Public Companies

6

Globalisation, Taxation and the Essence of Europe

NATALIA PUSHKAREVA

The discussion about developing countries' underrepresentation at global economic policy fora and the influence gap between developing and developed countries that results from it has been going on for quite some time, and many researchers and policy professionals across the world acknowledge the problem.[1] However, the issue is not exclusively specific to developing countries anymore.

This chapter discusses the recent case of Hungary unilaterally blocking – for some time, at least – introduction of the Global Minimum Tax in the EU, and its meaning for international tax competition in general. It analyses the consequences of such decisions for the relationship between the Member States, and uses a variation of the concept of the 'Winner's Curse' to illustrate how exercising coercive decision-making powers in a unilateral setting when making international tax choices can lead to suboptimal outcomes for the group as a whole.

The chapter concludes that due to the presence of the Unilateralist's Curse and related biases, a unanimous voting system is very likely to result in sub-optimal outcomes for the group, and so is a majority voting system in which GDP plays a significant role in how votes are allocated. A qualified majority voting system based on the allocation of one vote to each country is much more likely to produce balanced results. In cases where unanimity is required, the author argues that a disagreeing member should be provided with an opportunity to support their position with evidence.

---

[1] RC Christensen, M Hearson, and T Randriamanalina, 'At the Table, Off the Menu? Assessing the Participation of Lower-Income Countries in Global Tax Negotiations' (Brighton, Institute of Development Studies, ICTD Working Paper 115, 2020); L Parada, 'Global Minimum Taxation: A Strategic Approach for Developing Countries' (2024) 15 *Columbia Journal of Tax Law* 187; R de la Feria, 'The Perceived (Un)Fairness of the Global Minimum Corporate Tax Rate' in W Haslehner (eds), *The 'Pillar Two' Global Minimum Tax* (Cheltenham, Edward Elgar, 2024).

I. The Case of Hungary

In June 2022, Hungary, which has the lowest corporate income tax rate in Europe at 9 per cent[2] and whose currency is one of the weakest in the European area, blocked an EU directive that would impose a 15 per cent minimum tax on multinational corporations. EU regulations require the unanimity of Member States on 'sensitive matters' which include tax policy, and after initial consent to implementation of the reform, Hungary voted against the introduction of the global 15 per cent minimum tax, blocking the deal for the entire EU as not serving Hungary's national interests.

In particular, the Hungarian Government was concerned that the levy would diminish the competitiveness of Hungarian firms, endanger tens of thousands of domestic jobs, and increase inflation. Another concern was the competitiveness of Europe as a region in general: according to the country's Foreign Minister, Péter Szijjártó, 'Europe is in deep enough trouble without the global minimum tax.'[3] He also openly acknowledged experiencing significant political pressure to accept the Pillar Two proposal.[4] Hungary's Finance Minister, Mihály Varga, expressed the opinion that passing the minimum tax at this time would only worsen the economic challenges the country is currently facing. According to Varga, 'Interest rates and inflation are rapidly increasing, supply chains are also disrupted … All these unfavourable developments call for significant losses for businesses and households. Under such circumstances, introducing the global minimum tax at such an early stage would cause serious damage to the European economies.'[5]

Many European jurisdictions reacted quite negatively to Hungary's attempts to protect its own interests. Given that the European Commission was at the time still holding back billions of euros in COVID-19 relief funds in a dispute over the rule of law, the Hungarian Government was already in a challenging financial position. The country's stance against the introduction of the global minimum tax, together with tensions over other policy areas, lead to the US terminating the 1979 US-Hungary tax treaty, which in turn has contributed to the pressure on the Forint, the local currency, causing it to drop to record lows despite a significant increase in the central bank rate.

The French Finance Minister Bruno Le Maire claimed that 'Minimum taxation will be implemented in the coming months without or with Hungary', adding

---

[2] Tax Foundation, '*Taxes in Hungary*', taxfoundation.org/location/hungary/#:~:text=Hungary%20 has%20the%20lowest%20corporate,%2Dthan%2Daverage%20CFC%20rules.

[3] J Liboreiro, 'Hungary blocks EU deal on 15% minimum corporate tax' (*Euronews*, 17 June 2022) www.euronews.com/my-europe/2022/06/17/hungary-blocks-eu-deal-on-15-minimum-corporate-tax.

[4] GrantThornton, 'U.S threatens Hungary tax treaty over pillar 2' (*GrantThornton*, 19 July 2022) www.grantthornton.com/insights/newsletters/tax/2022/hot-topics/jul-19/u-s-threatens-hungary-tax-treaty-over-pillar-2.

[5] Deloitte, 'Hungary's opposition to global minimum tax has implications for Biden administration' (*Deloitte*, 18 June 2022) www.taxathand.com/article/24485/European-Union/2022/Hungarys-opposition-to-global-minimum-tax-has-implications-for-Biden-administration.

that he and colleagues are working 'on alternative solutions which would allow countries which are willing to adopt a European text ... without Hungary'.[6] At the same time, the European Parliament stated that 'unanimity decision making in the EU requires a very high level of responsibility, in line with the principle of sincere cooperation, as set out in the EU Treaty. For the longer term, member states should consider the benefit of transitioning to qualified majority voting, and the Commission should relaunch the idea to gradually introduce majority voting on tax matters'.[7]

Several EU jurisdictions, namely France, Germany, Italy, Spain, and the Netherlands, have been considering the so-called 'enhanced cooperation' mechanism, which would allow member countries to go ahead with a reform without having secured the unanimity that is usually required for making decisions on tax policy matters in Europe.[8] A minimum of nine EU jurisdictions will need to reach a consensus on the tax bill according to this procedure, and decisions will be considered even in the presence of other EU jurisdictions that might be against it.[9]

In response, Hungary's Economic Affairs Panel adopted a political declaration titled 'About the rejection of political pressure against the protection of Hungary's economic interests', in which it accused the European Parliament of putting excessive pressure on EU members opposing the introduction of the global minimum tax, which is in conflict with their interests.[10] The Panel asserted that 'Clearly overstepping its authority, the European Parliament would force Hungary to surrender its economic interests'.[11]

II. Sincere Cooperation? Unions, Competition and International Tax

A. What Constitutes Sincere Cooperation?

Given that the core values of European Union include freedom, democracy and equality, EU Member States can be subject to significant political pressure if they

---

[6] G Leali, 'EU can cut Hungary out of minimum tax rate deal, Bruno Le Maire says' (*Politico*, 30 June 2022) www.politico.eu/article/eu-to-implement-minimum-tax-rate-without-hungary-le-maire-says/.

[7] European Parliament Press Release 'As Hungary blocks global tax deal, MEPs denounce national vetoes', (*European Parliament*, 06 July 2022) www.europarl.europa.eu/news/en/press-room/20220701 IPR34359/as-hungary-blocks-global-tax-deal-meps-denounce-national-vetoes.

[8] European Commission, 'European Commission: Decision making on EU TAX Policy', taxation-customs.ec.europa.eu/taxation-1/decision-making-eu-tax-policy_en.

[9] EUR-LEX, 'Enhanced cooperation', eur-lex.europa.eu/EN/legal-content/glossary/enhanced-cooperation.html.

[10] G Szakacs, 'Hungary parliament panel reiterates opposition to global minimum tax' (*Reuters*, 11 July 2022) www.reuters.com/markets/europe/hungary-parliament-panel-reiterates-opposition-global-minimum-tax-2022-07-11/.

[11] ibid.

make a decision to protect their national interests in times of crisis rather than comply with regulations that do not necessarily benefit them, which is what is being positioned as 'sincere cooperation'. The principle of **sincere cooperation** is fundamental to the EU. According to *Article 4* of the TEU:

> '2. The Union shall respect the **equality of Member States** before the Treaties as well as their **national identities**, inherent in their fundamental structures, political and constitutional, inclusive of regional and local self-government. **It shall respect their essential State functions**, including ensuring the territorial integrity of the State, maintaining law and order and safeguarding national security ...
>
> 3. Pursuant to the principle of **sincere cooperation**, the Union and the Member States shall, in full mutual respect, *assist each other in carrying out tasks which flow from the Treaties.*
>
> The Member States *shall take any appropriate measure, general or particular, to ensure fulfilment of the obligations arising out of the Treaties* or resulting from the acts of the institutions of the Union.
>
> The Member States shall *facilitate the achievement of the Union's tasks* and *refrain from any measure which could jeopardise the attainment of the Union's objectives.'*[12]
>
> The Union should promote democracy, mutual respect, equality and the rule of law and 'shall respect the equality of Member States before the Treaties as well as their national identities, inherent in their fundamental structures, political and constitutional.'[13]
>
> Did it manage to do so when attempting introduction of the global minimum tax in Europe?

Over the years, the EU harmonised multiple policies within the Union, assuming that Member States have common interests that the EU could protect more effectively. However, some areas, such as taxation, remain key parts of Member States' national sovereignty, and the interests of different countries, even within the EU, might be quite diverse when it comes to tax policy. While some EU economies are more effective in collecting taxes at sustainable rates and funding adequate welfare for their citizens, others choose to stay 'competitive' for international business by providing low effective corporate tax rates and multiple opportunities for 'tax optimisation' to attract foreign direct investment ('FDI'). European economies differ in several fundamental ways, including their size and structure, political factors, levels of inequality, and integration in international trade, to name a few, which indicates that their optimal tax policy strategies might differ as well on many occasions.

The case of Hungary was presented to the public as a conflict between the principle of 'sincere cooperation', under which countries are supposed to 'facilitate the achievement of the Union's tasks and refrain from any measure that could jeopardise the attainment of the Union's objective', and a Member State trying to protect its national interests, including national jobs, economic growth, and

---

[12] Consolidated Version of the Treaty on European Union [2012] OJ C326/13, Art 4.
[13] ibid, (italic emphasis added).

well-being of its citizens, which will all be likely hurt if the Global Minimum Tax proposal is adopted, which created a lot of tension. Many, however, made the argument that the real reason behind Hungary's objection to the global minimum tax had nothing to do with the protection of its national interests, firms, and jobs.[14] In fact, at the beginning of the entire discussion, Hungary was supportive of the reform.[15] The actual reason the country opposed the introduction of the global minimum tax at the EU level by exercising its veto right, as many reasonably believe, was using the unanimity requirement for adopting tax policy reforms in the EU to gain political leverage for getting its way in other policy areas.

Some researchers, such as Tim van Brederode, assessed the effects the introduction of the Global Minimum Tax would have on the Hungarian economy, and came to the conclusion that the country's government had no rational reasons for taking such a strong negative position on the reform, and the public argument in support of the Hungarian veto is rather weak.[16] In particular, van Brederode argues, during Ecofin meetings earlier in the same year, Hungary voted in favour of the minimum tax directive, and the Hungarian Finance Minister only expressed his concerns about 'the huge pressure economies and companies are under from the war in Ukraine and rising inflation' after it became clear that Poland was ready to agree to the deal, meaning its acceptance at EU level.[17] Zoltán Kovács, Hungary's secretary of state for international communication and relations, also shared his worries about the disadvantageous effects on EU competitiveness and the potential job losses the global minimum tax might have after other EU jurisdictions accepted the deal.[18]

After the reform was proposed, the EU Tax Observatory modelled[19] the consequences the introduction of the Global Minimum Tax would have on every EU member, and the calculation for Hungary predicted that the country would collect around €600 million in additional tax revenues should the global minimum tax be implemented. As for the impact the introduction of the global minimum tax would have on Hungarian jobs, Van Brederode noted that while a sudden increase in corporate tax rates or dogmatic anti-avoidance measures causes

---

[14] eg, The Greens / EFA in the European Parliament 'Hungary's Blackmail Attempts Shows Urgent Need To Drop National Vetoes' (*The Greens / EFA in the European Parliament*, Press Release, 6 December 2022), www.greens-efa.eu/en/article/press/hungarys-blackmail-attempts-shows-urgent-need-to-drop-national-vetoes.

[15] T van Brederode, 'From Impasse to Unanimity: Understanding Hungary's Position on Pillar 2' (*Global Tax Governance Blog*, 7 September 2022) globtaxgov.weblog.leidenuniv.nl/2022/09/07/from-impasse-to-unanimity-understanding-hungarys-position-on-pillar-2/; Reuters, 'Hungary agrees to global tax deal, finance minister says' (*Reuters*, 8 October 2021) www.reuters.com/business/finance/hungary-agrees-global-tax-deal-finance-minister-says-2021-10-08/.

[16] Van Brederode (n 15).

[17] ibid.

[18] eg, Hungary Today, 'State Secretary: Global Minimum Tax Would Put Europe at a Competitive Disadvantage' (*Hungary Today*, 22 June 2022) hungarytoday.hu/state-secretary-kovacs-global-minimum-tax/.

[19] M Barake, P-E Chouc, & T Neef & G Zucman, 'Revenue Effects of the Global Minimum Tax: Country by Country Estimates' (*EU Tax Observatory Note No.2*, October 2021) www.taxobservatory.eu//wwwsite/uploads/2021/10/Note-2-Revenue-Effects-of-the-Global-Minimum-Tax-October-2021-1.pdf.

economic distortion on the labour market, which impacts labour reducing wages in the long-run the current low unemployment rate in Hungary[20] had a positive effect, and generally benefited labour wages.[21] Van Brederode concluded that it is likely that the implementation of Pillar Two would result in both gains and losses for Hungary.[22] While the exact impact the reform would have on the Hungarian economy depends on multiple factors, such as inflation and FDI policies, among others, it is quite likely that the benefits will outweigh the costs, the researcher states. Thus, the public reasons Hungary has voiced to justify the veto were likely not its true reasons.[23]

Nevertheless, whatever the reasons behind the Hungarian veto in this particular case were, it is arguable that Member States should have the freedom to disagree with an EU tax proposal where they have legitimate reasons to do so, and their position should be taken into account. If we accept the Union's right to go ahead with a policy proposal in the face of a member's opposition, whether the benefits of EU membership are worth the loss of autonomy for all Member States becomes less obvious. If the Union, whose goal is to promote members' wellbeing, is vested with coercive powers that it can use for the implementation of initiatives that are likely to damage some of its members, what is such a union's nature? Can such behaviour really be considered 'sincere cooperation' on behalf of other Union Member States? What makes one Member State, or a group thereof, entitled to advance their economic interests at the expense of other, often smaller, lower-income and more vulnerable members of the group?

While it is true that membership in an international organisation or a union comes with both benefits and costs, it is often the case that large, industrialised economies benefit disproportionately more from tax policies adopted at the international level, while lower-income countries benefit *somewhat* at best, which contributes to a rise of inequality, discontent, conflicts, and increases the risk of unilateral actions and non-cooperation in the long run.[24] These consequences are not quite in line with ideas of solidarity and enhanced collaboration the EU has been built on.

B. The Changing Contracts

Both the tax policy and the tax research communities have recently dedicated a lot of attention to the changing nature of the 'social contract' between a state

---

[20] Hungarian Central Statistical Office, www.ksh.hu/?lang=en.

[21] van Brederode (n 15).

[22] van Brederode (n 15).

[23] Ironically, by the time of this chapter's finalisation, Hungary became the first EU jurisdiction to implement the Global Minimum Tax in practice. Magyar Közlöny, Magyarorszhag Hivatalos Lapja (*Magyar Közlöny*, 30 November 2023) magyarkozlony.hu/dokumentumok/59ba20495cd587e54decf5b 41b0e6f9e4bba3926/megtekintes.

[24] M Schmelzer, 'A Club of the Rich to Help the Poor? The OECD, "Development", and "The Hegemony of Donor Countries"' in M Frey et al. (eds), *International Organisations and Development, 1945–1990* (London, Palgrave MacMillan, 2014).

and a citizen. Not that long ago, such a contract was considered 'given', whole and inflexible; taxpayers were linked to their jurisdiction very strongly. With globalisation and digitalisation, we observed not only the increased mobility of taxpayers and, thus, their increased ability to choose the social contract that suits them best, but also the 'unbundling' of the social contract into bits and pieces and creating a designer Lego constructor out of them.[25] This has impacted the entire nature of the relationship between a citizen and the state, creating a market-like competition for taxpayers between jurisdictions, which in its current form is harmful for many and unsustainable in the long-term.

However, another important change is happening concurrently. The nature of the 'contract' between the states themselves is also transforming, changing the nature of international organisations and unions. As relationships between countries become more complex, they unavoidably include elements of both cooperation and competition. To a certain degree, this is not a problem: some cooperation is required for regulating and managing competition, keeping it under control, and making sure that its harmful consequences are minimised. However, in some situations, like the Hungarian case, the conflict between the interests of a country and an organisation, between cooperation and protecting national interests, is more evident. In this case, the actions of the parties reveal their true expectations from each other, and the nature of their de-facto relationship.

The ways in which the rules of the 'contract' between the states are implemented matter too. In the Hungarian case, we observed political pressure and manipulations from the EU, as well as attempts to exclude Hungary from decision making and claim that the country is not cooperative, ie, not fulfilling its obligations as an EU member, while it expressed seemingly reasonable concerns about the effects a specific tax policy will have on its economy and people. Reaching agreement on the policy lobbied by the leaders of the group is positioned as a 'common good' that will benefit everyone and contribute to fighting global tax avoidance, which is not necessarily true in all cases. Such claims are often not supported by much analysis or argumentation. While there is uncertainty about the exact impact the introduction of the global minimum tax will have on the global tax competition, it is very likely that at least some economies will suffer losses in the short- and probably middle-term, including, potentially, Hungary, as well as a number of developing countries, many of which heavily rely on CIT tax incentives for attracting direct foreign investment.[26] In addition, introducing

---

[25] T Dagan, 'Klaus Vogel Lecture 2021: Unbundled Tax Sovereignty – Refining the Challenges' (2022) 76 *Bulletin For International Taxation* 1.

[26] eg, A Redonda, 'The Global Tax Deal and Tax Incentives: What if the Cure Is Worse Than the Disease?' (*Council of Economic Policies*, 18 March 2022) www.cepweb.org/the-global-tax-deal-and-tax-incentives-what-if-the-cure-is-worse-than-the-disease/; M Andersen, B Kett, & E von Uexkull, 'Corporate Tax Incentives and FDI in Developing Countries' in *Global Investment Competitiveness Report 2017/2018: Foreign Investor Perspectives and Policy Implications* (Washington D.C., World Bank Group, 2017) 73–9.

the tax requires legislative changes and puts an additional burden on tax administrations.[27] Thus, it is understandable that some countries might have reasonable doubts about implementation of Pillar II, even if in case of Hungary, the stance against it was mostly motivated by political reasons.

Concerns about the effectiveness of the introduction of GMT have been repeatedly discussed by leading experts in tax and development around the world, as well as international organisations.[28] The accusation of not cooperating 'for the greater good' in this case is far-fetched and based on the premise that GMT is: (1) effective; and (2) the only way to address aggressive tax competition. Acceptance of the inevitability of tax competition between countries and its regulation, instead of trying to find a single, one size-fits-all solution to combat it, could be much more constructive.[29]

C. Is 'Cooperation' a Nicer Word for Paternalism?

In the past couple of decades, globalisation has resulted not only in increased mobility and productivity, but also in increased interdependence of countries through myriads of invisible connections and, thus, in their increased fragility and openness to external shocks. The rhetoric acknowledging that 'global problems require global solutions' has been adopted almost without questioning whether it is true or at all practically possible. Especially in times of crises, when countries' resources are particularly scarce and many people start questioning states' ability to fulfil their part of the social contract, international organisations often use the political momentum to argue in favour of 'global solutions', enhanced cooperation, redistribution, mutual support, 'fairness', and inclusive policy making, supporting the vulnerable states in addressing fundamental issues they are facing. Such 'solutions' presented by global policy fora, however, are sometimes not the only, or even not the best, ways to address such challenges for some actors.[30] They are often designed by organisations dominated by developed economies, and, in fact, benefit them disproportionately, but are presented by institutions as the only solution that can address the issue in question and benefit all.[31]

The idea of 'fairness' and the expectation of international cooperation on tax matters often change to serve the needs of the countries setting the rules. No recent reform of international organisations intended to improve the inclusion

---

[27] eg, D Bunn, 'What the OECD's Pillar Two Impact Assessment Misses' (*Tax Foundation*, 23 January 2023) taxfoundation.org/global-minimum-tax-revenue-impact-assessment/.

[28] eg, A Christians, T Lassourd, K Mataba, E Ogbebor, A Readhead, S Shay, & ZP Tinhaga, *A Guide for Developing Countries on How to Understand and Adapt to the Global Minimum Tax International Institute for Sustainable Development* (Winnipeg, Manitoba, International Senior Lawyers Project, 2023); Bunn (n 27).

[29] T Dagan, *International Tax Policy: Between Competition and Cooperation* (Cambridge, CUP, 2018).

[30] R de la Feria (n 1).

[31] ibid.

of developing countries can be called a huge success. The two-phased Voicing Reform at the World Bank took place in 2008–2011, right after the global financial crisis, and was initially focused on increasing IBRD shareholding, realigning IBRD shareholding, and the addition of a third executive director for African countries.[32] The second phase of the reform focused on realigning voting powers within the Bank by transferring voting rights from developed countries to developing jurisdictions, especially 'dynamic emerging market economies', which have been playing an increasingly important role in the global economy.[33] Overall, the main result of the voice reform process was the transfer of *some* voting power from the US, Japan, and a number of European countries to the most dynamic and economically important developing economies, such as China. A total shift of voting power of only 4.59 percentage points from developed countries to DTCs was achieved, which is a very modest voting power realignment.[34] 'Voting power to GDP' ratios in the World Bank remain considerably unbalanced, despite the principle that voting power should 'largely reflect economic weight'.[35] Low-income countries as a group actually lost some of their voting power in the second phase of the voice reform process, thus partially eroding the gains they made in the first phase.[36]

The IMF's major reform aimed at increasing the representation of developing countries took place in 2006–2010 and attempted to make the allocation of quotas and shares more responsive to changes in global economic realities and enhance the participation of low-income countries. The reform was expected to result in a significant redistribution of quotas and voting shares in the IMF, benefiting developing countries in particular. The proposed quota increases for developing countries ranged from 12 to 106 per cent per country, with the largest gains going mainly to the fast-growing and most 'promising' emerging markets. However, *ex post*, the reform was criticised for falling short of achieving its targets and not being radical enough to ensure an actual transformation.[37]

Both reforms aimed at increasing representation of developing countries in key international organisations fell short of what was promised and focused on

[32] Development Committee Joint Ministerial Committee of the Boards of Governors of the Bank and the Fund on the Transfer of Real Resources to Developing Countries, *Development Committee Communiqué* (Washington D.C., World Bank Group, 13 April 2008).

[33] Development Committee, 'World Bank Group voice reform: enhancing voice and participation of developing and transition countries in 2010 and beyond' (Washington D.C., World Bank Group, DC2010-0006) 6.

[34] J Vestergaard, 'The World Bank and the emerging world order: Adjusting to multipolarity at the second decimal point' (Copenhagen, Danish Institute for International Studies, DIIS Report 2011:05, 2011).

[35] N Pushkareva, 'Representation, Taxation and Policy Entrepreneurship' in CJ Coyne, AR Hall & E Norcross (eds), *Knowledge and Entrepreneurship in Public Policy* (Lanham, Maryland, Lexington Books, 2024).

[36] Vestergaard (n 34).

[37] See, eg, 'Rethinking International Institutions: A Global South Agenda', *Centre for Global Governance and Policy Jindal School of International Affairs & Jindal Global Law School O.P. Jindal Global University* (O. P. Jindal Global University, 2011).

the 'richer' and 'larger' developing economies becoming important players on the international arena, as their actions thus could have serious consequences for more advanced countries. More and more countries – now not only developing ones but also, as the case of Hungary illustrates – some EU Member States feel unrepresented in collective global decision-making processes, and are choosing to introduce unilateral measures or simply resort to non-compliance instead of the 'global solutions' they are sceptical of.

As of now, it is fair to say that the 'losers' of the international tax policies produced by global fora in recent years were mainly developing, lower-income jurisdictions. A big part of the problem is that in many cases, their representatives face multiple barriers when participating in the tax policy making process, or are unable to participate at all. For instance, OECD meetings are held physically and in Paris, which makes it difficult to attend them for developing countries. When developing countries do manage to attend OECD meetings, they mostly attend plenaries which mainly approve policies designed by working groups (see the table below), which are mostly attended by representatives of developed economies.[38] Plenary itself rarely presents participants with an opportunity to have a say on policy design; policies that make it to this stage are effectively already 'pre-approved' and are very likely to be adopted as they are.[39] This is confirmed by an analysis that revealed that attendance rate for the Steering Group meetings is 50 per cent for OECD Member States, while the corresponding number for lower-income countries is only 12.5 per cent.[40] For Working Parties, where most of the technical work regarding shaping tax policies takes place, such numbers are 77.4 vs. 5.4 per cent for developed and lower income countries, respectively.[41] Thus, opportunities for developing countries to influence the content of international tax policies and protect their interests 'within the rules of the game' are very limited: this remains a 'rich countries' domain. Developed countries, to the contrary, got a chance to use their economic and political power to influence the content of tax policies designed at international institutions, as well as reframe the procedures of decision making, sometimes to the point of allowing them to ignore the interests of lower-income jurisdictions of the group completely, as in the case of Hungary. Not unexpectedly, many developing and lower-income countries, feeling powerless in their attempts to change the rules to their benefit, engaged in creative application of the said rules instead, which in many cases included the implementation of unilateral solutions undermining the spirit of cooperation as well as policy unity, and worsening international tax competition.

Such a lack of cooperation on tax policies is problematic on several levels. On top of contributing to international inequality, such dynamics undermine trust between states, and in this particular example even trust in the principles of the

---

[38] Christensen, Hearson and Randriamanalina (n 1).
[39] ibid 11.
[40] ibid 12.
[41] ibid 12.

European Union, which unavoidably has an impact on the relationship between the members of an international organisation or a union as well as cooperation dynamics. Coercive implementation of rules by international organisations can also be detrimental to the social contract between their Member States and their citizens, as the latter observe their state failing to make sovereign tax policy choices that would promote the country's interests.

All of these relationships, as different as they might look at first sight, are supposed to be based on trust and expectation of fair and equal representation,[42] which is hardly compatible with the 'we will go ahead, with or without you' attitude. De-facto terms of the 'contract' countries become part of when joining international organisations or unions – such as understanding of what constitutes 'sincere cooperation' – seem to vary from the legal agreement in such cases. Moreover, the entire nature of such unions seems to be more fluid in crisis times in particular, redefining unions' 'terms and conditions' as well as participants' de-facto rights and obligations. Over the long-term, such coercive decision-making mechanisms displaying disrespect to some of the organisation's members and building policy proposals and advocacy on false but attractively-sounding assumptions can be equally destructive to trust and cooperation as are uncoordinated tax rates or special tax regimes. Finding a balance between respecting member states' positions and ensuring effective decision-making process is not an easy task in a multilateral world. In fact, even when countries and unions do have concern for the 'common good' at heart, problems are likely to arise.

III. The Unilateralist's Curse

A. The Concept

The 'winner curse' is a concept very well known in auction theory. This is a phenomenon where the winning bid in an auction has a high likelihood of being higher than the actual value of the good sold.[43] In an auction, each bidder makes an independent, blind estimate, and the bidder with the highest estimate 'wins'. We also know that according to Condorcet's jury theorem, the average estimate of a group of people with above 50 per cent likelihood of guessing correctly and with uncorrelated errors will tend to be close to the correct value, and will tend to move closer to the true value as the size of the group increases.[44] That also means that, if the average estimate is likely to be an accurate estimate of the bid's

---

[42] T Dagan (n 25).

[43] R Thaler, 'Anomalies: The Winner's Curse' (1988) 2 *The Journal of Economic Perspectives* 191.

[44] M de Condorcet, *Essai sur l'application de l'analyse à la probabilité des décisions rendues à la pluralité des voix* [Essay on the Application of Analysis to the Probability of Majority Decisions] (Imprimerie Royale, 1785).

value, the winner's guess about the bid's value is very likely overestimated. The larger the number of bidders, the more likely it is that at least one of them has overestimated the value of the bid. Thus, the 'winner's curse' is that even though the auction's winner technically 'wins', in reality they often end up overpaying.

In their article 'The Unilateralist's Curse and the Case for a Principle of Conformity' Bostrom, Douglas, and Sandberg proposed the concept of the 'unilateralist's curse'.[45] The unilateralist's curse and the winner's curse have similar set-ups. The difference between the two lies in the goals of the agents and the nature of the decisions to be made. In the winner's curse, each agent aims to make a bid if and only if doing so will be valuable for them. In the unilateralist's curse setting, however, the decision-maker chooses whether to undertake an initiative with an eye to the common good, that is, seeking to undertake the initiative if and only if it contributes positively to the common good. Also, in the 'unilateralist's curse', the action or decision of one member of the group is enough to implement the initiative unilaterally for a group of actors (or to block its implementation), hence the name. In this set up, a number of agents each have the power to undertake an initiative that would have significant effects on other group members. Bostrom, Douglas, and Sandberg demonstrated that in such a situation, if each agent acts on their own personal judgement as to whether the initiative should be undertaken, the initiative will be undertaken significantly more often than is optimal due to some members of the group overestimating the value of its implementation. Similarly, if there is unilateral veto power and every actor has the power to block policy initiatives, they would be blocked more often than optimal.

B. The 'Unilateralist's Curse' and International Tax Policy Making

As can be seen from the previous paragraph, one of the key differences between the 'winner's curse' and the 'unilateralist's curse' is the motivation of the actors. In the 'winner's curse' setting, actors are driven by their self-interest, while in the 'unilateralist's curse' setting, they care about the common good, and make the decision only if they believe it will benefit all members of the group.

International tax policy making presents a complex context for analysis, especially when it comes to analysing actors' motivation. While the outcomes of recent tax reforms are often presented as the 'common good', the actions of many actors, especially more privileged ones, reveal that in reality, countries are mostly concerned about their own wellbeing and thus are likely to vote for a certain policy only if perceived benefits *for them* from such a policy's implementation exceed associated risks, including political ones, and may be if it *somewhat* improves redistribution outcomes for *some* lower-income countries as a bonus.

---

[45] N Bostrom, T Douglas & A Sandberg, 'The Unilateralist's Curse and the Case for a Principle of Conformity' (2016) 30 *Social Epistemology* 350–371.

However, both benefits and costs associated with the implementation of a specific tax policy are, to a certain degree, unknown to decision makers *ex ante*, and are replaced by their estimates, which unavoidably contain an error of unknown magnitude. If we accept that the average estimate of a group of people with an above 50 per cent likelihood of guessing correctly and with uncorrelated errors will tend to be close to the correct value, it logically follows that there will be 'overbidders' in the group who would overestimate the benefits of a particular decision. The larger the group, the higher the number of 'overbidders'. In fact, Bostrom, Douglas, and Sandberg discovered the presence of 'unilateralist's bias': in the 'unilateralist's curse' setting, even for a group as small as only five actors, there is a very high chance that the initiative in question will be undertaken due to the presence of 'overbidders' in the group, even if the initiative's true value is negative.

In some cases, for instance, in tax policy voting at the European Union level, the mechanisms employed in international tax policy decision making do require the unanimity of all parties involved and thus indeed align with the unilateralist's curse setting in the sense that a vote by one country can prevent the implementation of a particular tax policy for the entire region. Many would argue that during the global minimum tax holdout, Hungary acted as the 'unilateralist' of the group. While this is technically true given the design of the voting mechanism, the assumption of common good motives does not hold here. Although the global minimum tax may be good for some EU jurisdictions, Hungary exercised its right of veto to *allegedly* protect its national interests, as it claimed that was in the country's best interests. Nevertheless, the danger of one actor – even a benevolent one – blocking a tax policy proposal due to miscalculating its benefits and risks is likely in such cases and needs to be addressed. On most occasions, however, the setting in which decisions on international tax policies are made is not unilateral in a strict sense, as such decisions are often made based on majority rule.

Another important consideration is that the original unilateralist's curse setting assumes that decisions are made by actors independently, while in international taxation it is often not so. While countries are sovereign to make decisions on their tax policies formally, in practice we know that many factors affect countries' choices of who, what, and how to tax, and the tax policies of other countries, especially those competing with the country in question, do play a role.[46] Many countries, especially the lower-income ones, also openly admit experiencing significant political pressure to accept particular international tax proposals.[47] In this case, when making the decision, the country is not only comparing the revenue effects of implementing the policy vs. leaving things as they are, but rather

---

[46] M Devereux, B Lockwood, & M Redoano, 'Do countries compete over corporate tax rates?' (2008) 92 *Journal of Public Economics* 1235.
[47] eg, Christensen, Hearson and Randriamanalina (n 1).

the potential benefits of the policy's implementation with the political costs of not doing so, which can include trade sanctions, withholding funds due to the country, etc. Such costs are not easy to estimate and depend on many factors, which are defined by a country's involvement in international trade, its membership in various unions, and many other factors that make it more integrated into the international community but also more prone to various kinds of international pressure.

Finally, the original 'unilateralist's curse' setting assumes that the initiative voted on has an equal, objective value – whatever that is – to all the actors taking part in the voting process. In international taxation, however, the preferences of countries differ based on multiple factors, including the size and structure of their economies, geography, politics, the position such countries have in the value-added chains of multinational corporations, and many other reasons, including the unique challenges they are facing. Thus, consensus on international taxation is not easy to build, as unavoidably different tax policies have different values for different jurisdictions. We also know that the tax policy preferences of 'developed' and 'developing' countries often differ, as they have different policy priorities and face different challenges when it comes to international taxation, and that global tax policy discussions are mainly dominated by 'developed' economies protecting their own financial interests, while lower-income jurisdictions often find it very challenging to voice their opinions and concerns or even be present during such negotiations.

Every tax policy choice also entails multiple less obvious and visible consequences related to close economic integration and globalisation – they are empowering in some aspects but also limiting sovereignty in others. Every policy presents a trade-off: closer ties with other economies result in economic benefits but at the same time mean the country is more prone to 'internal' pressure from within the group, and other Member States have multiple mechanisms for limiting its freedom and can use various leverages to push the country in the 'right' direction. These kinds of trade-offs are often more abstract and 'potential' before they materialise, hard to predict and quantify, even though we do see some consistency in what leverages are being used. The best prediction of such risks we can get *ex ante* is a subjective valuation by the country.

Given that the European Union currently has 27 members, and even the 'enhanced cooperation' mechanism requires the agreement of at least nine European jurisdictions, the chance that some of them are significantly overestimating tax policy's value when making the decision is high. In this case, ignoring the estimations of other group members and going ahead with the policy can produce suboptimal results for the group as a whole. The same applied, of course, to situations where a country underestimates the benefits of the reform, but statistically, the bias is on the side of overestimation. As follows from the findings of Bostrom, Douglas, and Sandberg, for 27 agents, which is the number of members the EU has now, in 'unilateralist's curse' setting, the likelihood of an erroneous decision (ie, going ahead with the initiative when in fact its value is negative) is dangerously close to 100 per cent.[48] Even for nine actors, which is the case for the 'enhanced cooperation' mechanism, the probability of erroneous action is at 80 per cent.[49] Given that the international tax policies developed in recent years and the global minimum tax generally disproportionately benefit the 'rich', large, industrialised, capital-exporting economies, this set up puts lower-income jurisdictions in a very vulnerable position if they are pushed to accept decisions of other group members almost unilaterally.

It is true that decisions in tax policy are not strictly unilateral in the sense Bostrom, Douglas, and Sandberg discuss: no one actor technically can set tax policy rules in other jurisdictions directly. However, countries' tax policy choices are highly affected by other countries' decisions and, in many cases, by political pressure from international organisations. The magnitude of the effects of both unilateral actions of particular countries and political pressure from international organisations is hard to estimate, but both are significant, meaning that, especially in larger groups and international organisations, suboptimal outcomes are very likely in the presence of the unanimity voting requirement. A qualified majority voting system, on the contrary, has the potential to produce better outcomes. Where a switch to majority voting is not possible, it seems reasonable to provide parties disagreeing with a unilateral decision made on the group's behalf, be it accepting a policy or vetoing it, with a formal objection supported by data and analysis, thus empowering them to adequately protect their interests if needed.

It can be argued, however, that majority voting undermines national sovereignty over tax policy matters as it will unavoidably result in some cases where some countries will be outvoted even though their positions are well-justified and, possibly, even shared by a substantial minority. Some previous research also argues that where the issues to be voted on are of a dichotomous nature (such as pass/fail on tax policies), whether the voting system is based on unanimity or majority often does not have a significant impact on outcomes, while the amount of information that group members have about each other's preferences makes a big difference.[50]

IV. Conclusions

The international tax context is not exactly multilateral, and there is a risk that policies will be implemented due to some actors in the group overestimating their value. However, the principle of '*sincere cooperation*' should not be

---

[48] Bostrom, Douglas and Sandberg (n 45) 355.
[49] ibid.
[50] C Miller, 'Group Decision Making Under Majority and Unanimity Decision Rules' (1985) 48 *Social Psychology Quarterly* 1, 53.

interpreted in a way that requires Member States to commit to initiatives clearly going against their national interests. The value of implementing a particular tax policy as well as the costs and risks associated with refusing to do so are not the same for all group members and, in fact, can differ significantly.

Creating a unilateral setting entails a risk of hold outs, and not always for a good reason. However, the opposite scenario is hardly desirable either. Assessing the benefits and costs associated with a specific tax policy in a specific setting requires a subjective valuation that will have an error of an unknown magnitude. Typically, the country's government would have the best information and understanding of the local context required for making such an assessment. Assessment of the benefits and costs of policy implementation by other actors or states is thus potentially more erratic.

It is thus desirable for countries to have the option of providing a reason for rejecting a certain policy proposal in the event that there are serious grounds for their position. If implementation of the policy does indeed entail significant risks for some members of the group, that should be respected, and they should not be pushed to consent to the policy in cases where that would jeopardise the wellbeing of their citizens. An agreement on a policy option acceptable to all actors needs to be achieved in such cases based on the data provided by them. That will reduce the risks of using hold outs for political pressure while protecting less powerful group members from being pushed to accept policies putting them in an even more vulnerable position.

While the exclusion of developing countries from the tax policy-making process is hardly news, it seems that some lower-income 'developed' countries are facing similar issues of their interests being overlooked in the unions they are part of. Exercising coercive powers when making international tax decisions is detrimental to trust between the union and its members, as well as between Member States and their citizens, and is likely to result in suboptimal outcomes for the entire group.

Both *ex ante* and *ex post*, the effects of the implementation of particular tax policies are often misrepresented by simplified, overgeneralising, or frankly false claims. Groups of actors are likely to include actors overestimating the benefits of the implementation of specific initiatives, and in a unilateral-like setting, when some actors of the group are experiencing significant pressure from others who might be overestimating the policy's benefits, this is likely to lead to suboptimal outcomes for the group as a whole, making the cost of excluding several actors from the policy-making process larger than the long-term benefit from such exclusion. Introducing a requirement to provide a justification, ideally based on data analysis, supporting a veto on tax policy matters can help ensure that the less privileged states still have the freedom to disagree with tax policies, putting them in a vulnerable position, while making it significantly harder using the veto mechanism as a political leverage.

7

Sustainability Reporting and Corporate Taxation

VASILIKI KOUKOULIOTI

Taxes are fundamental to the existence of a civilised society.[1] They can therefore significantly contribute to achieving sustainability, as specified in the United Nations 2030 Sustainable Development Goals (SDGs) Agenda.[2] The SDGs are not tax goals per se, but they describe a framework that taxation can contribute to shaping.[3] Fiscal policies can serve a twofold purpose: on the one hand, they finance domestic resource mobilisation, on the other, they support behavioural shifts to influence socio-economic outcomes. The first purpose would entail fair, transparent, and efficient tax systems with a special focus on developing countries, while the latter would include the implementation of gender responsive tax policies (SDG 5), tax incentives to attract infrastructure investment (SDG 9), carbon taxes (SDG 13), or taxes on harmful and unhealthy products (SDG 3).

A significant obstacle to achieving sustainable development has been base erosion and profit shifting (BEPS) practices by multinational corporations. While all countries are impacted by global corporate income tax (CIT) losses estimated at 4–10 per cent of global CIT revenues,[4] the scale and economic impact of BEPS are higher in developing countries as a percentage of their GDP, due to structural limitations and greater reliance on corporate taxes.[5] Bird and Davis-Nozemack

---

[1] 'Taxes are what we pay for civilized society', Justice Holmes in *Compania General De Tabacos De Filipinas v Collector of Internal Revenue* (1927) 275 US 87, 100. See, also, Franklin D Roosevelt, 'Message to Congress on Tax Evasion Prevention' (online by Gerhard Peters and John T. Woolley, *The American Presidency Project*, 1 June 1937) www.presidency.ucsb.edu/documents/message-congress-tax-evasion-prevention, '[w]hen our legitimate revenues are attacked, the whole structure of our Government is attacked. "Clever little schemes" are not admirable when they undermine the foundations of society.'

[2] United Nations, General Assembly Resolution A/RES/70/1, 'Transforming our world: the 2030 Agenda for Sustainable Development' (21 October 2015).

[3] See R Pilke and P Räsänen, 'Practicing or Preaching? Linking Taxation and Sustainable Development in EU Foreign Policy' (2018) 23 *European Foreign Affairs Review* 203, 205.

[4] OECD, *Measuring and Monitoring BEPS, Action 11–2015 Final Report* (Paris, OECD/G20 Base Erosion and Profit Shifting Project, OECD Publishing, 2015).

[5] The OECD calculated in 2010 that at the aggregate global level half of the sum needed to finance the Millennium goals could come from more effective taxation in developing countries. V Atisophon,

have thus defined tax avoidance, not just as a financial problem for tax authorities, but as a 'sustainability problem' with 'organizational and societal consequences', proposing that this approach could better help mitigating it.[6]

Inevitably, there has been a significant increase in demand for corporate sustainability information in recent years, especially from the investment community, but also due to fast-changing citizen awareness, consumer preferences, and market practices.[7] Corporations have been increasingly confronted with stakeholder pressure to introduce environmental, social, and governance (ESG) considerations in their decision making. Various initiatives, ranging from institutional investors integrating ESG factors and responsible investment principles into their policies and investment decisions[8] to the development of several sustainability reporting standards,[9] demonstrate that stakeholder demands on ESG issues have risen.

However, compared with other areas of corporate responsibility, disclosures and commitments on tax remain less developed and standardised. A 2021 global analysis using a dataset of 1,300 listed companies across both developed and emerging markets found that only a third (34 per cent) of these companies have commitments or policies on tax transparency in place, compared to 87 per cent for climate change and 98 per cent for health and safety.[10] Nevertheless, certifications and recommendations for best practices that could build an objectively measured tax sustainability profile are starting to emerge, adopting different approaches on the importance and purpose of tax reporting and the relevance of tax information to sustainable development.

The purpose of this chapter is to explore the landscape of tax sustainability reporting and critically assess the suitability of tax metrics to measure corporations' contribution to sustainability. Section I identifies general and tax-specific challenges in using tax information to assess how sustainable and responsible a

---

J Bueren, G de Paepe, C Garroway and JP Stijns, 'Revisiting MDG cost estimates from a domestic resource mobilisation perspective' (*OECD Development Center Working Papers* 306, 2011).

[6] R Bird and K Davis-Nozemack, 'Tax Avoidance as a Sustainability Problem' (2018) 151 *Journal of Business Ethics* 1009.

[7] Directive 2022/2464 of the European Parliament and of the Council of 14 December 2022 amending Regulation (EU) No 537/2014, Directive 2004/109/EC, Directive 2006/43/EC and Directive 2013/34/EU, as regards corporate sustainability reporting [2022] OJ L322, Preamble, para 11.

[8] See, eg, United Nations Principles for Responsible Investment (PRI), comprising of six principles and relevant actions developed by an international group of institutional investors reflecting the increasing relevance of environmental, social and corporate governance issues to investment practices, 'What are the Principles for Responsible Investment?' (UN Principles for Responsible Investment) www.unpri.org/about-us/what-are-the-principles-for-responsible-investment.

[9] See, eg, the United Nations Guiding Principles Reporting Framework on human rights reporting; the Global Reporting Initiative, developed by the Global Sustainability Standards Board (GSSB-GRI) on economic, environmental, and social impacts reporting; the Sustainability Accounting Standards Board (SASB) on reporting of financially-material environmental, social, and governance issues.

[10] E Bourne, C Dodsworth and J Kooroshy, 'Global Trends in Corporate Tax Disclosure' (*FTSE Russel*, 10 June 2021) content.ftserussell.com/sites/default/files/global_trends_in_corporate_tax_disclosure_final.pdf.

corporation is. Section II attempts to address these challenges by suggesting adjustments to existing tax metrics and anticipating a general shift in the regulatory role these metrics might play. Finally, section III concludes with some more general considerations on the future of tax sustainability reporting.

Throughout the chapter, terms, such as corporate social responsibility, sustainability and ESG interact and overlap. Though different, they will be mostly used interchangeably to capture the idea of corporate behaviour to enhance long-term societal value.

I. Problems of Using Tax for Sustainability Reporting

Though concerns have been raised on whether corporate social responsibility (CSR) should guide tax behaviour, it is currently undeniable that tax and CSR are becoming closely interlinked.[11] The narrow view of the corporation as a profit generation machine, as per Friedman's infamous statement, sounds anachronistic.[12] In this context, Avi-Yonah constructs a compelling argument to prove that, under any of the three views of the corporation, CSR is acceptable, and hence corporations have an affirmative obligation not to engage in tax minimisation practices.[13] Under the artificial entity view, the corporation is viewed as a creature of the state and should therefore engage in CSR as part of its societal mission without imposing additional burdens on the state. Under the real entity view, the corporation is an entity separate from both the state and its shareholders and is encouraged to engage in CSR by avoiding tax minimisation practices as part of its obligations to the state. Lastly, under the aggregate view, whereby the corporation is the mere aggregate of its individual members or shareholders, taxes are a detriment to shareholder value and should therefore be minimised. However, Avi-Yonah considers this view contradictory, because if applied by all corporations, the state would be deprived of adequate resources to fulfil the social responsibility functions born exclusively by it – corporations should therefore engage in CSR also under the aggregate view.

Addressing CSR is also in the interests of enterprises. Actions that can clearly and demonstrably benefit shareholders in the long run, for example, actions to prevent environmental disasters or compliance with ethical rules, even though

---

[11] See, eg, C Panayi, 'Is Aggressive Tax Planning Socially Irresponsible?' (2015) 43 *Intertax* 544 (providing a more critical approach towards CSR and tax).

[12] '[T]here is [...] only one social responsibility of business – to use its resources and engage in activities designed to increase its profits'. M Friedman, 'A Friedman Doctrine – The Social Responsibility of Business Is to Increase Its Profits' (*New York Times Magazine*, 13 September 1970) www.nytimes.com/1970/09/13/archives/a-friedman-doctrine-the-social-responsibility-of-business-is-to.html, (citing M Friedman, *Capitalism and Freedom* (Chicago, University of Chicago Press, 1962) 133).

[13] R Avi-Yonah, 'Corporate Taxation and Corporate Social Responsibility' (2014) 1 *New York University Journal of Law & Business* 11.

costly in the short run, can protect against corporate calamities.[14] Engaging in CSR activities entails the management of relationships with a variety of stakeholders and should hence be treated as an investment strategy that can lead to the long-term minimisation of risks rather than a cost. Going beyond legal obligations can contribute to a company's competitiveness, as measured by CSR's impact on risk and reputation management, which has become increasingly important as enterprises face more public scrutiny.[15] CSR activities can also improve a company's productivity (both directly, because of a better working environment) and indirectly (by attracting the attention of consumers and investors) for example, when listed in an ethical stock market index like the MSCI KLD 400 Social Index. Though companies' tax obligations remain within the confines of the letter and the spirit of the law, tax regulation is inevitably imperfect and ambiguous and thus should not be exclusively relied upon to achieve better tax governance.[16]

Therefore, the expectation that corporations engage in socially responsible activities would entail not only refraining from tax planning activities that undermine the sustainability of the tax systems where they operate, but also undertaking investment decisions that are guided by sustainability considerations in the markets where they operate, instead of exclusively by regulatory obligations. This trend is demonstrated by the rise of reporting standards that introduce types of self-regulation and voluntary reporting of tax strategies, in particular how a corporation's approach to tax corresponds to its sustainability commitments. In this way, the existing tax reporting initiatives have already paved the way towards defining and measuring responsible tax conduct by reference to, not only legal obligations, but also privately set standards that might go beyond the law.

Nevertheless, though it is now uncontested that tax is a core sustainability metric, the tax sustainability reporting landscape is characterised by lack of harmonisation and a plethora of sustainability standards that can create confusion and negatively impact different stakeholders.

A. Sustainability Reporting Confusion

The increasing demand for sustainability information has given rise to a plethora of sustainability reporting standards on ESG-related issues. While financial reporting is intensely regulated, non-financial reporting, or better sustainability reporting,[17]

---

[14] ibid 15.

[15] 'Communication from the Commission on the European Competitiveness Report' 2008 [SEC (2008) 2853] COM/2008/0774 final.

[16] H Gribnau, 'Why Social Responsible Corporations Should Take Tax Seriously' in KK Egholm Elgaard, RK Feldthusen, A Hilling and M Kukkonen (eds), *Fair Taxation and Corporate Social Responsibility* (Copenhagen, ExTuto Publishing, 2019).

[17] See, eg, Directive 2022/2464 (n 7), recital 8, on why the term 'sustainability information' is preferable: 'Many stakeholders consider the term "non-financial" to be inaccurate, in particular because it implies that the information in question has no financial relevance. Increasingly, however,

has not been standardised yet. Not-for-profit organisations, advocacy groups, and policy institutions have developed voluntary sustainability reporting standards and frameworks, each addressing the needs of different users.[18] The current landscape has been commonly referred to as the 'alphabet soup' of ESG reporting standards.[19] Repeated calls for harmonisation were answered in September 2020, when five leading global organisations announced a statement of intent to work towards developing a comprehensive corporate reporting system.[20] More recently, the International Sustainability Standards Board (ISSB), launched in November 2021 by the International Financial Reporting Standards at the COP26 climate summit, proposed two standards on climate and general sustainability-related disclosures, which will form a comprehensive global baseline of sustainability disclosures for the financial markets.[21]

While the ISSB initiative moves in the direction of ESG reporting unification, a different institution is developing its own set of standards, raising the question of whether unification can actually be achieved. The European Union has repeatedly identified the need for harmonisation and standardisation for the better functioning of the internal market and has moved quickly in this direction by introducing legislation, including the EU Taxonomy Regulation,[22] the Sustainable Finance

---

such information does have financial relevance. Many organisations, initiatives and practitioners in the field of sustainability reporting refer to "sustainability information". It is therefore preferable to use the term "sustainability information" in place of "non-financial information"'.

[18] Examples of standards are the Global Reporting Initiative (GRI) and Sustainability Accounting Standards Board (SASB). Examples of frameworks are the Carbon Disclosure Standards Board (CDSB), the International Integrated Reporting Council (IIRC), the Carbon Disclosure Project (CDP) and the Task Force on Climate-related Financial Disclosures (TCFD).

[19] H Blomme, and J Basha, 'Unpuzzling the Sustainability Reporting Alphabet Soup' (2021) *Accountancy Plus, The Official Journal of CPA Ireland*, 9. See, also, S Watkins, 'The ISSB's battle to sort the alphabet soup of ESG reporting' (*Financial Times Professional*), professional.ft.com/en-gb/blog/the-issbs-battle-to-sort-the-alphabet-soup-of-esg-reporting/#:~:text=The%20International%20 Sustainability%20Standards%20Board,decide%20on%20a%20single%20framework.

[20] Carbon Disclosure Project, Climate Disclosure Standards Board, Global Reporting Initiative, International Integrated Reporting Council and Sustainability Accounting Standards Board, 'Statement of Intent to Work Together Towards Comprehensive Corporate Reporting' (September 2020) sasb. org/wp-content/uploads/2023/01/Statement-of-Intent-to-Work-Together-Towards-Comprehensive-Corporate-Reporting.pdf.

[21] International Financial Reporting Standards S1 General Requirements for Disclosure of Sustainability-related Financial Information, *International Sustainability Standards Board* (June 2023) www.ifrs.org/content/dam/ifrs/publications/pdf-standards-issb/english/2023/issued/part-a/issb-2023-a-ifrs-s1-general-requirements-for-disclosure-of-sustainability-related-financial-information. pdf?bypass=on; International Financial Reporting Standards S2 Climate-related Disclosures, International Sustainability Standards Board (June 2023) www.ifrs.org/content/dam/ifrs/publications/pdf-standards-issb/english/2023/issued/part-a/issb-2023-a-ifrs-s2-climate-related-disclosures.pdf? bypass=on.

[22] Regulation (EU) 2020/852 of the European Parliament and of the Council of 18 June 2020 on the establishment of a framework to facilitate sustainable investment, and amending Regulation (EU) 2019/2088, recital para 12: 'The criteria for determining whether an economic activity qualifies as environmentally sustainable should be harmonised at Union level in order to remove barriers to the functioning of the internal market [...]. Such harmonisation would therefore facilitate cross-border sustainable investment in the Union.'

Disclosure Regulation (SFDR),[23] the recently adopted Corporate Sustainability Reporting Directive (CSRD),[24] and the soon-to-be adopted Corporate Sustainability Due Diligence Directive (CSDD).[25] In particular, the CSRD stresses that '[t]he development of mandatory common sustainability reporting standards is necessary to reach a situation in which sustainability information has a status comparable to that of financial information.'[26] However, despite these efforts, the landscape does not seem much clearer at the EU level either. The EU sustainability reporting framework is an amalgam of reporting obligations stipulated in different legal documents. In November 2022, asset managers in Europe, including Amundi and AXA, degraded their most sustainable funds, holding tens of billions of dollars, as a response to the uncertainty provoked by the EU sustainability rules that failed to provide the industry with a clear definition of sustainability.[27] This uncertainty more likely will be further exacerbated when the ISSB framework is finalised, raising questions about the interaction of this new set of standards with the mandatory EU sustainability reporting standards.

The lack of a single sustainability disclosure standard, on the one hand, and the growing demand for sustainable investments, on the other, has increased the importance of and reliance on ESG rating agencies.[28] These third-party data providers allow investors to screen corporations based on their ESG performance. Some of the largest international ESG rating providers are S&P Global, Sustainalytics, Morningstar, and Moody's.[29] However, while the market for sustainability information is growing rapidly, research has shown that ESG ratings from different providers disagree to such an extent that there is no certainty as to how good a company's ESG performance is.[30] Divergence is mainly documented in 'how'

---

[23] Regulation (EU) 2019/2088 of the European Parliament and of the Council of 27 November 2019 on sustainability-related disclosures in the financial services sector, recital para 9: 'It is therefore necessary to address existing obstacles to the functioning of the internal market and to enhance the comparability of financial products in order to avoid likely future obstacles.'

[24] Directive 2022/2464 (n 7), recital para 33: 'Information should also be harmonized, comparable and based on uniform indicators where appropriate, while allowing for reporting that is specific to individual undertakings and does not endanger the commercial position of the undertaking.'

[25] 'Proposal for a Directive of The European Parliament and of The Council on Corporate Sustainability Due Diligence and amending Directive' (EU) 2019/1937, COM/2022/71 final, Explanatory Memorandum, section 3: 'large companies across the board asked for greater harmonisation in the area of due diligence to improve legal certainty and create a level playing field'.

[26] Directive 2022/2464 (n 7) recital 37.

[27] A Klasa, 'European asset managers blame regulatory confusion for downgrade of ESG funds' (*Financial Times*, 22 November 2022) www.ft.com/content/d74445d5-1275-4a1e-a118-70f2750ce7c9.

[28] According to UN Principles for Responsible Investment 2020, more than 3,000 investors representing over $100 trillion in assets have committed to integrating ESG information into their investment decisions. UN Principles for Responsible Investment (2020) Annual Report, www.unpri.org/about-the-pri/annual-report-2020/6811.article.

[29] A Demartini, 'Provision of Non-Financial Data: Mapping of Stakeholders, Products and Services' (Autorité des marchés financiers, December 2020) www.amf-france.org/sites/institutionnel/files/private/2020-12/mapping-esg-publication.pdf.

[30] F Berg, JF Kölbel and R Rigobon, 'Aggregate Confusion: The Divergence of ESG Ratings' (2022) 26 *Review of Finance* 1315; AK Chatterji, R Durand, DI Levine and S Touboul, 'Do ratings of firms converge? Implications for managers, investors and strategy researchers' (2016) 37

rating agencies choose to measure, which can distort the purpose of ratings to capture objective observations that can be ascertained.[31] The divergence issue partly stems from the fact that 'sustainability' is an essentially contested concept. If there is no way to define sustainability without a thoroughly agreed upon moral theory, it is not surprising that there is little agreement among rating agencies.[32] Apart from the lack of agreement on a moral theory level, the sustainability reporting confusion is exacerbated by the fact that the ESG ratings market remains largely unregulated, with only some isolated attempts in different jurisdictions.[33] Japan has developed the world's first code of conduct for ESG evaluation and data providers,[34] the UK has announced a package of measures to improve trust and transparency in the market for sustainable investment products,[35] and the EU has issued a proposal for a regulation on the transparency of ESG rating activities.[36] Most of these regulatory initiatives attempt to address the lack of transparency about data sources and methodologies used, the management of conflicts of interest, the protection of confidential information, and the need for comparability and standardisation. Nevertheless, regional ESG standardisation will still not address the lack of harmonisation.

The landscape of tax reporting for sustainability purposes is equally complex. Taxation was initially not considered a core metric for ESG purposes, until the United Nations Sustainable Development Goals acknowledged taxes as the essential 'fuel' to build a more equal and prosperous society and to achieve sustainable development.[37] It was for this reason that only recently have non-governmental organisations and advocacy groups started developing tax standards covering various tax topics, including tax governance, tax planning, transparency, and relationships with authorities.[38] The first ESG standard for tax was developed in 2019 by the Global Reporting Initiative (GRI 207 standard) and comprises

---

Strategic Management Journal 1597; S Kotsantonis and G Serafeim, 'Four Things No One Will Tell You About ESG Data' (2019) 31 *Journal of Applied Corporate Finance* 50.

[31] Berg et al. (n 30) 1327–1341.

[32] See, WB Gallie, 'Essentially Contested Concepts' (1956) 56 *Proceedings of the Aristotelian Society* 167.

[33] International Organization of Securities Commissions, 'Environmental, Social and Governance (ESG) Ratings and Data Products Providers – Final Report' (2021) www.iosco.org/library/pubdocs/pdf/IOSCOPD690.pdf.

[34] Financial Services Agency, 'The Code of Conduct for ESG Evaluation and Data Providers' (December 2022) www.fsa.go.jp/news/r4/singi/20221215/02.pdf.

[35] Financial Conduct Authority, 'Sustainability Disclosure Requirements (SDR) and investment labels' *Policy Statement PS23/16* www.fca.org.uk/publication/policy/ps23-16.pdf.

[36] European Commission, 'Proposal for a Regulation of The European Parliament and of The Council on the transparency and integrity of Environmental, Social and Governance (ESG) rating activities', COM (2023) 314 final.

[37] United Nations, 'Transforming' (n 2). Pursuant to target 17.1: 'Strengthen domestic resource mobilization, including through international support to developing countries, to improve domestic capacity for tax and other revenue collection.'

[38] P Hongler, F Regli and T Berndt, 'Tax Reporting and Sustainability' (*Institute of Public Finance, Fiscal Law and Law & Economics, Working Paper*, 2021), ile.unisg.ch/wp-content/uploads/2021/06/WP-06-Hongler-Regli-Berndt.pdf.

four elements: i) an approach to tax; ii) tax governance, control, and risk management; iii) stakeholder engagement and management of concerns related to tax; and iv) Country-by-Country-Reporting (CbCR).[39] In 2020, the World Economic Forum (WEF) published a White Paper on Measuring Stakeholder Capitalism outlining three different tax metrics: total tax paid, tax collected by the company on behalf of other taxpayers, and total tax paid by country for significant locations.[40] More recently, in 2021, the Fair Tax Mark accreditation introduced a Global Multinational Business Standard of responsible tax conduct based on the principle of paying 'the right amount of tax (but no more) in the right place at the right time, according to both the letter and the spirit of the law' and providing 'sufficient public information'.[41]

In the EU, sustainability reporting legislation has so far mainly focused on the environmental aspect of ESG reporting, leaving taxation either unmentioned or at the periphery of sustainability considerations.[42] However, both the CSRD preamble[43] and the minimum safeguards provided for in the EU Taxonomy Regulation[44] stress the importance of the OECD Guidelines for Multinational Enterprises. These Guidelines stipulate two key expectations for enterprises that: (a) they should comply with the letter and spirit of tax laws; and (b) they should treat tax governance and tax compliance as important elements of their oversight and broader risk management systems.[45] A more direct reference to taxation can be found in the SFDR, which includes in the definition of 'sustainable investment' the requirement that investee companies are tax compliant.[46] Though this legislation acknowledges that taxation has a role to play in achieving sustainability, it provides no further guidance on which tax behaviour is considered sustainable and what corporations should report, especially when asked to comply with the spirit of the tax law.

---

[39] Global Reporting Initiative, 'Global Reporting Initiative-207' (2019).

[40] World Economic Forum, 'Measuring Stakeholder Capitalism: Towards Common Metrics and Consistent Reporting of Sustainable Value Creation, White Paper' (September 2020) www3.weforum. org/docs/WEF_IBC_Measuring_Stakeholder_Capitalism_Report_2020.pdf.

[41] Fair Tax Foundation, 'Global Multinational Business Standard, Guidance Notes' (2021) fairtaxmark. net/wp-content/uploads/2022/10/Global-MNC-standard-criteria-print-version.pdf.

[42] eg, the EU Taxonomy Regulation establishes criteria for determining whether an economic activity qualifies as environmentally sustainable, while leaving at a later stage '[f]urther guidance on activities that contribute to other sustainability objectives, including social objectives', Regulation (EU) 2020/852 (n 22), preamble no. 6 and Art 1. Also, the CSRD provides for the adoption of Sustainability Reporting Standards covering ESG factors without any reference to taxation. Directive 2022/2464 (n 7) Art 1 para 8.

[43] Directive 2022/2464 (n 7), preamble para 45.

[44] Regulation (EU) 2020/852 (n 22) Art 18.

[45] OECD 'OECD Guidelines for Multinational Enterprises' (2011) www.oecd.org/daf/inv/mne/ 48004323.pdf. See, also, Platform on Sustainable Finance, 'Final Report on Minimum Safeguards' (October 2022) 49 finance.ec.europa.eu/system/files/2022-10/221011-sustainable-finance-platform-finance-report-minimum-safeguards_en.pdf, (suggesting that the identification of procedures for establishing compliance with the minimum standards can follow the analytical process by considering the OECD MNE Guidelines).

[46] Regulation (EU) 2019/2088 (n 23) Art 2 point 17.

At the same time, though not directly linked to sustainability reporting, tax transparency initiatives can inform stakeholders about a corporation's tax strategy and hence its tax contribution. However, the landscape is characterised by multiple, sometimes deviating, reporting obligations and increased complexity.[47] Under BEPS Action 13 minimum standard, corporations with consolidated group revenue of at least €750 million are required to prepare a country-by-country (CbC) report with data on the global allocation of income, profit, and taxes paid among tax jurisdictions in which they operate, and share it with tax administrations in these jurisdictions (obligatory tax authority CbCR).[48] However, if any of these jurisdictions are in the EU, the CbC reports should be made public (obligatory public CbCR).[49] At the same time, there are a number of voluntary public CbCR frameworks by various standard-setters, such as GRI 207, whose scope is much wider, covering corporations of any size, type, sector, or geographic location, provided they report under GRI standards and identify tax as a material topic.[50] Tax transparency reporting requirements are expected to further increase as a result of ongoing policy and legislative initiatives. The ISSB is due to announce its sustainability disclosure standards, and it is not clear yet whether tax and CbCR will be among a new set of non-financial reporting requirements, in which case they will apply to all corporations using IFRS. There is also the question of whether ISSB will align its approach to tax reporting with the one followed by the CSRD. Lastly, the EU's new business tax agenda would encompass a new proposal requiring certain large companies to publish their effective tax rates, which might be connected to CbCR data.[51]

In this landscape, ESG rating agencies introduce an additional layer of complexity. Tax metrics are surprisingly under-represented in ESG ratings, with a study finding that 50 per cent of major agencies, including Moody's ESG and Morgan Stanley Capital International (MSCI), did not include a tax indicator in their ESG rating system.[52] Where tax metrics are used to rate ESG performance, the average correlation level is only 0.04, meaning that there is significant

[47] For a comparative overview of CbC tax reporting obligations under BEPS Action 13, EU public CbCR Directive and GRI-207, see S Verloove, P Hoving and R Aviles Gutierrez, 'EU Public Country-by-Country Reporting' (2022) 29 *Intl. Transfer Pricing J.* 3.

[48] OECD 'Transfer Pricing Documentation and Country-by-Country Reporting' (2015) *Action 13–2015 Final Report, OECD/G20 Base Erosion and Profit Shifting Project.*

[49] Under this Directive, in-scope corporations should report on income tax information, including their activities, number of employees, total net turnover, profit before tax, income tax due in the country, tax actually paid, and accumulated earnings. Directive (EU) 2021/2101 of the European Parliament and of the Council of 24 November 2021 amending Directive 2013/34/EU as regards disclosure of income tax information by certain undertakings and branches [2021] OJ L429.

[50] Global Reporting Initiative, 'Comparison of GRI 207: Tax 2019 & OECD Action 13 BEPS Country-by-Country Report' www.globalreporting.org/standards/media/2537/comparison-gri-207-tax-2019-oecd-beps.pdf.

[51] European Commission, 'Communication from the Commission to the European Parliament and the Council', Business Taxation for the 21st Century, COM (2021) 251 final.

[52] Berg et al. (n 30) 1325.

divergence in the scope, measurement, and weight of tax metrics among different agencies.[53] Apart from the divergence, tax metrics are also considered insufficient in scope, because they do not cover the OECD MNE Guidelines.[54]

The plethora of sustainability standards and the lack of a generally accepted methodology to measure and manage sustainability-related risks have important implications for most stakeholders. Investors are unable to take sufficient account of sustainability-related risks and opportunities in their investment decisions, potentially creating inefficiencies in global capital markets and posing a threat to financial stability.[55] In particular, divergent disclosure standards and divergent results from market-based practices (ESG rating agencies) make it difficult to compare different financial products and thus create an uneven playing field for such products. Similarly, researchers using ESG rating schemes to conduct empirical analysis might risk drawing conclusions that are not accurate.[56] Corporations, especially those with cross-border activities, are confronted with different reporting requirements and, hence, increased compliance burdens, costs, and complexity. At the EU level, such divergent measures and approaches in reporting standards could undermine the internal market, in particular the right of establishment and the free movement of capital, and distort competition.[57] At the same time, because of the uncertainty about ESG targets, corporations have a decreased incentive to invest in improving their ESG performance or might waste resources and hence reduce social welfare by relying on invalid, irrelevant, or even contradictory metrics.[58] The confusion and lack of sustainability information create an accountability deficit and damage citizen trust in corporations. Non-governmental organisations, civil society actors, communities affected by corporations' activities, and other stakeholders are less able to hold corporations accountable and enter into a dialogue with them on the impact of their activities on sustainability matters.

An additional unavoidable effect of the lack of harmonisation, and the consequent subjectivity to sustainability requirements is the increased risk of 'greenwashing' practices by corporations and investors. Such practices include misleading or fraudulent disclosures about one's ESG performance and efforts for the purpose of influencing customers, capital inflows, and investment choices.[59] The literature also uses the term 'CSR decoupling' to characterise situations where external CSR elements, ie, public and highly visible initiatives, are not matched by internal CSR elements, ie, inward-looking practices that involve real actions.[60]

---

[53] ibid 1329.

[54] Platform on Sustainable Finance (n 45).

[55] Directive 2022/2464 (n 7), preamble para. 14; Chatterji (n 30) 1598.

[56] Chatterji (n 30) 1598.

[57] Directive 2022/2464 (n 7), preamble para. 16; and Regulation (EU) 2019/2088 (n 23) preamble para. 9.

[58] Chatterji (n 30) 1598.

[59] World Economic Forum, 'ESG: ESG Regulation and Policy-Making' (2024) intelligence.weforum.org/topics/a1G680000004EI1EAM/key-issues/a1G680000004EYTEA2.

[60] CSR decoupling is further discussed in section I.B.iii.

Regulatory initiatives in different jurisdictions are attempting to address the risk of 'greenwashing'. The US Securities and Exchange Commission (SEC) has set up a task force in March 2021 to identify ESG-related misconduct proactively.[61] Examples of SEC enforcement actions constitute charges against BNY Mellon for falsely representing or implying in various statements that all of its investment funds had received ESG quality reviews, and Vale S.A., a Brazilian mining company, for manipulating dam safety audits, obtaining false safety certificates and misleading all levels of stakeholders through the company's ESG disclosures.[62] The UK Financial Conduct Authority (FCA) confirmed in November 2023 a substantial package of measures to improve the trust and transparency of sustainable investment products and minimise greenwashing, ensuring that sustainability-related claims are fair, clear and not misleading.[63] Lastly, the EU has published legislation and reports on ESG benchmarks aimed at increasing transparency and preventing greenwashing.[64]

The lack of a consistent tax reporting system creates confusion and difficulties in accurately reporting and evaluating ESG performance, which, as a result, affects the validity and reliability of sustainability standards, blurs a clear understanding of a corporation's contribution to funding public benefits, and hinders the ability to identify sustainable corporations and ultimately to achieve the hypothesised benefits of sustainable practices.

B. Concerns on whether Taxes are an Appropriate Sustainability Metric

Despite the undeniable relevance of taxes in assessing the socially responsible behaviour of corporations, concerns can be raised about whether tax metrics can accurately measure the contribution of corporations to achieving the SDGs. These concerns relate to two intrinsic characteristics of corporate taxes that might render them unsuitable for accurately capturing their impact on the distribution of wealth in a society and, thus, on sustainability: first, that taxes only represent one side of the fiscal balance, the other being expenditures, and second, that the person liable to pay the tax might be different from the one ultimately bearing the tax, described as corporate tax incidence. Apart from these characteristics, taxes paid might be a misleading figure if taken out of context.

---

[61] US Securities and Exchange Commission, 'SEC Announces Enforcement Task Force Focused on Climate and ESG Issues, Press Release' (4 March 2021) www.sec.gov/news/press-release/2021-42.

[62] See US Securities and Exchange Commission, 'Enforcement Task Force Focused on Climate and ESG Issues' (US Securities and Exchange Commission, 11 April 2023) www.sec.gov/spotlight/enforcement-task-force-focused-climate-esg-issues.

[63] Sustainability Disclosure Requirements (n 35).

[64] Regulation (EU) 2019/2089 of 27 November 2019 amending Regulation (EU) 2016/1011 as regards EU climate transition benchmarks, EU Paris-aligned Benchmarks and sustainability-related disclosures for benchmarks; EU Technical Expert Group on Sustainable Finance, 'Report on Benchmarks' (September 2019).

i. Taxes Disregard the Spending Side

Taxes have been identified as the necessary 'fuel' to achieve sustainable development, since they can generate the funds required to finance government activities
in support of the SDGs.[65] Nevertheless, the collection of tax revenues is a necessary, but not sufficient, condition for sustainable development. In other words,
taxation, though a prerequisite for the accomplishment of most SDGs, cannot
be regarded in isolation from other policies that determine how tax resources
are mobilised domestically.[66] Tax measures, therefore, mainly interact indirectly
with the SDGs, in that their primary objective is to raise revenue. which can be
used at a second stage to pursue policy objectives that are in line with the SDGs.
Conversely, if tax resources are not channelled towards sustainable development
objectives, the mere collection of taxes does not suffice to achieve the SDGs.

Taxes can also interact directly with the SDGs, when a tax system's redistributive, and not just revenue-generating, function is accomplished. The
redistributive function of taxation is 'aimed at reducing the unequal distribution
of income and wealth that results from the normal operation of a market-based
economy'.[67] This can be achieved by a progressive tax system or wealth taxes.
Nevertheless, progressive taxation does not guarantee redistribution, as this
depends on spending policies. Murphy and Nagel in their seminal work argued
that, since pre-tax income or ownership is not generated and secured without any
help from the government, discussions about tax justice should focus on how the
after-tax income is distributed within a society.[68] To assess therefore the sustainability footprint of an activity both the allocation of burdens through taxes and
the distribution of benefits through spending policies should be considered.[69]

Similar considerations can be expressed about the role of international
taxation in the achievement of sustainable development. International tax law
concerns the allocation of taxing rights among countries and thus influences the
ability of less developed economies to raise tax revenues. In this context, Richard
and Peggy Musgrave developed the theory of inter-nation equity, advocating for
the allocation of more taxing rights to less developed countries.[70] However, in the

---

[65] International Monetary Fund, OECD, UN, World Bank Group, 'Taxation & SDGs. First Global
Conference of the Platform for Collaboration on tax', *Conference Report* (14–16 February 2018) ('taxes
generate the funds that finance government activities in support of the SDGs').

[66] United Nations, 'Transforming' (n 2) – Goal 17, para 17.1: 'Strengthen domestic resource mobilization, including through international support to developing countries, to improve domestic capacity
for tax and other revenue collection.'

[67] RS Avi-Yonah, 'The Three Goals of Taxation' (2006) 60 *Tax Law Review* 1, 3.

[68] L Murphy and T Nagel, *The Myth of Ownership: Taxes and Justice* (New York, OUP, 2002).

[69] 'What matters for distributive purposes in any society are the distributional consequences of taxing
and spending together, not taxes alone. Moreover, all taxes matter, not just income taxes.' I Grinberg,
'Comment on Miranda Stewart's 'Redistribution between Rich and Poor Countries'' (2018) 72 *Bulletin
for International Taxation* 4/5.

[70] Though the two authors had developed the issue of 'inter-nation equity' in various articles by
1972, the first extended discussion of the concept is found in their 1972 essay. RA Musgrave and

current nation-state system, both revenue collection and government expenditure are matters of national, not international, prerogative.[71] As a result, the dominant moral subject on the recipient side of the redistributive mechanism is the government, not the individuals.[72] In this context, the allocation of more taxing rights to less developed economies can help achieve sustainable development under the assumption of a benevolent and capable government on the recipient side that has the political will and capacity to make 'sustainable' use of its additional taxing rights. Absent this government, the fulfilment of inter-nation equity provides no guarantee that poverty will be eradicated, and inequalities will be reduced. On the contrary, a government might cause poverty and inequality or be unable, under the pressure of globalisation, to address the widening income disparities.[73] For example, it might be the case that a country decides not to fully exercise its tax jurisdiction by providing tax incentives to make its tax system more competitive and attractive to foreign investment, thus minimising the tax resources necessary to fulfil duties of justice towards its citizens.[74] It has also been argued that without the right domestic institutions, including the rule of law, administrative capacity, and a robust system of anti-fraud and anti-corruption measures, wealth transfer will not bring any benefits to the recipient country, or it may even cause harm when put into the hands of the wrong people.[75]

Coming back to the value of tax metrics in measuring a corporation's sustainable behaviour, the amount of taxes paid does not show whether tax revenues are channelled towards SDGs, and thus does not guarantee an SDG-friendly practice. It is a question of how these taxes are distributed domestically via spending policies, which are nevertheless not reported in the current tax reporting standards. Nevertheless, since the design of internal fiscal policies is in principle outside the control of corporations, this limitation can be addressed by adopting sustainability reporting focused on measuring good corporate tax citizenship. An alternative way to address this limitation is analysed in section II. Since corporations do have control over where they decide to invest, consideration for investment location characteristics that relate to spending policies could provide useful insights about their contribution to achieving sustainable development.

PB Musgrave, 'Inter-nation equity' in Richard Bird and John Head (eds), *Modern Fiscal Issues: Essays in Honor of Carl S. Shoup* (Toronto, University of Toronto Press, 1972) 63–85.

[71] NH Kaufmann, 'Fairness and the taxation of international income' (1998) 29 *Law and Policy in International Business* 145, 188.

[72] J Stark, 'Tax Justice Beyond National Borders – International or Interpersonal?' (2022) 42 *Oxford Journal of Legal Studies* 133.

[73] Developed countries experience the crisis of the welfare state. Developing countries have limited administrative capacity. See, eg, RS Avi-Yonah, 'Globalization, Tax Competition, and the Fiscal Crisis of the Welfare State' (2000) 113 *Harvard Law Review* 1573.

[74] L Abramovsky, A Klemm and D Phillips, 'Corporate Tax in Developing Countries: Current Trends and Design Issues' (2014) 35 *Fiscal Studies* 559.

[75] M Risse, 'How Does the Global Order Harm the Poor?' (2005) 33 *Philosophy and Public Affairs* 349, 373.

ii. *The Mystery of the Corporate Tax Incidence*

The progressivity of corporate taxation, and hence its redistributive function and its direct interaction with the SDGs, also depends on who bears the burden of corporate tax. This is described as the 'corporate tax incidence'.

Corporations, due to their nature as legal constructs, cannot bear the burden of taxes. It is rather individuals, in their capacity as owners, employees, suppliers, or consumers, that are the subjects of tax incidence.[76] If the corporate tax falls upon the owners in the form of lower dividends, it is more likely to be progressive, compared to when it is shifted to employees in the form of lower wages, to customers in the form of higher prices, or to suppliers in the form of reduced payments for inputs.[77]

In practice, it is difficult to identify the incidence of tax.[78] This would require imagining the counterfactual of what would have happened in the absence of taxes, which can vary among industries, businesses, and countries. Some commentators have, therefore, questioned whether it makes sense to think about fairness in the context of corporate taxation.[79] According to this view, if more taxes on corporations say nothing about the actual distribution of the burden of corporate tax among individuals, knowing this is instrumental to evaluating the progressiveness of a tax system, then corporate taxation might not be the right instrument to measure the redistributive function of a tax system, and hence the extent to which it contributes to achieving sustainable development. However, the view about the indeterminacy of corporate tax incidence does not explain why corporations persistently advocate for lower corporate tax rates or engage in tax avoidance activities. Research suggests that lower corporate tax rates are consistent with corporations' economic interests and that corporate shareholders and top executives frequently benefit from corporate

---

[76] RA Musgrave and PB Musgrave, *Public Finance in Theory and Practice*, 5th edn (New York, McGraw Hill, 1989) 237: '[T]he resulting chain of adjustments-the process of '"shifting the tax burden"' -may lead to a final distribution of the burden or economic incidence, which differs greatly from the initial distribution of liabilities or statutory incidence.'; ERA Seligman, *Double Taxation and International Fiscal Cooperation* (New York, The Macmillan Co., 1928) 105–106: '... the legislator does indeed not think of a particular person, but nevertheless believes that some person, who is the owner, will not only pay but bear the tax ...'.

[77] AJ Auerbach, 'Who Bears the Corporate Tax? A Review of What We Know' (2006) 20 *Tax Policy and the Economy* 1; MJ Graetz and AC Warren, 'Integration of Corporate and Shareholder Taxes' (2016) 69 *National Tax Journal* 677; S Bank, *From Sword to Shield: The Transformation of the Corporate Income Tax, 1861 to Present* (Oxford, OUP, 2010). It should be noted that this statement assumes that the owners are more likely to be in the upper part of the income distribution.

[78] There is substantial disagreement among researchers in the field. Most economists think that the burden is shared between labor and capital, without however agreeing on how much of the burden is shifted to workers. See, eg, RA Felix and JR Hines, 'Corporate taxes and union wages in the United States' (2009) 29 *International Tax and Public Finance* 6; M Devereux, L Liu and S Loretz, 'The elasticity of corporate taxable income: New evidence from UK tax records' (2014) 6 *American Economic Journal: Economic Policy* 19.

[79] MP Devereux, AJ Auerbach, M Keen, P Oosterhuis, W Schön and J Vella, *Taxing Profit in a Global Economy* (Oxford, OUP, 2019) 35.

tax cuts.[80] Also, conventional models of corporate tax incidence assign the vast majority of the burden of the corporate tax to capital or shareholders.[81]

These outcomes therefore suggest that it is enough for sustainability reporting to measure good tax behaviour. Also, similarly to the argument in section I.B.i., corporations do not in principle set corporate tax rates, but they can comply or fail to comply with tax laws, engage in profit shifting and tax avoidance or refrain from doing so, and thus undermine or enhance sustainability. In a globalised world, corporations can also decide on where to locate their activities with a view to minimising their tax burden. Further analysis on how sustainability reporting can be improved by incorporating investment location decisions follows in section II.

iii. *Complexity in Tax Decision-making*

Despite other corporate sustainability metrics, such as those measuring emissions or waste,[82] tax-related information is usually highly context-specific. As a general rule, the fewer emissions a corporation produces, the better, though organisation-specific metrics might be taken into consideration to help contextualise the organisation's efficiency as well as compare it with other organisations.[83] The same does not hold true for taxes: amount of taxes paid reveals little about a corporation's sustainability profile.

The choices corporations have on how to structure their business and determine their tax position are diverse, as is their fiscal and social impact. Depending on the business sector, different business decisions will determine what constitutes responsible tax behaviour: location and ownership of intangible assets in the digital sector, holding-company structures in the extractives sector or tax behaviour of clients in the accountancy and financial sectors.

Similarly, the same tax output can be interpreted differently depending on the circumstances in which it occurs. Total taxes paid by a corporation depend on its net profit margin, which can vary significantly depending on the industry,[84] as well as on the use of tax incentives and reliefs, which can either be general incentives available to its competitors or company-specific ones secretly negotiated

---

[80] See, eg, KA Clausing, 'Capital Taxation and Market Power' (SSRN, 2023) ssrn.com/abstract=4419599.

[81] See, eg, JR Nunns, 'How TPC Distributes the Corporate Income Tax' *Tax Policy Center* (13 September 2012) www.taxpolicycenter.org/sites/default/files/alfresco/publication-pdfs/412651-How-TPC-Distributes-the-Corporate-Income-Tax.PDF.

[82] See, eg, Global Reporting Initiative 305: Emissions (2016) www.globalreporting.org/standards/media/1012/gri-305-emissions-2016.pdf; Global Reporting Initiative 306: Waste (2020) www.globalreporting.org/standards/media/2573/gri-306-waste-2020.pdf.

[83] Examples of organisation-specific metrics are production volume and premises size.

[84] For example, based on data about US companies, the auto industry has an average net margin of 3.53%, while the software (system and application) industry can achieve one of 19.14%. 'Margins by sector (US)' (January 2024) pages.stern.nyu.edu/~adamodar/New_Home_Page/datafile/margin.html.

with the tax authorities in tax rulings.[85] Another relevant parameter is the place where these taxes are paid. Paying more taxes in developing countries is generally better, because they are more in need of tax revenues, but the contribution of these taxes to sustainable development depends on how they are spent domestically. For corporations, this might translate into whether they decide to invest in countries that implement redistributive policies or whether they undertake structures that result in reduced tax revenues in countries that are more in need of these revenues.

Apart from a careful factual assessment, detecting cases of tax abuse and aggressive tax planning requires an assessment of the subjective element of the transaction. In domestic and EU anti-tax avoidance legislation, such as the Anti-Tax Avoidance Directive (ATAD I),[86] and anti-tax avoidance soft law instruments, such as relevant BEPS Project Actions,[87] the taxpayer's or transaction's purpose is essential to identifying cases where the taxpayer circumvents the object and purpose of the law. This connects back to the OECD MNE Guidelines, which state that 'enterprises should comply with both the letter and spirit of the tax laws and regulations of the countries in which they operate'.[88]

For example, the UK Controlled Foreign Companies (CFC) regime provides that a UK resident company may be taxed on a proportion of the profits of a CFC resident in a lower tax jurisdiction if 'the main purpose, or one of the main purposes, of the arrangement' is to obtain a tax advantage.[89] Also, under the principal purposes test (PPT), one of the key provisions in the Multilateral Instrument (MLI) to assist tax authorities to prevent tax treaty abuse, treaty benefits, such as reduced withholding taxes on interest, royalties and dividends, are denied 'if it is reasonable to conclude, having regard to all relevant facts and circumstances, that obtaining that benefit was one of the principal purposes of any arrangement or transaction that resulted directly or indirectly in that benefit'.[90] These are two

---

[85] Tax incentives, such as IP box regimes, provided they fulfil the nexus requirement, can as a whole have positive and negative effects. Nevertheless, tax incentives provided in a secret and discretionary manner to specific companies can distort markets, undermine democratic processes and public perceptions of tax justice and provide opportunities for corruption.

[86] Council Directive (EU) 2016/1164 of 12 July 2016 laying down rules against tax avoidance practices that directly affect the functioning of the internal market [2016] OJ L193.

[87] The most relevant Actions are 3, 5, 6 and 7.

[88] OECD, 'OECD Guidelines for Multinational Enterprises' (2011) 60.

[89] Taxation (International and Other Provisions) Act 2010 (TIOPA 2010), Part 9A. The UK CFC regime is a complex set of rules with a series of 'gateways' and exemptions. The regime was reformed significantly in 2012, when the 'main purpose' test was introduced with the intention to make it consistent with EU law. For an analysis on the rationale of the reform, see HM Treasury, 'Consultation on Controlled Foreign Companies (CFC) reform' (2011), assets.publishing.service.gov.uk/government/uploads/system/uploads/attachment_data/file/81304/consult_cfc_detailed_proposals.pdf.

[90] OECD, 'Article 7 – Prevention of Treaty Abuse, Multilateral Convention to Implement Tax Treaty Related Measures to Prevent BEPS' www.oecd.org/tax/treaties/multilateral-convention-to-implement-tax-treaty-related-measures-to-prevent-beps.htm ('Multilateral Instrument' or 'BEPS MLI'). The PPT was developed under OECD/G20 BEPS Project-Action 6 as a minimum standard. See, OECD, 'Preventing the Granting of Treaty Benefits in Inappropriate Circumstances', Action 6–2015 Final Report (2015) *OECD/G20 Base Erosion and Profit Shifting Project*.

examples of anti-tax avoidance provisions that require a careful consideration of the intent behind a taxpayer's presence in a 'tax haven' or in a country with a beneficial tax treaty network before measures are taken against this taxpayer. However, the use of different terms to describe the subjective element[91] and the operation of the subjective element as a counterfactual to the transactions that would have taken place in the absence of any tax consideration create challenges in identifying tax-abusive practices and applying the relevant legislation consistently.[92]

These challenges are further exacerbated by the dynamic nature of tax policymaking. International tax standards vary depending on the policy body that generates them, and the (geo)political circumstances, in which they appear, so tax practices cannot be properly evaluated unless these conditions are considered. The evolution in the past 25 years of what is considered harmful tax competition provides pertinent proof. From targeting low corporate tax rates, tax havens, and preferential tax regimes[93] to introducing information exchange requirements[94] and the nexus approach,[95] the OECD has continuously revisited its approach to harmful tax competition and, as a result, its policy suggestions for anti-tax avoidance measures.[96] At the same time, the OECD and the EU have developed divergent attitudes towards tax good governance standards. The OECD shifted from a more confrontational approach against non-OECD members[97] to establishing the OECD/G20 Inclusive Framework on BEPS in 2016, inviting the participation of developing and emerging countries on an 'equal footing'.[98] The EU

---

[91] Examples of such terms include 'intention', 'purpose', 'motive', 'object' and 'aim'.

[92] P Piantavigna, 'The Role of the Subjective Element in Tax Abuse and Aggressive Tax Planning' (2018) 10 *World Tax Journal* 2.

[93] The key factors in identifying tax havens were: (i) no or nominal taxes, (ii) lack of transparency or effective exchange of information, and (iii) no substantial activities; and the key factors in identifying preferential tax regimes were: (i) no or low effective tax rates, (ii) application to geographically mobile income, (iii) provision to foreign taxpayers or activities as opposed to domestic taxpayers or activities ('ringfencing'), and (iv) lack of transparency or exchange of information with other jurisdictions. OECD, 'Harmful Tax Competition: An Emerging Global Issue' (1998).

[94] OECD, 'A Process for Achieving a Global Level Playing Field' (2004) *OECD Global Forum on Taxation*.

[95] The 'nexus approach' provides that a taxpayer can 'benefit from an IP regime only to the extent that the taxpayer itself incurred qualifying research and development (R&D) expenditures that gave rise to the IP income', meaning that the substantial activity that contributed to the IP income should be done at the jurisdiction offering the IP regime. OECD 'Countering Harmful Tax Practices More Effectively, Taking into Account Transparency and Substance', Action 5–2015 Final Report, Chapter 4 (2015) *OECD/G20 Base Erosion and Profit Shifting Project*.

[96] For a detailed historic analysis of how the concept of harmful tax competition has evolved, see L Faulhaber, 'The trouble with tax competition: From Practice to Theory' (2018) 71 *Tax Law Review* 311.

[97] The Forum on Harmful Tax Practices, established in 1998, was an exclusive OECD-member forum deciding inter alia on 'tax havens' blacklists.

[98] The Inclusive Framework (IF) initiative has been extensively criticised as not providing equal cooperation opportunities to all members, especially developing countries. See, eg, A Christians and L van Apeldoorn, *Tax Cooperation in an Unjust World* (Oxford, OUP, 2021). Nevertheless, recent empirical research suggests that lower-income countries' participation in the IF has allowed them to make some modest achievements to date. See RC Christensen, M Hearson and T Randriamanalina,

seems to have moved in the opposite direction. From a dialogue and consensus-based approach, where the objective was to 'reach agreement with as many third countries as possible on common principles of cooperation and transparency',[99] the EU moved to stronger instruments to 'reprimand' third countries that did not meet the EU tax good governance standards by inviting member states to adopt unilateral measures, such as national blacklists and termination of tax treaties,[100] and introducing an EU blacklist[101] and common defensive measures.[102]

Are tax metrics in a position to capture this complexity? Existing tax metrics in sustainability reports generally attempt to report compliance with the spirit and letter of tax laws by asking for total taxes paid by country,[103] including country-by-country information,[104] and the company's tax strategy.[105] While tax metrics should prioritise simplicity, their attempt to codify complex and dynamic legal provisions risks rendering them overly simplistic or even misleading. There are no industry-specific tax metrics, and this 'one-size-fits-all' approach disregards the industry-relevant contextualisation, thus making it difficult to evaluate and compare the information reported. It is also highly questionable whether tax metrics can document the subjective elements underpinning a transaction. Though a company's 'tax strategy' can help explain the rationale behind its business and tax decisions and its tax policy commitments,[106] it can also include strategically select information about positive aspects to deflect public scrutiny from negative effects and mislead public opinion about its performance and intentions.

For the same reasons, tax strategies and tax sustainability reporting in general, can also function as a legitimation tool. Critical research has identified that CSR reporting can be used to legitimise and 'greenwash' a company's activities

---

'At the Table, Off the Menu? Assessing the Participation of Lower-Income Countries in Global Tax Negotiations' (2020) *International Centre for Tax & Development Working Paper* 115 opendocs.ids. ac.uk/opendocs/bitstream/handle/20.500.12413/15853/ICTD_WP115.pdf?sequence=9.

[99] European Commission, 'Communication from the Commission to the Council, the European Parliament and the European Economic and Social Committee: Promoting Good Governance in Tax Matters', COM (2009) 201 final (28 April 2009).

[100] European Commission, 'Commission Communication of 6 December 2012 regarding Measures Intended to Encourage Third Countries to Apply Minimum Standards of Good Governance in Tax Matters', [2012] OJ L338.

[101] Inclusion in the EU blacklist would trigger defensive measures in the non-tax and tax area, ie, restriction of development aid and discouragement of foreign investment in the blacklisted country. See, Council of the European Union, 'The EU list of non-cooperative jurisdictions for tax purposes – Council conclusions' (2017) 15429/17 FISC 345 *Economic and Financial Affairs Council* 1088.

[102] European Commission, 'Communication from the Commission to the European Parliament and the Council on an External Strategy for Effective Taxation' (2016) COM (2016) 24 final.

[103] eg, World Economic Forum, Stakeholder (n 40), Pillar 4-Prosperity, core and expanded metrics.

[104] eg, Global Reporting Initiative and Fair Tax Mark.

[105] This is described using different terms, such as 'approach to tax' (GRI), 'tax policy' (FTM) and 'accountability and governance' (Bteam).

[106] FTM specifically refers to three commitments: a) seek to declare profits in the place where their economic substance arises; b) not use tax havens artificially and for the purposes of tax reduction; c) follow the spirit as well as the letter of the law, and not structure transactions and operations artificially for the purpose of avoiding tax.

and function as a marketing tool to increase support by stakeholders, including customers.[107] This has also increased instances of CSR decoupling.[108] Recent empirical research has evidenced a negative correlation between CSR and good tax behaviour, suggesting that responsible firms measured by different CSR disclosures are more involved in tax avoidance as compared to less responsible firms.[109] Interestingly, CSR decoupling seems to be employed to a greater extent by firms headquartered in countries with stronger national governance.[110] CSR reporting can therefore degenerate into an organisational façade for businesses to achieve self-interested goals, including low-cost virtue signalling as a way to conceal controversial tax strategies.[111]

Tax metrics measure compliance with the applicable tax provisions without challenging their suitability for achieving sustainable development. Tax compliance is recognised by some as sufficient to justify a responsible business conduct.[112] Avi-Yonah, on the other hand, has argued that tax compliance is not always enough and that corporations have an affirmative obligation not to engage in tax minimisation practices, even if these are legal.[113] This approach is reflected in some tax metrics that ask firms to comply with the spirit of the law.[114] However, no tax metric expects corporations to go beyond the law and devise their business in a way that addresses, possibly unfair, distributional outcomes within and among countries perpetuated by the current (international) tax order. There is indeed concern that this might raise questions about the nature of management's obligations to shareholders. For example, while some tax metrics stress

---

[107] A Schneider, 'Bound to Fail? Exploring the Systemic Pathologies of CSR and Their Implications for CSR Research' (2019) 59 *Business & Society* 1303, 1310–12.

[108] The term CSR decoupling, or ESG decoupling, is used to describe the misalignment between a firm's CSR, or ESG, disclosure and its actual CSR, or ESG, performance. See, eg, P Bromley and WW Powell, 'From Smoke and Mirrors to Walking the Talk: Decoupling in the Contemporary World' (2012) 6 *Academy of Management Annals* 1, 483.

[109] See, eg, T Zeng, 'Relationship between corporate social responsibility and tax avoidance: International evidence' (2019) 15 *Social Responsibility Journal* 244; MA Gulzar, J Cherian, MS Sial, A Badulescu, PA Thu, D Badulescu, and NV Khuong, 'Does corporate social responsibility influence corporate tax avoidance of Chinese listed companies?' (2018) 10(12) *Sustainability* 4549; and TM Montenegro, 'Tax Evasion, Corporate Social Responsibility and National Governance: A Country-Level Study' (2021) 13(20) *Sustainability* 11166.

[110] Montenegro uses national governance to describe government efficiency, regulatory quality, rule of law and corruption control, as well as the national quality of public company auditors working environments. The same relation between state progressiveness and tax avoidance/CSR decoupling has been evidenced in M Visser, D Reimsbach and G Braam (2022) 'Corporate social responsibility, tax avoidance and the political role of the state: A normative perspective and empirical evidence' paper presented at 44th Annual Congress of European Accounting Association, 11–13 May, Bergen, Norway.

[111] CH Cho, M Laine, RW Roberts and M Rodrigue, 'Organized hypocrisy, organizational façades, and sustainability reporting' (2015) 40 *Accounting, Organizations and Society* 78.

[112] See, eg, A Hilling and DT Ostas, *Corporate Taxation and Social Responsibility* (Stockholm, Wolters Kluwer, 2017). The authors distinguish between compliance (obeying the law) and cooperation (improving the law), and argue that compliance with the tax law suffices as good CSR, while cooperation is called for when laws have a high degree of moral salience.

[113] Avi-Yonah (n 13).

[114] eg, Fair Tax Mark. This principle is provided in the OECD MNE Guidelines.

the importance of only using legitimate tax reliefs aligned with a company's business,[115] no tax metric expects companies to minimise the use of tax incentives, especially when it comes to developing countries, despite the general agreement among policymakers that most incentives, especially tax holidays, undermine public revenues without commensurate benefit in terms of investment, employment, and economic activity.[116] Additionally, no tax metric reports comparative data on tax revenues foregone by different countries, richer and poorer, as a result of a firm's tax-driven business decisions,[117] or the percentage of overall government tax revenue contributed by a corporation.[118] In general, countries' different needs in tax resources are not treated as a relevant parameter to assess corporate sustainability, even though the UN 2030 SDG Agenda has underlined the special needs and implementation challenges with which developing countries are confronted, hence calling for actions to address their special needs.[119] Instead of considering countries' special needs, most sustainability reports seem to reproduce entrenched racial biases. By not clarifying how they define 'tax havens', they possibly imply the use of the EU or national blacklists.[120] Nevertheless, such blacklists have historically targeted states like Dominica and Panama, while excluding wealthier ones like Switzerland, Luxembourg, and the United States.[121] Dean and Waris tell the details of the culture story underpinning tax havens, where nations with predominantly Black or Brown populations have been treated disparately and punished for peculiar at best and racially driven at worst reasons.[122]

---

[115] Examples of these tax metrics are Fair Tax Mark (Part 4: Tax Notes Disclosures) and Bteam (Principle 5: Seeking and accepting tax incentives).

[116] International Monetary Fund (IMF), 'Revenue Mobilization in Developing Countries' (2011); IMF/OECD/UN/World Bank, 'Supporting the development of effective tax systems: a report to the G20' (2011).

[117] Christian Aid, Oxfam and Action Aid, 'Getting to Good – Towards Responsible Corporate Tax Behaviour' (2015), on why and how approaching tax responsibility beyond legal compliance benefits companies and the developing countries in which they operate.

[118] Oxfam and United Nations Global Compact, 'The Poverty Footprint – A People-centred Approach to Assessing Business Impacts on Sustainable Development, Poverty Footprint Indicators Guide' (2015), d306pr3pise04h.cloudfront.net/docs/issues_doc%2Fhuman_rights%2FPoverty+Footprint+ Indicator+Guide_21+Sept+2015_final.pdf.

[119] eg, Goal 10a calls for the implementation of the principle of special and differential treatment for developing countries, and Goal 10b encourages official development assistance and financial flows, including foreign direct investment, to States where the need is greatest. United Nations, 'Transforming' (n 2).

[120] OECD, 'Towards Global Tax Co-operation' (2000) Report to the 2000 Ministerial Council Meeting and Recommendations by the Committee on Fiscal Affairs, Progress in Identifying and Eliminating Harmful Tax Practices 17; Council of the EU, 'Council Conclusions on the revised EU list of non-cooperative jurisdictions for tax purposes' (14 February 2023) 6375/23 FISC 19 ECOFIN 143.

[121] The United States, despite being identified as a high-risk country in facilitating tax avoidance, was never included in any EU blacklist, due to economic dependencies and fears of retaliation. See, L Hakelberg, *The Hypocritical Hegemon – How the United States Shapes Global Rules against Tax Evasion and Avoidance* (Cornell University Press, 2020) 5–6.

[122] S Dean and A Waris, 'Ten Truths About Tax Havens: Inclusion and the 'Liberia' Problem' (2021) 70 *Emory Law Journal* 7.

A notable exception is the Fair Tax Mark, which uses the Tax Justice Network Corporate Tax Haven Index.[123]

The current design of tax metrics is therefore inappropriate to measure corporations' contribution to sustainability. The disregard for the spending side of the fiscal account and the difficulty in determining the corporate tax incidence challenge the suitability of corporate taxes to measure their contribution to sustainable development. Also, the complex interaction of business decisions with taxes cannot be captured by 'out-of-context' and 'one-size-fits-all' tax metrics. The identified challenges are not nonetheless insurmountable. Careful consideration of the specificities of tax, including accounting for the special characteristics of the investment locations, apart from the amount of taxes paid, could help create more reliable corporate tax sustainability metrics. The following section develops some ideas for their improvement.

II. How can Corporate Tax Sustainability Reporting be Improved

The first step towards addressing the challenges of existing tax sustainability reporting standards is their harmonisation. Alignment under a single tax reporting standard and generally accepted metrics and methods for measuring, valuing, and managing sustainability-related risks could enhance consistency and improve the comparability and reliability of corporate tax sustainability information.[124] Tax sustainability reporting harmonisation will also make sustainability divergence more intelligible and foster competition.[125] The current attempts at unification, though promising, might be creating further confusion. Among these are the International Sustainability Standards Board (ISSB) intention to deliver a comprehensive global baseline of sustainability-related disclosure standards,[126] a statement of intent by five global organisations to work together towards comprehensive corporate reporting,[127] the EU legislative initiatives to create uniform standards of mandatory corporate sustainability disclosures,[128]

---

[123] In this index, many developed countries, such as Switzerland, Luxembourg and the UK, are not only included but they also rank high. Tax Justice Network, 'Corporate Tax Haven Index – 2021 Results' cthi.taxjustice.net/en/.

[124] See, eg, Berg et al (n 30) 1319. These benefits have been also mentioned in the preamble of Directive 2022/2464 (n 7).

[125] Berg et al (n 30) 1343.

[126] International Financial Reporting Standards, 'General Sustainability-related Disclosures' www.ifrs. org/projects/completed-projects/2023/general-sustainability-related-disclosures/#final-stage.

[127] CDP, CDSB, GRI, IIRC and SASB, 'Statement of Intent' (n 18).

[128] See, eg, Directive 2022/2464 (n 7) and Directive 2014/95/EU of the European Parliament and of the Council of 22 October 2014 amending Directive 2013/34/EU as regards disclosure of non-financial and diversity information by certain large undertakings and groups Text with EEA relevance [2014] OJ L193.

and the European Sustainability Reporting Standards (ESRS) developed by EFRAG, a private association advising the European Commission.[129] A possible source of tax metric divergence and under-representation is the lack of consensus on the role of taxation in achieving sustainable development. In this context, the UN 2030 SDG Agenda could provide a starting point on how taxes can interact directly and indirectly with the SDGs and, more specifically, which tax behaviour should be considered responsible for sustainability purposes.

Harmonisation, however, will not solve the inherent limitations relating to using taxes in sustainability reporting. As analysed, even though sustainable development relies both on tax and spending policies, the latter are not considered for sustainability reporting purposes (sub-section I.B.i.), while the 'mystery' of the corporate tax incidence questions the very suitability of corporate taxes to measure a corporation's contribution to sustainable development (sub-section I.B.ii.). At the same time, existing tax metrics so far have focused only on compliance with the letter and the spirit of the law, sometimes adopting overly simplistic or divisive approaches (sub-section I.B.iii.). Most importantly, tax sustainability reporting disregards the special assistance developing countries need to achieve sustainable development. Despite these challenges, this section suggests that there are ways to overcome these challenges if tax sustainability metrics re-evaluate their principles and standards.

As a starting point, consideration should be given to the countries where corporations decide to invest, since different countries have different development characteristics and needs. Developing countries, in particular, are confronted with special challenges that warrant special treatment. This has been acknowledged in various instances. The United Nations Framework Convention on Climate Change introduced the principle of common but differentiated responsibilities (CBDR) and respective capabilities.[130] The 'differentiated responsibilities' component of the CBDR principle suggests that both historic responsibility for current environmental problems, and the capability to address these problems should determine how responsibility is shared among countries.[131] Similarly, the UN SDG 10 on the reduction of inequality within and among countries invites all stakeholders to '[i]mplement the principle of *special and differential treatment for developing countries*, in particular least developed countries, in accordance with World Trade Organization agreements' and '[e]ncourage official development assistance and financial flows, including *foreign direct investment*, to States

---

[129] Platform on Sustainable Finance, 'Final Report' (n 45) 15: 'The European Sustainability Reporting Standards (ESRS) and disclosure requirements are expected to result in an improved comparability, availability, and quality of corporate sustainability-related information. This creates a more reliable basis of data for the assessment of the sustainability of companies, which also allows to draw more reliable comparisons between companies.'

[130] United Nations Framework Convention on Climate Change art 3(1), (9 May 1992) S. Treaty Doc No. 102-38, 1771 *United Nations Treaty Series* 107.

[131] See D Bell, 'Global Climate Justice, Historic Emissions, and Excusable Ignorance' (2011) 94 *Monist* 391, 391.

where the need is greatest, in particular least developed countries, African countries, small island developing States and landlocked developing countries, in accordance with their national plans and programmes' (emphasis added).[132] In international tax policy, where rules are nominally reciprocal but substantively asymmetrical, there have been proposals for less uniformity and for a framework that acknowledges and accounts for the differences that exist among states.[133]

There are different ways in which tax sustainability metrics could account for differences among countries when measuring a corporation's sustainable behaviour. Tax metrics could measure whether a tax responsible company progressively reports a larger portion of its income in poorer countries, while being consistent with transfer pricing rules and the group's operations. This could be achieved by reporting changes to transactions and ownership structures, for example, locating high-value functions or the development and management of intangibles in economies with greater fiscal needs.[134] Additionally, tax metrics could measure not only whether a tax responsible company seeks a tax-level playing field, by avoiding opaque processes and abstaining from company-specific tax incentives, but also whether it progressively attempts to minimise the impact of foregone revenues, as a result of transactions and structures, on poorer countries. Hence, by acknowledging the differences in countries' fiscal needs, tax metrics could attempt to report on the international equity of a company's tax liabilities.

Nevertheless, as analysed in sub-section I.B.i., progressively paying more taxes in poorer countries provides no guarantee that companies contribute to sustainable development in these countries.[135] This depends on how tax revenues are spent domestically, which is determined by sovereign governments when they devise their domestic spending policies. Some country-specific characteristics could therefore provide guarantees that taxes paid will either directly or indirectly contribute to sustainable development. To this effect, institutional accountability and the rule of law are relevant to achieving sustainable development.[136] These factors entail the quality of domestic institutions, including the rule of law, administrative capacity, prevention of fraud, corruption, and bribery, and effective and accountable institutions, as well as the quality of tax institutions, including tax

---

[132] United Nations, 'Transforming' (n 2).

[133] SA Dean, 'More Cooperation, Less Uniformity: Tax Deharmonization and the Future of the International Tax Regime' (2009) 84 *Tulane Law Review* 125.

[134] Though narrow and widely criticised as unsuitable for measuring economic performance and social progress, GDP per capita could be an indicator to determine countries' fiscal needs. See, for the criticism, JE Stiglitz, A Sen and JP Fitoussi, *The Measure of Economic Performance and Social Progress Revisited: Reflections and Overview* (N° 2009–33, OFCE, *Centre de Recherche en Économie de Sciences Po*, December 2009).

[135] Rawls has remarked with respect to this that 'merely dispensing funds will not suffice to rectify basic political and social injustices'. See, J Rawls, *The Law of Peoples, with The Idea of Public Reason Revisited* (Cambridge, MA, Harvard University Press 2001) 108.

[136] See, eg, Goal 16, United Nations, 'Transforming' (n 2); and, OECD, 'Development Co-operation Report 2014: Mobilising Resources for Sustainable Development' (OECD Publishing 2014).

administrative reforms, alignment with international standards on exchange of information, level of tax morale, and effectiveness of tax collection mechanisms. The level of human development can also provide evidence that tax resources are used to support ongoing development efforts. A country's protection of human rights and commitment to eradicating inequality can help reveal societal injustices usually masked under economic growth metrics, especially in more affluent countries, and hence distinguish 'worthy' from 'unworthy' recipients of a bigger share of national gains.[137] Introducing such metrics however would require careful consideration of complexities. On the one hand, the most disadvantaged countries will tend to score poorly on these metrics, and this might discourage investment in them. On the other hand, such metrics could encourage developing countries to compete for capital with better governance rather than tax breaks.

General social development indices, such as the Gini index[138] or the Human Development Index (HDI),[139] could be used together with more specific ones measuring the sustainability of a tax system. Researchers have developed a tax system sustainability evaluation model and a tax sustainability index to measure the sustainability of EU countries' tax systems in accordance with the main goals of the Europe 2020 strategy.[140] Their evaluation model measures how the tax system of a particular country contributes to the sustainability of a country's four basic pillars, economy, society, environment, and institutions, further divided into policy areas, in order to meet the needs of the current generation without compromising the needs of future ones.[141] The evaluation is conducted by identifying the tax tools which can be used to achieve the policy goals and assessing through a set of questions whether the tax system of the assessed EU Member State applies these tools. It is worth noting, though, that devising such pillars would present more challenges once one moves outside the EU to nations with much less homogeneity in terms of internal policies and ideological commitments.

Tax sustainability reporting that would include metrics about institutional accountability, human development, or tax system sustainability in the countries

---

[137] 'Simply put, in a world where North Korea can spend money without asking Japan for any authorization and can even use it to prepare for a war against Japan, the Japanese will not be willing to engage in any cross-border redistribution of wealth, regardless of North Korean poverty and the reasons for it', I Benshalom, 'The New Poor at Our Gates: Global Justice Implications for International Trade and Tax Law' (2010) 85 *New York University Law Review* 1, 5–6.

[138] The Gini coefficient compares cumulative proportions of the population against cumulative proportions of income they receive, and it ranges between 0 in the case of perfect equality and 1 in the case of perfect inequality.

[139] United Nations Development Programme, 'Human Development Report 2010 – The Real Wealth of Nations: Pathways to Human Development' (2010), Introduction by A Sen, vi. See also RF Kennedy's 1968 speech at the University of Kansas noting that GDP 'measures everything in short, except that which makes life worthwhile' www.jfklibrary.org/learn/about-jfk/the-kennedy-family/robert-f-kennedy/robert-f-kennedy-speeches/remarks-at-the-university-of-kansas-march-18-1968.

[140] M Dobranschi, D Hampel, J Janová, D Nerudová and P Rozmahel, 'Tax System Sustainability Evaluation: A Model for EU Countries' (2019) 54 *Intereconomics* 3, 138.

[141] World Commission on Environment and Development, *Our Common Future: World Commission on Environment and Development* (Oxford, OUP, 1987).

where taxes are paid would be able to report more accurately the impact of corporate tax payments on sustainable development. Such metrics could therefore document the sustainability of the choices corporations make among a range of equally legally acceptable and commercially justifiable options. The UN Blueprint for Business Leadership on the SDGs acknowledges these options businesses have and urges them to adopt responsible taxation practices and distribute the economic value they generate across stakeholders to alleviate inequality, even by 'distributing profits above a certain threshold to community'.[142]

III. Conclusion and the Way Forward

This chapter is concerned with the question of whether corporate taxes are an appropriate metric to measure sustainability. Tax payments are small pieces in a complex regulatory and political puzzle, and they should thus be observed within the wider context of the domestic and international distribution of burdens, benefits, and resources. To achieve this, corporate tax sustainability metrics should shift from a 'one-size-fits-all' approach to one that accounts for both industry and investment location characteristics. This could entail the introduction of industry- or country-specific metrics, including those relevant to economic development needs and the level of institutional accountability at the investment locations.

Reforming the current tax sustainability reporting landscape will also provide more incentives to corporations to measure the sustainability of their tax behaviour. An increasing number of corporations are publishing sustainability reports, including information on taxes paid and tax strategies, based on either a specific standard or a combination thereof.[143] But this trend is far from being considered an established, universal practice. The lack of a single standard and the consequent complexity and administrative burden involved in navigating the different available options could explain the reluctance of some corporations to report on tax sustainability. Research using the real option theory has proven that companies 'delay' investment in sustainable tax behaviour because the benefits of such investment are uncertain.[144] This observation fits well with corporate governance

---

[142] United Nations Global Compact, 'Blueprint for Business Leadership on the SDGs' (2018) blueprint.unglobalcompact.org/.

[143] See, eg, Shell, 'Tax Contribution Report 2022' (2023) reports.shell.com/tax-contribution-report/2022/_assets/downloads/shell-tax-contribution-report-2022.pdf; NN Group N.V., 'Total Tax Contribution Report 2022' (2023) www.nn-group.com/article-display-on-page-no-index/total-tax-contribution-2022.htm; Phillips, 'Country Activity and Tax Report 2022' (2023) www.results.philips.com/publications/ar22/downloads/pdf/en/PhilipsCountryActivityAndTaxReport2022.pdf; and AngloAmerican, 'Tax and Economic Contribution Report 2022' (2023), www.angloamerican.com/~/media/Files/A/Anglo-American-Group-v5/PLC/investors/annual-reporting/2022/tax-and-economic-contribution-report-2022.pdf.

[144] A Van de Vijver, D Cassimon and PJ Engelen, 'A Real Option Approach to Sustainable Corporate Tax Behavior' (2020) 12(13) *Sustainability* 5406.

research, which predicts that if there is no paradigm shift in the future that would force multiple institutional gatekeepers to change their orientation, sustainable corporate governance will likely fail unless it is framed as advancing shareholder interests.[145] Additionally, tax sustainability standards seem redundant: they measure compliance with the letter and the spirit of the law, a role already assigned to substantive rules and compliance and enforcement mechanisms. On the other hand, if they also aspire to measure sustainability beyond the law, questions might arise, including what a sustainable tax rate is, which jurisdictions should be treated as tax havens, or which proportion of a corporation's total tax bill should be paid to poorer countries.

Despite these considerations, sustainability is becoming increasingly relevant in tax debates, the same as in environmental or human rights ones. Corporations are no longer justified in making tax decisions, ignoring their societal impact and undermining the achievement of sustainable development. It is therefore imperative to include tax in ESG metrics after careful consideration of the complexities of tax systems. Tax metrics will thus be able to provide more accurate measures of sustainable behaviour and bring wider societal change.

---

[145] DS Lund and E Pollman, 'The Corporate Governance Machine' (2021) 121 *Columbia Law Review* 2563.

PART IV

Individual Taxation Across Borders

8

Taxation of Cross Border Migrations: Re-evaluating the Allocation between Home Country and Host Country

TAMIR SHANAN AND DORON NAROTZKI

In 1923, when the League of Nations asked four renowned economists to propose allocating taxing rights between countries for cross-border transactions, an emphasis was given to the country that hosted the economic activity. It received the first bite of the apple (taxing rights), whereas the taxpayer's country of residence was entitled to receive an inferior right to tax active income that was generated overseas and, in some instances, the first right to tax passive income. In our view, the time has come to revisit such an allocation of taxing rights. Such allocations should be applicable to all countries, and not necessarily focused on developing or developed countries as the migration does not concentrate solely on specific countries. The economic reality of our world has changed greatly, but the international tax system still relies on the rules of a bygone era. The main concepts the international income tax systems relied upon were 'the ability to pay' and the 'benefit' principles. These tax rules were primarily focused on avoiding double taxation. However, less attention was given to double non-taxation and tax evasion issues.[1] At the time the international income tax systems for such transactions were formed, capital (both physical and human) was relatively static. Nowadays capital is significantly more mobile.

Our chapter calls to re-examine the existing rules for taxing cross-border migrants and to redefine the countries of destination's obligations (the countries where the migrants move to and establish their new homes at, ie, 'host countries') and the countries of origination (the country from which the migrant flew, ie, 'home countries').

---

[1] MJ Graetz, 'Taxing International Income: Inadequate Principles, Outdated Concepts, and Unsatisfactory Policies' (2001) 54 *Tax Law Review* 261, 323–36; PB Musgrave, *Taxation of Foreign Investment Income: An Economic Analysis* (Baltimore, Johns Hopkins Press, 1963); PB Musgrave, *United States Taxation of Foreign Investment Income* (Cambridge, International Tax Program, Harvard Law School, 1969); MA Desai & JR Hines 'Evaluating International Tax Reform' (2003) 56 *National Tax Journal* 409.

The issue of cross-border migration is often raised in the context of brain-drain (which focuses on the movement of highly skilled people from developing countries to developed countries). However, the World Bank estimates that just more than half (52 per cent) of the world's cross-border population migrated from low-income countries to high-income countries (South to North flows or developing to developed flows) whereas the other half are cross-border migrants who move to developing countries (including south to south flows and north to south flows).[2] For instance, in 2018

> the number of international migrants and refugees was estimated to be 266 million persons, of whom 240 million (90%) were economic migrants. Around 46% of migrants from developing countries went to high-income countries. However, the share of migrants from developing countries going to other developing countries was larger than the share going to the 'North,' as defined by high-income countries belonging to the OECD.[3]

About two-thirds of cross-border migration in Sub-Saharan Africa and 58 per cent of cross-border migration in Europe and Central Asia is intra-regional. India, Russia, South Africa, and several other developing countries are among the top host countries for migrants.[4]

Nevertheless, the vast literature[5] about cross-border migration focuses on 'brain drain' and neglects to analyse the impacts of people's movement from developed countries to other developed countries or to developing countries, and even more so, the movement of people from developing countries to other developing countries.[6] Most literature about 'brain drain' explores the ways in which developed countries should 'compensate' developing countries for the losses they incur from the movement of their 'best and brightest,' highly skilled nationals, but this issue represents only one part of this economic conundrum.[7]

The time has come to revisit the tax rules for taxing cross-border migration. This is especially true considering these rules were defined almost a century ago based on the work of the League of Nations and on the bilateral tax treaties at the time, when the number of cross-border migrants was significantly lower, and their

---

[2] CW de Wenden, 'New Migrations' (2016) 23 *International Journal on Human Rights* 18; World Bank, *Leveraging Economic Migration for Development: A briefing for the World Bank Board* (Board Report, 2019) 12–24; A Mckeown 'Global Migration 1846-1940' (2004) 15 *Journal of World History* 155.

[3] M McAuliffe & A Triandafyllidou, *World Migration Report 2022* (International Organisation for Migration, PUB2021/032/L, 2021); T Givens, R Navarre, & P Mohanty, *Immigration in the 21st Century: The Comparative Politics of Immigration Policy* (Routledge, 2020).

[4] P Giannoccolo, The Brain Drain: A Survey of the Literature (April 7, 2009) available at SSRN: ssrn.com/abstract=1374329; S Commander, M Kangasniemi & L Winters, 'The Brain Drain: Curse or Boon? A Survey of the Literature, Challenges to Globalization' in R Baldwin and L Winters (eds), *Challenges to Globalization: Analyzing the Economics* (Chicago, University of Chicago Press, 2004).

[5] S Dodani & R LaPorte, 'Brain Drain from Developing Countries: How Can Brain Drain be Converted into Wisdom Gain?' (2005) 98 *Journal of the Royal Society of Medicine* 487; See also WJ Carrington & E Detrgiache, 'How Extensive Is Brain Drain?' (1999) 36 *Finance & Development* 46.

[6] McAuliffe & Triandafyllidou (n 3).

[7] Y Brauner, 'Brain Drain Taxation as Development Policy' (2010) 55 *Saint Louis University Law Journal* 221.

economic impact was far less meaningful. This chapter will explore the different patterns of cross-border migrants and the existing rules for taxing cross-border migrants (both by the host and home country). Then, we will analyse the proposals raised by Professor Jagdish Bhagwati 50 years ago and address the rationale behind not incorporating them within the international tax practices/rules.[8] The fundamental idea of his proposal was that the host (developed) countries would impose a surtax on skilled migrants, collect the tax, and then transfer it to the home (developing) countries. Professor Bhagwati's underlying rationale for this tax was the need to compensate developing countries for the losses those countries experienced by individuals who were born, raised, and often professionally trained there but eventually left to a developed country to find more lucrative employment opportunities (higher salaries, better working conditions, etc). This system aimed to improve the home countries' standard of living (more stable lives in the developed countries and better educational opportunities for the migrant's children).

Professor Bhagwati's proposal barely impacted the way migration is taxed. Over the years, the literature about the taxation of international migrants suggested that the home countries did not solely suffer costs but also gained benefits.[9] Our chapter will analyse these costs and benefits and advocate for cooperation between the host and home countries in a way that would not sacrifice the host countries' right to tax and would recognise the home countries' contribution.

The second contribution this chapter has to the existing literature is regarding the relationship between migrants and their home countries. Our proposal would recommend not solely focussing on residency in shaping the taxing relations between migrants and their home countries. We would call for putting more emphasis on the taxpayer's domicile as a proxy for determining a country's right to tax.[10] We believe that the existing physical presence test, which establishes residency in cases where one resides 183 days or more in a certain jurisdiction, is less relevant and in any event, is recognised under the existing tax rules as such countries are entitled to tax such cross-border income because they are considered the source countries. Similarly, it is our view that citizenship in many instances may be economically not meaningful enough, and in other instances, it may be puzzling when one has multiple citizenships.[11] Our research explores the economic and

---

[8] J Bhagwati and K Hamada, 'The Brain Drain, International Integration of Markets for Professionals and Unemployment: A Theoretical Analysis' (1974) 1 *Journal of Development Economics* 19; J Bhagwati and K Hamada, 'Domestic Distortions, Imperfect Information and The Brain Drain' (1975) 2 *Journal of Development Economics* 265.

[9] RD Pomp, 'The Experience of the Philippines in Taxing its Nonresident Citizens' (1985) 17 *New York University Journal of International Law and Politics* 245; see also Brauner (n 7) 225, 232; M Beine et al., 'Brain Drain and Human Capital Formation in Developing Countries: Winners and Losers' (2008) 118 *Economic Journal* 631, 648.

[10] Such relationship has been referred to in the literature as one's 'social membership' see J Carens, *The Ethics of Immigration* (Oxford, OUP, 2013); D Bamford, 'Duties in an International World: The Importance of Past Residence and Citizenship' (2022) 17 *Problema. Anuario de Filosofía y Teoría del Derecho* 143.

[11] See R Mason, 'Citizenship Taxation' (2016) 89 *Southern California Law Review* 169; MS Kirsch, 'Taxing Citizens in a Global Economy' (2007) 82 *New York University Law Review* 443; EA Zelinsky,

tax implications of migration for skilled and unskilled migrants, migration from one country to another (not necessarily from developing countries to developed countries), and suggests a model that assists countries with ways to tax those individuals in a fairer manner that will lean on social justice, social contracts, and ties between the individual and her domiciliary community and not solely between countries or on technical standards as it is currently.[12]

One possible solution to this challenge is to strengthen the 'domiciliary' concept, which defines fiscal residency more broadly and does not solely focus on the country where the individual resides that calendar year. For instance, under this concept, an immigrant who studies for a graduate degree in a host country and decides to work for several years after graduating there does not cease to have her domicile in her home country merely because she is temporarily residing abroad. Similarly, an individual who decides to travel the world and move from one place to another with no fixed or permanent anchor does not, in our opinion, cease to have her domicile in her home country merely because she is temporarily residing abroad. We would also explore the different proposals to replace the existing rules with an alternative personal jurisdiction regime that relies on the taxpayer's citizenship (which was adopted by the United States over a century ago for specific historical reasons and has also been adopted by several other countries, including Eritrea, Philippines, and more recently by Hungary and Lithuania).[13]

Our chapter proposes a model that captures unrealised and untaxed economic 'rent' that derives from know-how and skills that may possibly be attributed to a certain extent to their home countries. We also propose a model that can be easily adopted, administered, and monitored by the home countries and will enhance global fairness between countries, migrants, and the host and home countries.

I. Types of Migration

Based on estimates of the global migration phenomenon, there are approximately one billion migrants in the world, which represents approximately one seventh of the global population.[14] Roughly a quarter of these one billion migrants are cross-border migrants. This accounts for roughly 3.6 per cent of the world's population.

'Citizenship and Worldwide Taxation: Citizenship as an Administrable Proxy for Domicile' (2011) 96 *Iowa Law Review* 1289; C Blum & PN Singer, 'A Coherent Policy Proposal for U.S. Residence-Based Taxation of Individuals' (2008) 41 *Vanderbilt Law Review* 705, 705; R Avi-Yonah, 'The Case Against Taxing Citizens' (2010) 58 *Tax Notes International* 389.

[12] Bhagwati & Hamada, 'The Brain Drain' (n 8); see also extension of the model Bhagwati & Hamada, 'Domestic Distortions (n 8).

[13] Avi-Yonah (n 11); RS Avi-Yonah, 'Taxing Nomads: Reviving Citizenship-Based Taxation for the 21st Century' in T Dagan and R Mason (eds), *Taxing People: The Next 100 Years* (Cambridge, CUP, forthcoming, 2024).

[14] World Health Organization, '*Refuge and Migrant Health*' (WHO), www.who.int/health-topics/refugee-and-migrant-health#tab=tab_1.

However, this relatively minor percentage is misleading, as their economic presence in high-income developed countries is much more apparent. These migrants represent approximately one eighth of a high-income nation's population, and since many of these cross-border migrants reside in close-proximity, their presence in these communities is much more significant.[15] Cross-border migrants and their annual economic impact are colossal and estimated at billions of dollars.[16]

Further, about 60 per cent of international migrant workers were able to increase their compensation dramatically (as they are compensated ten times higher than in developing countries). This increase in earnings affects these migrants' loved ones who were left behind as they continue to transfer hundreds of billions of dollars annually (cross-border remittance).

The number of cross-border immigrants has more than tripled in the past five decades,[17] and it seems that this trend will continue. It is estimated that by 2030, for every young person (15–24 years of age), there will be three seniors (65+) in many developed countries (for example, Germany, Italy or Japan).[18] Whereas the ratio of seniors to young people in developing countries will be the complete opposite (for example, in Uganda, the ratio will be 1:9, in Nigeria 1:7, in India and Mexico 1:2).[19] These demographic changes will probably increase migration pressures in developed countries as their tax bases will likely narrow and the costs of care for the elderly will rise. In contrast, these demographic changes will also hypothetically increase migration pressures in developing countries, as they will find it difficult to offer their young population job opportunities and will likely suffer increasing poverty. These projections point to a significant increase in migration pressures in the coming decades, especially from South Asia and Sub-Saharan Africa to North America and to European countries.[20]

Migration waves impact countries' demography, economy, culture, and even politics.[21] The literature about international migrations classifies migration into two basic groups: voluntary migration and involuntary migration.[22] Voluntary

---

[15] McAuliffe & Triandafyllidou (n 3) 21–39.

[16] This estimate is based on the result of multiplying the average salaries in the developed countries and the number of migrant workers, and including the amounts remitted by migrants to their friends and families. See also McAuliffe & Triandafyllidou (n 3) 39.

[17] In 2020, around 153 million international migrants in the world in 1990, around 84 million international migrants in the world in 1970 and these numbers were much smaller 50 years earlier when the rules for taxing cross-border transaction were formed almost a century ago based on the League of Nations work and on the bilateral tax treaties there were negotiated and signed. See McAuliffe & Triandafyllidou (n 3) 23–24.

[18] World Bank, *Leveraging Economic Migration for Development: A briefing for the World Bank Board* (Board Report, 2019).

[19] ibid 9–11.

[20] ibid 3–7.

[21] Migration and its economic impact have been studied and described by numerous scholars, for example, see GJ Borjas 'Economic Theory and International Migration' (1989) 23 *The International Migration Review* 457.

[22] M Verkuyten, HG Altabatabaei, & W Nooitgedagt, 'Supporting the Accommodation of Voluntary and Involuntary Migrants: Humanitarian and Host Society Considerations' (2018) 9 *Social Psychological and Personality Science* 267.

migrants are individuals who decide to leave their families, friends, and communities in their home countries and establish new lives abroad. The main drivers for voluntary migration include income improvement, professional opportunities in the destination countries, medical and healthcare services, social security, marriage opportunities, family reunification, an escape from social exclusion and inequality, and a desire to move away from corruption. Whereas the main drivers of involuntary migration are persecution (political or other), state instability (armed conflict), and natural or ecological disasters.

Our paper will focus on the first group but not on the second, as the relationships between individuals who were persecuted are much more complex, and it seems that the issue of the allocation of taxing rights regarding countries that force their taxpayers to leave is, in most instances, unjustified. For convenience, we would therefore suggest distinguishing between the following three migration categories:

A. 'Involuntary Migration' (Refugees, Asylum Seekers, and Displaced Persons)

As indicated earlier, the first category of migrants refers to all cases of migrants who were forced to leave their home country.[23] The size of this group changes from one year to another, as it also includes migrants who try to escape armed conflicts (for example, the millions of Ukrainian citizens who left Ukraine after the invasion of the Russian Federation). This also includes the migration of women or members of the LGBTQ community who are discriminated against, along with individuals who left their home countries due to natural or ecological disasters (volcano eruptions, earthquakes, drought). Based on the most recent immigration report, forced or displaced migrants make up about 10 per cent of all cross-border migrants, and in 2020, there were approximately 28 million forced migrants.[24]

B. Voluntary Migration

This category can be subdivided into the following two main clusters: 'traditional migrants' and 'temporary migrants'.

i. 'Traditional Migration'

Many of today's international migration streams began with recruitment and employment after WWII. This category includes migrants who leave their home

---

[23] World Bank (n 18) 8–12.
[24] McAuliffe & Triandafyllidou (n 3) 45–55.

country to provide themselves and their family members with better life conditions, medical care, education opportunities, and career opportunities. The migrants in this category, after they become established, often assist their family members, who were left behind in their home countries, to leave for the host country. This category refers to migrants who wish to become members of the community in the host country and to abandon their economic and social ties in their home country (even though many of them do not renounce their home country citizenship and acquire citizenship or denizen status (permanent residence status) in the host country).[25]

ii. 'Temporary Migration'

The main characteristic in this category is the temporary status of the migrants during their stay in the host country. It refers to migrants who leave their home countries for a specific motivation or purpose with the intention that, afterward, they will return to their home country or move to another country. Nevertheless (and despite their transitory or temporary status), the migrants in this category often spend more than 183 days a year in a certain taxing jurisdiction (generally in the host country). A study conducted by the World Bank found a significant percentage of cross-border migrants leave their host country and move back to their home country or to another country within a decade.[26]

A minority of temporary migrants do not even have a fixed base in the host countries, as they spend several weeks or months at each location they visit (travelling to more than three or four countries a year). These migrants are generally referred to as nomads or digital nomads.[27] Most temporary migrants, unlike traditional migrants, do not make the efforts to adopt the languages, customs, identities, and cultural practices of the host countries to become full members of the societies.

There are several categories within the term 'temporary migration', and each category has different demographic, economic, and other characteristics, all of which do not abandon their domicile during their stay in the host country. Foreign students are often one example of temporary migrants who leave their home countries for a certain period to acquire education, even if they decide to spend several years after graduating to acquire professional skills. Other categories

---

[25] See Y Brauner, 'Mobility of Individuals, the Brain Drain, and Taxation in the Digital Age' in S Kostic et al., (eds), *International Taxation of Individuals in the 21st Century* (IBFD, 2024).

[26] C Dustmann and JS Görlach, 'The Economics of Temporary Migrations' (2016) 54 *Journal of Economic Literature* 98. For example, based on research conducted in 2016, half of all individuals who migrated to European countries left these countries within 10 years. Similarly, approximately 20% of migrants who move to Australia, Canada, New Zealand, or the United States leave these countries back home or to a different home country.

[27] A subcategory of temporary migrants that poses significant challenges to the existing tax laws refers to highly skilled individuals that travel around between countries 'with no strings attached' having no fixed base (staying a couple of months and less than 183 days in each location) in any country and continue to work remotely, relying on internet access to their western employers. Avi-Yonah 'Taxing Nomads' (n 13).

of temporary migrants are employment migrants, medical-care migrants, senior/ retired migrants,[28] and the previously discussed digital nomads.[29]

One caveat we wish to make regarding our proposal is that this chapter focuses on the biggest category of voluntary migrations, 'traditional migration'. However, we believe that our recommendation can also apply to involuntary migrants and temporary migrants (including digital nomads). Before we explain the weaknesses in the existing rules for determining fiscal residency and the unfair allocation that results from these rules, we would like to shed some light on the economic aspects of cross-border migration.

II. Economic Impacts of Cross-Border Migration

The economic impact of approximately 300 million cross-border migrants is significant, even though they account for less than four per cent of the world population. Their economic impact goes beyond themselves and impacts the migrant's family and friends who were left behind, countries of destination, and countries of origin. Surprisingly enough, even though cross-border migration is a global phenomenon, about 2/3 of all international migrants live in 20 countries (while most live in only five countries: the United States, Germany, Saudi Arabia, Russia, and United Kingdom).[30] Additionally, 1/3 of all international migrants come from ten countries, with most of them coming from only five countries: India, Mexico, China, Russia, and Syria.[31]

This chapter will try to present the costs and benefits of migration for the country of origin, the country of destination, and the migrant. Further, this chapter will assert that it is too difficult to assess the long-term impact of cross-border migrations on the home and host countries as the effects on both are mixed.

A. Costs and Benefits for the Country of Origin

Initially, the economic literature assumed that cross-border migration negatively impacted the home countries due to the loss of their educated talent pool to

---

[28] de Wenden (n 2) 3–5 presents new trends of migrations, one of which is the elderly migration: 'North-to-South migration flows, for their part, are also generating new trends in migration. "Britishland", where the British go to retire in Western France (Normandy, Bretagne and Aquitaine), is one example of this. Relatively well-off retirees are also migrating to Spain (the Germans and the British), southern Portugal (the British), Greece, Morocco, Tunisia and Senegal (the French). The same phenomenon can be found in the Caribbean, this time with retirees from the U.S. and Canada.'

[29] Avi-Yonah, 'Taxing Nomads' (n 13).

[30] United States 51 million, Germany 13 million, Saudi Arabia 13 million, Russia 12 million, United Kingdom 10 million; See McAuliffe & Triandafyllidou (n 3) 21.

[31] India 17.5 million, Mexico 11.8 million, China 10.8 million, Russia 10.8 million, Syria 8.2 million; see McAuliffe & Triandafyllidou (n 3) 21.

developed countries, with very little gains, from these migrants' departure. The home countries also suffered losses that included sunk educational costs, medical costs, losses of future potential gains that these migrants could have generated in their countries of origin,[32] and the high recruitment costs that migrants and those who think of migrating bear.[33]

The need to compensate home countries, whose citizens relocate and move to another country, for the loss of untaxed, unrealised gains was addressed by the many countries that adopted exit taxes. These exit taxes attempt to capture unrealised, untaxed appreciated gains of assets based on their appreciation during the period the individual owned the property just before he/she abandoned his/her tax residency or renounced his/her citizenship. However, these exit taxes unfortunately do not capture human capital appreciation. At the time of migration, emigrants generally do not benefit from the increase in wages, and in any event, many of the economic benefits that derive from the know-how and intellectual property they acquired or developed prior to the relocation can easily be deferred. Also, emigrants do not benefit because the 'appreciation' period (unlike the holding period of a movable property) is less explicit and poses greater collection challenges for the home countries.[34]

However, later economic studies identified several benefits that the country of origin receives from cross-border migration. One example is the incentivisation of education by the countries' citizens. This results from a desire to migrate overseas.[35] This opportunity, as Brauner states, creates the motivation for 'too many' individuals to acquire skills, leaving them with more rather than less educated and skilled workers.[36] Another argument in this context deals with the circular waves of emigration many of the cross-border migrants make. Based on different studies, it seems that a significant percentage of the cross-border migrants return to their home country after less than a ten-year period with know-how, skills, and professional connections that enable them to attract capital and invest in these home (developing) countries.[37] Other studies show that cross-border migrants invest in their home countries and that such investments positively impact their growth and development.

Another benefit that the economic literature has raised over the years is the remittance of significant funds earned by cross-border migrants in the host countries.[38]

---

[32] See Brauner (n 25).

[33] ibid.

[34] AG Abreu, 'Taxing Exits' (1996) 29 *U.C. Davis Law Review* 1087; WL Dentino & C Manolakas 'The Exit Tax: A Move in the Right Direction' (2012) 3 *William & Mary Business Law Review* 341; WT Worster, 'The Constitutionality of the Taxation Consequences for Renouncing U.S. Citizenship' (2010) 9 *Florida Tax Review* 921; E Farkas-DiNardo, 'Is the Nation of Immigrants Punishing Its Emigrants: A Critical Review of the Expatriation Rules Revised by the Jobs Creation Act of 2004' (2005) 7 *Florida Tax Review* 1; RA Westin, 'Expatriation and Return: An Examination of Tax Driven Expatriation by United States Citizens, and Reform Proposals' (2000) 20 *Virginia Tax Review* 75; CE Steuerle, 'Alternatives to the Expatriate Tax' (1995) 57 *Tax Notes* 567.

[35] See Brauner (n 25).

[36] ibid.

[37] ibid.

[38] ibid.

In 2020, the International Organization for Migration (IOM) found that the funds that were remitted by cross-border migrants to their families in their home countries amounted to more than $700 billion, and this figure was apparently even smaller than the amount the year before (probably because of the impacts of the COVID-19 pandemic).[39] It is fairly difficult to claim that the overall net effects of cross-border migration are necessarily negative to the country of origin.[40]

B. Costs and Benefits for the Country of Destination

Regrettably, unlike studies that attempted to quantify the economic effects of cross-border migration on home countries, little research has been devoted to the economic effects of the host countries. We assume that a reasonable justification for the scarcity of such research is because many assumed that, to the extent that such cross-border migration was not worthwhile to some individuals, these countries would close their borders to such immigration. The World Bank mentions the following points regarding the benefits of cross-border migration: it reduces labour-market constraints, increases the availability of goods and services, reduces prices for consumers, and reduces the economic burdens of caring for the elderly by allowing people who could not afford it otherwise to retire and get assistance in ageing at home. However, the presence of cross-border migrants tends to push out unskilled and uneducated local populations, which increases governmental subsidies and increases poverty to a certain extent.[41]

C. Costs and Benefits for the Cross-Border Migrant

Other than for involuntary migrants, it is relatively clear that those who benefit the most from cross-border migration are the migrants and their families. However, in addition to the gains the migrant receives, two reports prepared by the World Bank (2016 and 2019) also discuss the different costs they bear. Such costs include high (and often even inflated) recruitment fees. Moreover, in addition to the high overhead costs that the migrant incurs to migrate and find a position, many migrants are required to accept jobs below their education or qualifications. Many of them face inferior working conditions (they are discriminated against by employees as they are more dependent on them). These migrants may find themselves underpaid and face lower job security than local workers. Their special status sometimes even forces them to work in unsafe working conditions, and despite that, their social and medical coverage is sometimes limited.[42]

---

[39] ibid.
[40] ibid.
[41] ibid.
[42] ibid.

The economic impact on the migrants is extremely apparent. As we indicated before, cross-border migrants seek to improve their professional opportunities while increasing their quality of life. The World Bank reports that there is a significant income gap between the average income in high-income developed countries and the average income in low-income developing countries. They found for the period 2013–2017 that the average income earner in a high-income country earned f54 times the amount of income earned by an average income earner in a low-income country. The report also indicated that even if the developing countries continued to grow faster than the developed countries, it would still take more than 100 years to close such income gaps.[43]

Based on various pieces of literature and research devoted to the impact of cross-border migration on developed and developing countries quest for growth, it seems fairly difficult to assess the ultimate costs the developing countries suffer and whether the gains the developed countries benefit are at the expense of the developing countries. Given this ambiguity, we advocate for an international tax system that allows the country of origin and the country of destination to tax the migrants' economic enrichment, at least in the early years after the migrant leaves her home country.

The coming chapter will explore the existing rules that allocate taxing rights under customary international tax rules, particularly in bilateral tax treaties.

III. Tax Bases and Jurisdiction to Tax under Existing Rules

The allocation of taxing rights between the home country and host country was determined almost a century ago based on the 1923 League of Nations committee's recommendation.[44] The committee endorsed the benefit approach ('economic allegiance'), which gave the source countries the primacy right to tax cross-border income while resident countries had an inferior right to tax as they had to credit foreign taxes paid to the source country. Accordingly, the source countries had the first right to tax active income. The compromise between the capital exporting and importing countries was achieved with respect to passive income.

Based on the 1923 report, bilateral tax treaties were negotiated and signed, and after the second world war, each of the United States, the Organization for Economic Cooperation and Development (OECD) and the United Nations prepared model tax conventions that were utilised for treaty negotiation purposes and intended to eliminate double taxation as well as prevent tax evasion. Each of

---

[43] Ibid.
[44] League of Nations, *Report on Double Taxation. Submitted to the Financial Committee by Professors Bruins, Einaudi, Seligman and Sir Josiah Stamp* (Geneva, League of Nations E.F.S.73.F.19, 1923); See also Avi-Yonah (n 11); MJ Graetz and MM O'Hear, 'The "Original Intent" of U.S. International Taxation' (1997) 46 *Duke Law Journal* 1021.

the three bilateral treaty models favoured source countries based on the 'benefit approach' that was endorsed by the 1923 report. Also, each of the three tax treaty models determined that, for tax treaty purposes, an individual is considered a resident of the relevant country if, under the laws of that country, she is liable to tax by reason of her domicile or residence.[45]

The main difference between the two concepts 'residency' and 'domiciliary' is that residency, at least in common law countries, is often used in reference to matters such as voting, taxation, schools, etc. Typically, residency is based on physical presence in that particular country.[46] Whereas domicile is linked to the intention of the taxpayer to stay, live, and return to a particular country and represents one's home base and her 'relationship' with a specific location or jurisdiction.[47] In civil law countries, both terms are used to base the personal attachment of a taxpayer to a particular country, and such attachment can be based on physical presence, use of possession of a home, economic activity, familial connections, social interests, or on other factors.[48]

Arguably, the tax treaty models do not give preferential treatment in the tiebreaker rules that determine residency to a personal attachment to a particular country unless such attachment was based on domiciliary or residency. However, if we carefully analyse the tiebreaker rules that were incorporated in Article IV, it seems that the physical presence test supersedes. The tiebreaker rules propose several connecting factors in a specific order, and if the first connecting factor is only satisfied in one country, then the other country 'loses' its status as the 'residence' country for purposes of the application of the tax treaty. The four tiebreaker rules, in the exact order they appear in the treaty model, are: a permanent home that is available to him; personal and economic relations (centre of vital interests); habitual abode; and nationality.[49]

The tax treaty wording of 'permanent home available to him' has been interpreted as 'something more than just a place to sleep and keep home some belongings on a *temporary* basis [… and] of such quality that it is of the vital interest for the individual.'[50] Such interpretation implies, in our view, that the quality of the permanent home is determined by the intensity of the taxpayer's use. The intensity of use is based on the physical presence of the taxpayer in that particular

---

[45] See D Narotzki, 'Tax Treaty Models – Past, Present, and a Suggested Future' (2017) 50 *Akron Law Review* 383.

[46] Note 'Conflict of Laws: Domicile and Residence' (1927) 25 *Michigan Law Review* 795. See also Note 'Domicile, Acquisition of Domicile' (1926) 39 *Harvard Law Review* 654.

[47] *Udny v. Udny* [1869] 1 LR Sc and Div 441, LR 1 HL 441 ('settling down'); *Ennis v. Smith* [1852] 55 US 400 ('actual residence in the place'); *Graham v. Graham*, 9 N. D. 88, 81 N. W. 44 (N.D. 1899) ('residence in fact'); *McCarthy v. McCarthy*, 122 A. 529 (R.I. 1923) ('actual abode'). See also, 'The Domicile of Persons Non Sui Juris' (1909) 22 *Harvard Law Review* 220; See also, 'Intention Requisite to Effect a Change of Domicile' (1910) 23 *Harvard Law Review* 211.

[48] K Vogel et al., *Klaus Vogel on Double Taxation Conventions*, 4th edn (Alphen aan den Rijn, Wolters Kluwer Law & Business 2015) 270–277.

[49] ibid 277–280.

[50] ibid 271.

country, as it does not have any minimal requirement as to the ownership of such home or to the minimal period it was used by the taxpayer.

The following two tiebreaker rules, 'centre of vital interests' and 'habitual abode', also rely heavily on the physical presence of the taxpayer and his immediate family in a specific country.[51] Additionally, the application of the tax treaties requires that each calendar year, the taxpayer's residency be determined (and such determination is made independently, regardless of prior years' determination). As such, the first three tiebreaker rules rely heavily, in our view, on the physical presence of the taxpayer. For tax treaty purposes, the taxpayer's residency may change easily from one year to another based on her physical presence during that year. The only tiebreaker criterion that is less 'flexible' and not subject to the taxpayer's 'control' is the fourth tiebreaker criterion, which is based on the taxpayer's nationality. Unlike the first three tiebreaker rules, 'nationality' is a long-lasting personal link, not easily acquired or lost. Also, nationality is not determined in accordance with the taxpayer's physical presence in a particular country.[52]

We believe that the existing rules for determining residency for tax treaty purposes put too much emphasis on the temporary physical presence of the taxpayer during a taxable calendar year. This uneven emphasis becomes apparent when we consider the inherent preference that each of the three treaty models has in allocating taxing rights for employment income and business profits between the source and residence countries. Both Article VII (Business Profits) and Article XV (Employment Income) allocate all taxing rights to the source country, which supposedly hosts the economic activity in its territory. This binary allocation (exclusively to the source country) in addition to the weight that the physical presence factor has in determining taxpayer's residency should be re-examined.[53]

This emphasis on physical presence was perhaps justified a century ago, when it was more difficult to migrate, and the economic reality was very different. It was almost impossible to work or render services remotely. Hence, we believe the time has come to recognise the contribution of the taxpayer's country of origin (home country) and to reflect this contribution in international tax practices and rules.

IV. Bhagwati Proposal

This basic idea of the so-called 'brain drain tax,' as first introduced by Professor Bhagwati, is that skilled migrants typically earn economic rents that rely on skills and know-how, which they received in their home country (especially when the training and education relies on state funding), due to their relocation benefit

---

[51] ibid 270–277.
[52] ibid 277–280.
[53] ibid 257–258.

because the host-country did not invest any of its own resources in order to receive skilled professionals.[54] Furthermore, such relocation of skilled professionals from developing countries to developed countries also results in shortages of skilled professionals in the developing countries and puts these countries at a further disadvantage.[55] Bhagwati's proposal focused solely on aspects of horizontal fairness as it was aimed mainly at promoting global fairness between developing and developed countries. His proposal focused on the phenomena of skilled migrants leaving developing countries and moving to developed countries.[56]

However, this chapter further develops this idea and explores the jurisdiction to tax individuals, specifically the fundamental principle of 'residency' under the existing international norms, which leads to the development of vertical fairness. This chapter also wishes to develop a fair relationship between the host and home, which will be based on a fair allocation of taxing rights between them without putting an excessive administrative or economic burden on them while also increasing cross-border transparency.

A. Physical Presence Test

Most countries incorporate a physical presence test in the way that their domestic tax systems define residency for tax purposes. The most typical definition focuses on the taxpayer's physical presence during a calendar year. This physical presence test relies on migrants residing in a country for a minimal period of six months or 183 days within a calendar year. The idea behind the physical presence test is that using a connecting personal factor for allocating taxing rights does not need an explanation and suggests that such physical presence connects the taxpayer socially, economically, and more. Moreover, since individual taxpayers can only be in a single place at any given time, this factor can be easily detected and measured and is less manipulable. However, this connecting factor can be easily orchestrated in advance by the taxpayer. Furthermore, in the last decade, technological and communicational breakthroughs have made it clear that a territorial relationship is of less importance than before, and consequently, physical presence is not sine qua non for taxation.[57]

The physical presence test, as a personal connecting factor in determining fiscal residency, can change from one year to the next and does not pay enough attention to the taxpayer's previous attachments to other countries. One can reside 40 years in a certain country and then move the following year to a different country, thereby becoming subject to tax in the new country without regard to the

[54] Bhagwati & Hamada, 'The Brain Drain' (n 8); see also extension of the model Bhagwati & Hamada, 'Domestic Distortions' (n 8).
[55] ibid.
[56] ibid.
[57] See Brauner (n 25).

40 years of residence in the prior country. Also, since the 1923 report already put an emphasis on the territorial connection to the country that hosts the profitable activity, it is unclear what this connecting factor adds since, in any event, active income is taxed at source, and except for remote work, source rules in any way give preference to the host country.[58]

B. Citizenship/Nationality

It is not surprising that, over the years, only a handful of countries have defined fiscal residency based on citizenship or nationality. The United States was the first to adopt this criterion for historical reasons (to make sure the wealthy people who escaped the draft and did not participate in the civil war would at least contribute indirectly by paying their fair share in taxes).[59] Within this limited category, other countries, including Eritrea and the Philippines, abandoned the citizenship test after realising that enforcing taxation on their citizens who reside overseas is impractical. Recently, several eastern European countries added this criterion in addition to other factors.[60]

Over the years, many scholars have criticised the United States because it creates situations in which individuals who are children of US citizens living abroad and have no meaningful ties with the United States are considered US persons and suffer double taxation.[61] Lately, an additional criticism was raised by different scholars who identified a new phenomenon in which countries treat nationality as a traded commodity and offer wealthy individuals local investments or a flat annual fee. By offering these individuals or entities, they are able to escape reporting under the OECD/G20 common reporting standards.[62]

We do accept that in many instances citizenship may serve well as a proxy for taxpayer's residency, and as Kirsch and Avi-Yonah noticed, an additional benefit of using nationality as a connecting factor is that it generally takes traditional migrants between five and ten years before they acquire citizenship in their (new) host country and a similar extensive period to lose it.[63] However, as in the case of *Cook v. Tait*,[64] there are instances in which the taxpayer has several

---

[58] ibid.

[59] Avi-Yonah (n 11); Graetz & O'Hear (n 44).

[60] eg, Hungary and Lithuania adopted the citizenship's taxpayer as an alternative criterion for establishing fiscal residency for tax purposes.

[61] T Dagan & T Fisher, 'State Inc.' (2017) 27 *Cornell Journal of Law and Public Policy* 661; SV Kostic, 'International Taxation and Migrations' in Y Brauner (ed), *Research Handbook on International Taxation* (Cheltenham, Edward Elgar, 2020) 353.

[62] OECD, 'Residence/Citizenship by Investment Schemes' www.oecd.org/tax/automatic-exchange/crs-implementation-and-assistance/residence-citizenship-by-investment/ (accessed 4 April 2024).

[63] MS Kirsch, 'Taxing Citizens in a Global Economy' (2007) 82 *New York University Law Review* 443; Brauner (n 7); Avi-Yonah, (n 11).

[64] *Cook v. Tait*, 265 U.S. 47 (1924) ('the basis of the power to tax was not and cannot be made dependent upon the situs of the property in all cases, it being in or out of the United States, nor was not and

citizenships, other instances in which the country of citizenship has no material meaning and allocating to it the taxing rights seem arbitrary, and in extreme situations, instances in which the taxpayer was persecuted or forced to leave (asylum seekers, refugees etc). Using the citizenship factor to attribute income to such country can be unjust.

C. Domiciliary

Domicile is one of the personal connecting factors in determining fiscal residence. Initially, in the first OECD model convention in 1963, the heading of Article IV was not 'Residence' but rather 'Domicile.' However, the term domicile is not homogeneously defined in all countries, and it is used in common law systems differently than in civil law systems. It also has different meanings depending on the context (international law, family law, property law, and so forth), which is probably one of the reasons why tax systems found it challenging to rely on such indistinct standards and felt that residency represented a balanced approach to determining taxing rights.[65] Unlike civil law systems, where the term domiciliary is used as a synonym for fiscal residency, common law countries adopt the concept of domiciliary to represent not just an immediate or temporary relationship with a particular country but rather one that follows the 'heart' and a continuing attachment.[66]

In English-speaking common-law countries, domicile is linked to the taxpayer's intention to stay, live, and return to a certain state. People are domiciled where they have or are at least deemed to have their permanent home.[67] Except for the fact that domicile is an undefined standard that is hard to administer and difficult to adjudicate whether one should be viewed as a resident or not, there are five benefits, in our view, that make it the ultimate personal connecting factor. First, a taxpayer can never be left without a domicile, which is acquired at birth. Second, a taxpayer cannot have more than a single domicile (unlike multiple residencies or multiple citizenships). Third, a domicile takes into account the taxpayer's previous background and is determined not only on the immediate circumstances but also requires 'intention.'[68] Fourth, it is determined based on different factors that impact the taxpayer and are less easily controlled (manipulable) by the

---

cannot be made dependent upon the domicile of the citizen, that being in or out of the United States, but upon his relation as citizen to the United States and the relation of the latter to him as citizen. The consequence of the relations is that the native citizen who is taxed may have domicile, and the property from which his income is derived may have situs, in a foreign country, and the tax be legal, the government having power to impose the tax.').

[65] FM Keesling, 'The Importance of Citizenship, Residence and Domicile in Federal Income Taxation' (1943) 31 *California Law Review* 283, 287.

[66] ibid 287: 'It is axiomatic that an individual can at any one time have but one domicile and that a domicile once acquired is retained until a new one is established.'

[67] Vogel (n 48) 257, 267.

[68] 'Intention Requisite to Effect a Change of *Domicile*' (1910) 23 *Harvard Law Review* 211.

taxpayer. Fifth and finally, a change of domicile takes a while and does not happen immediately when a migrant moves to a new country.[69]

The main criticism against using domicile as a personal connecting factor is that it poses significant challenges in administering it (as it relies on the taxpayer's intent). However, since domicile of origin is acquired by every human being by birth, if our proposal is adopted, any transition or change in domicile would take five to ten years. During such a period, one needs to have a fixed base in a country, live there for several years, and be subject to taxation on a worldwide basis at progressive rates. Then, it seems that administering this factor in cross-border settings should not be that challenging.

Therefore, it is our opinion that international tax rules should replace the existing connecting factors and adopt domiciliary as the personal connecting factor.

V. Our Proposal

Our proposal calls for a change in the allocation of taxing rights between the home and host country. Such a change can be easily achieved if the host country cooperates with the home country. Fifty years ago, a change in this direction (regarding developing countries) was raised by Professor Bhagwati and several of his colleagues. However, their efforts were futile.[70] The idea that the host countries would impose a foreign migrant surtax, collect the tax revenues, and remit them to their home countries was not taken up. The fact that countries open their borders to cross-border migration signals, in our view, that they gain benefits from such phenomenon and that is why we believe they should cooperate and exchange the foreign migrants' information, at least during the first five to ten years. The resistance of countries to exchanging information has dramatically diminished during the past decade after the inclusion of CRS, FATCA, and the implementation of the multilateral instrument by 100 countries.[71]

Nevertheless, unlike the Bhagwati proposal, our recommendation does not include the imposition of a surtax, collection, or remittance of the tax proceeds.[72] We recommend that the host country only transfer the fiscal information of the foreign migrants to their home countries during a certain period and before the taxpayers change their domicile.

---

[69] Keesling (n 65) 287. See also, 'Intent in Domicile' (1928) 37 *Yale Law Journal* 1125, 1125–32.

[70] Bhagwati and Hamada, 'The Brain Drain' (n 8); see also extension of the model Bhagwati & Hamada, 'Domestic Distortions' (n 8).

[71] OECD, 'Multilateral Convention to Implement Tax Treaty Related Measures to Prevent BEPS' (OECD, November 2016) www.oecd.org/tax/treaties/multilateral-convention-to-implement-tax-treaty-related-measures-to-prevent-beps.htm.

[72] Bhagwati and Hamada, 'The Brain Drain' (n 8); see also extension of the model Bhagwati & Hamada, 'Domestic Distortions' (n 8).

Second, we recommend that taxpayers' fiscal residency be based on their domicile. In our view, relying on domiciliary is fairer as it recognises the contribution of the home country, as abandonment of domiciliary is a process that takes a while (several years). Such a process can only be completed after the taxpayer acquires a domicile in another country, which subjects the taxpayer to tax on a global basis. Lastly, basing the fiscal residency on domicile would make sure that taxpayers (and even nomads) cannot abandon their fiscal residency before they acquire a new fiscal residency in a different country. We also recommend considering some restrictions regarding the acquisition of domicile in 'tax havens' or in countries that have very little social and economic meaning with the taxpayer.

Third, in computing the taxpayer income tax liability, we recommend that the host country have the primacy taxing right. However, the country of origin should be considered the resident country regardless of the country in which the taxpayer resides, at least in the first five to ten years (possibly until she abandons her citizenship and acquires a new citizenship in the host country). To make sure that the migrant has enough income or capital to support her living (and in case she is married to support her family's cost of living), a taxable deduction should be granted by the country of origin. The idea is that if the taxpayer's income does not meet the minimal income that allows living with dignity in the host country, no additional taxation should be imposed by the home country. The American income tax system, in a way, offers a similar idea by providing an exclusion that exceeds the standard cost of living.[73] Such exclusion also reduces administrative burdens for taxpayers who earn relatively little and exempts them from filing tax returns that would, in any event, be exempt in the United States.

Fourth, even though developed countries' ability to enforce the collection of taxes is much more challenging, and with respect to citizens who live abroad even more so, we believe that developed countries would be able to enforce such taxes by forcing their citizens living abroad to renew their passports relatively frequently. Also, to the extent that the host countries would require the migrants to show that they have no tax liabilities in their home countries before granting them new citizenship or renewing their working visas, the ability of the home countries to enforce the imposition of such taxes would be accomplished to a greater extent.[74]

Fifth, we recommend that the period in which the home countries would be able to participate and share the taxes from the foreign income tax their citizens living overseas would be limited to a certain period between five (5) and

---

[73] 26 U.S.C. s 911.
[74] Absent such assistance, the ability of the developing countries is doubtful. This is probably the reason why the Philippines attempts tax its foreign citizens were repealed. See Pomp (n 9).

ten (10) years. First, during this period, the ties between the migrant and her home country are stronger and tighter. Second, the legitimacy of imposing such taxes during the first couple of years after the migration is a compensatory mechanism for the country of origin's investment in the taxpayer and her family. However, as time goes by, such legitimacy lessens, and as know-how becomes obsolete, the contribution of the home country to the economic attributes of the taxpayer becomes more and more distant, and the taxes imposed on the migrants by the home country can be adjusted and reduced during this period. Lastly, this proposal does not automatically apply to refugees, asylum seekers, and displaced persons. The taxpayers that were persecuted in their home countries and had to leave (to escape for their lives) the home country should be entitled to no tax revenues.

VI. Concluding Remarks and Recommendation

It is important, in our view, to offer a new paradigm for taxing migrants and not solely concentrate on the relations between developed and developing countries, as was done previously. Moreover, as the western world ages, more countries will moderate their migration restrictions and offer new opportunities to individuals from low-income countries, and by 2030, the estimate is that more than half a billion migrants will move from their home countries.

Accordingly, the migration reality was very different and relatively unimportant when the rules for taxing cross-border income and gains were drafted. Human capital was relatively static, and immigration for employment was not as common. Over the past several decades, and even more so after the global pandemic, it seems that the mobility of human capital is on the rise.

The existing rules determine an individual's residency each calendar year separately, and when an individual is deemed to have more than a single tax residency, the current tiebreaker rules under both the UN, the OECD, and the US treaty model acknowledge residency for the country in which one has her habitual abode. Most migrants abandon the habitual abode they had in their home country, and as a result, they become residents for tax purposes in the destination country. This outcome deprives the home country of its ability to tax its citizens after she left and disregards the costs it invested in her medical, social welfare, and education that, to some extent, made her the taxpayer she is. The allocation of all taxing rights to the country of residence under Article XV of the DDT is unfair. A new allocation of taxation rights could benefit the home country without harming the host country at all.

Lastly, we would also like to note that our proposal makes sure that no migrant will be subject to double taxation from one end or double non-taxation from the other end, since based on the domiciliary concept, one cannot be without a domicile from one end but cannot also have multiple domiciles at the same time. Therefore, our proposal makes sure that nomads, for example, that spend less than 183 days in each country would still be subject to taxation in their home countries even if the host countries would exempt them or find it difficult to enforce their taxing rights over their income. Ultimately, our proposals will result in a more equitable international tax regime that allows origin countries and migrants to reap the benefits of their labour.

9

Caught between Two Sovereigns: The International Taxation of Cross-Border Individuals

BERNARD SCHNEIDER

The income taxation of individuals has historically been based on residence. Until recently, this was straightforward conceptually and in practice for almost all individuals. However, the international tax system is as out of date for expatriate and migrant individuals as it is for multinational corporations. The existing system of residence assumes limited migration, voluntary or otherwise. In addition, it assumes a 'clean break' from one jurisdiction to another, with a clear point of transition from one jurisdiction to the other and generally no further changes in jurisdiction. This was the situation at the time of the 1920s Compromise, until at least the Second World War. Since then, however, the situation has changed. Population movements after the war were augmented by migration driven by the Cold War and political crises, as well as by economic migration. Subsequently, advances in communications and transportation have made it easier, and cheaper, for individuals to move. It has also made it easier for migrants, and even their descendants, to maintain contact with their jurisdiction of origin. Thus, not only are people more mobile today, but this 'new mobility' is often marked by multiple or serial migrations. Whereas once migration was uni-directional and generally irreversible, today expatriates and migrants may make multiple moves in their lifetime. All of this has led to an increase in the number of changes in jurisdiction and the consequent possibility of overlapping tax residency.[1] This new mobility has also led to changed attitudes towards expatriates and ethnic diasporas, reflected among other things in greater acceptance of dual citizenship and broader transmission

---

[1] In fact, the question of residence is relevant for wealth taxation and information exchange, as well as income taxation. It is does not follow from the discussion of the residence of individuals for income tax purposes that the definition of residence for wealth taxation and information exchange should necessarily be the same. However, these aspects of the residence of individuals are outside the scope of this discussion.

of citizenship by descent, at least in some countries. However, it has not generally been reflected in the rules governing the taxation of migrants and cross-border individuals, which remain stuck in the era of the 1920s Compromise.

The chapter considers the justifications for establishing jurisdiction over individuals and examines state practice in the area of residence. It examines the normative bases of the existing regimes for taxing individuals in the cross-border context and considers the implications of notions of fairness for our understanding of the cross-border taxation of individuals.

There are several factors to consider in terms of the determination of the residence of individuals. Within a jurisdiction, the primary considerations include horizontal and vertical equity; as between jurisdictions, there is the question of the equitable distribution of taxing rights between jurisdictions, based on the level of connection between the individual and the jurisdiction. From the perspective of the individual, however, assuming broadly similar bases and rates of taxation, the primary consideration is not where he or she pays tax but rather ensuring that he or she is not subject to taxation in more than one jurisdiction – that is, avoiding double taxation on the basis of residence. This is particularly important because the consequence of tax residence typically is taxation on a worldwide basis, that is, on income from anywhere in the world.

Assuming 190 central-level tax jurisdictions in the world, there are 17,955 possible unique combinations (and thus 17,955 possible tax treaties).[2] It is generally understood that there are over 3,000 tax treaties currently in force.[3] Thus, only about a sixth of all possible treaty pairs exist. Therefore, any comprehensive remedy for the problem of double residence needs to be found outside the framework of double tax treaties. In principle, this could be done via a multilateral agreement along the lines of the Multilateral Convention to Implement Tax Treaty Related Measures to Prevent Base Erosion and Profit Shifting. However, it seems unlikely that there will be any movement in this direction, given that the taxation of individuals has been largely ignored in the discussions of the last decade on reform of the international tax system. Thus, the most likely, or least unlikely, venue for these changes is at the domestic level.

I. The Creation of Double Residence

The jurisdictional basis for the taxation of individuals is tax residence. The largely consistent use of the term 'residence' to justify the taxation of individuals

---

[2] The formula for combinations is $n!/r!(n-r)!$, where n is the number of different items and r is the number of items that can be selected for any combination, items cannot be repeated in a given combination and the order of items does not matter.

[3] See, eg, M Lang, *Introduction to the Law of Double Taxation Conventions*, 3rd edn (Amsterdam, IBFD, 2021) 3.

(as opposed to income earned by individuals) masks a very broad range of definitions and specific rules across jurisdictions. The different approaches can be categorised as follows:

1) Nationality or immigration status – The right to live and work in a country is often considered a sufficient basis for taxation, in some jurisdictions, whether or not that right is actually being exercised, ie, even if the individual is outside the jurisdiction.

   While this category sounds uniform, in fact it is not, as both citizenship and immigration status are granted differently by different jurisdictions. In some jus soli countries like Canada and the United States, citizenship is granted to all born in the territory, regardless of circumstances or parentage.[4] Other countries limit citizenship by birth to children of parents who are themselves citizens or permanent residents.[5] At the same time, countries grant citizenship by descent on varying bases. Thus, for example, Canada grants citizenship automatically (ie, by operation of law, and without any requirement to register the birth) to the children of at least one citizen parent who is not himself or herself a citizen by descent.[6] By contrast, Singapore grants citizenship to the child of at least one citizen parent but requires registration within one year of the birth of the child.[7] The approach to dual and multiple citizenship also varies. Some countries accept multiple citizenships, either formally[8] or informally.[9] Others do not and require dual citizens at birth to elect one citizenship when reaching the age of majority and/or require those who want to naturalise in the jurisdiction to give up their foreign citizenship.[10]

---

[4] For Canada, see Citizenship Act, RSC, 1985, c C-29, s 3(1)(a); for the United States, see 8 US Code s 1401(a). The language of the US statute incorporates the language of the Citizenship Clause of the Fourteenth Amendment of the US Constitution, and the principle of birthright citizenship is generally, although not universally, understood to be constitutionally mandated, see, eg, CL Eisgruber, 'Birthright Citizenship and the Constitution' (1997) 72 *New York University Law Review* 54.

[5] See, eg, the United Kingdom; an individual born in the United Kingdom 'shall be a British citizen if at the time of his birth his father or mother is – (a) a British citizen; or (b) settled in the United Kingdom', British Nationality Act 1981, c 61, s 1(1). 'Settled in the United Kingdom' is defined by the Act as being in the United Kingdom 'without being subject under the immigration laws to any restriction on the period for which he may remain', which includes permanent residents and certain other specific categories (such as refugees and asylees), British Nationality Act 1981, s 50(2).

[6] Citizenship Act, ss 3(1)(b) and 3(3)(a). This rule has recently been held to violate the Charter of Rights and Freedoms, *Bjorkquist et al v Attorney General of Canada*, 2023 Ontario Superior Court 7152, and its future is uncertain.

[7] Constitution of the Republic of Singapore, art 122(2)(a).

[8] In Canada, the Canadian Citizenship Act, 1976, SC 1974-75-76, c 108 (consolidated as the Citizenship Act, RSC, 1985, c C-29), removed the provisions restricting dual nationality that were present in the predecessor law, the Canadian Citizenship Act, 1946, SC 1946, c 15.

[9] An individual naturalising in the United States renounces his or her allegiance 'to all foreign powers and potentates' in the naturalisation oath. However, there is no attempt to enforce this renunciation by, for example, ensuring that the individual has renounced his or her original citizenship in front of officials of the country in question. In turn, some countries ignore the language of the US naturalisation oath as having no legal effect under their domestic law.

[10] Singapore is an example of a jurisdiction with both these rules, see Constitution of the Republic of Singapore, arts 122(4) and 127(4), respectively.

Similarly, jurisdictions grant different types of immigrant statuses that may be considered sufficient to justify taxation, and they do so on different bases – employment, marriage to a citizen or permanent resident, membership in the ethnic diaspora etc.

2)   Domicile – An individual's domicile is generally considered to be the place to which he or she belongs or considers his or her permanent or ultimate home.[11] This is often linked to place of birth or emigration, but it may be determined by other factors, such as the domicile of the individual's parents.[12] It is thus possible for an individual to be domiciled in a jurisdiction without actually being present there, and in extreme cases without ever having been there.

3)   Subjective residence tests – Some 'thick' concepts of tax residence consider a cluster of factors in determining whether the individual has a sufficient relationship to the jurisdiction. This sufficient relationship is sometimes referred to as the centre of the individual's personal and/or economic life. Factors can include the location of one's family, the availability of a place to live, the location of banks and other financial accounts, a driving licence, professional accreditation, etc. Because in most jurisdictions the consequence of residence is taxation on a worldwide basis, these factors tend to be substantial.

4)   Objective residence tests – These residence tests generally limit themselves to counting days of physical presence, or in some cases workdays, either in one year or over several years.

Thus, tax residence may be based on a substantive relationship with the jurisdiction or on physical presence. The former, in turn, can be related to a specific status, such as nationality or immigration status, or a bundle of connections between the individual and the jurisdiction that justifies taxation of the individual on what is, in most jurisdictions, a worldwide basis. Considered from a different perspective, status and physical presence can be considered objective tests, while residence based on a bundle of connections entails a more subjective test.

Residence based on an individual's status can change in the absence of any change in the daily life of the individual; indeed, in some cases, the individual's status may change without any affirmative action on his or her part. For example,

---

[11] For example, for US Estate Tax purposes, an individual acquires a domicile in a place by living there, even for a brief period of time, with no definite present intention of leaving; 26 Code of Federal Regulations s 20.0-1(b)(1).

[12] For example, in the United Kingdom, every individual is attributed a domicile of origin at birth. This domicile is the father's domicile if the child is legitimate and the mother's if not, not domicile in the country in which the child was born. An individual may acquire a domicile of choice by leaving the country of their domicile of origin and taking up residence in another jurisdiction with the intention of making that their place of permanent or indefinite residence. However, if the domicile of choice is lost, the domicile of origin revives unless and until a new domicile of choice is acquired. Glen Loutzenhiser, *Tiley's Revenue Law*, 10th edn (Oxford, Hart Publishing, 2022) 1143.

the acquisition of permanent residence or the right to emigrate to a jurisdiction could arise by operation of law, for example, by marriage or, in the case of minors, by the naturalisation or immigration of the minor's parent or parents.

Residence can also be acquired or lost based on a change in the circumstances of the individual, for example, a change in physical presence or activities in the jurisdiction that brings the individual either above or below the threshold for tax residence. In the cleanest situation, this involves a 'clean break' from one jurisdiction followed by an unambiguous attachment to another, which together constitute an identifiable change of residence from one jurisdiction to another for tax purposes. From the point of view of the individual, this is the ideal situation, at least in the sense that he or she is clearly tax resident in one and only one jurisdiction.

However, a move from one jurisdiction to another may not be so clear or definitive. This can be because the individual's circumstances after the move do not clearly indicate that he or she is no longer resident in the first jurisdiction, or it may arise due to different definitions of tax residence that overlap. The broader and/or more subjective the definitions of residence, the more likely are the chances of overlap and hence dual residence. In addition, there are two possible points of transition, entry into and exit from the jurisdiction, either physically or in terms of status. Some jurisdictions make entry easier than exit. It is thus possible to enter one jurisdiction for tax purposes without having yet exited another.

II. The Prevalence of Double Residence

There are of course no definitive statistics on the number of individuals who are subject to double taxation on the basis of residence, but we can attempt to estimate this on the basis of the existing data.

With regards to migrants, the Population Division of the UN Department of Economic and Social Affairs estimates that the number of persons living outside of their country of origin reached 281 million in 2020.[13] This is roughly equal to the size of the entire population of Indonesia, the world's fourth most populous country,[14] or about 3.6 per cent of the world's population.[15] Between 2000 and 2010, the number of international migrants increased by 48 million, with another 60 million added between 2010 and 2020.[16] Thus, although the overwhelming majority of people live in the same country where they were born, the number of people who do not has been steadily increasing.

---

[13] United Nations Department of Economic and Social Affairs [UN DESA], Population Division, 'International Migration 2020 Highlights', Report ST/ESA/SER.A/452 (2020) 5; International Organization for Migration [IOM], 'World Migration Report 2022' (2021) 2.
[14] UN DESA (n 13) 5.
[15] IOM (n 13) 2.
[16] UN DESA (n 13) 5–6.

Much of this increase in the last two decades has been due to labour or family migration.[17] Furthermore, most of these migrants have gone to high-income countries.[18] Humanitarian crises in many parts of the world also contributed; in 2020, the number of persons worldwide who were forcibly displaced across national borders stood at 34 million, double the number in 2000.[19] Thus, refugees and asylum seekers account for a relatively small share, 12 per cent, of the total number of international migrants globally.[20] Low- and middle-income countries hosted over four-fifths of the world's refugees and asylum seekers in 2020.[21]

In 2020, nearly half of all international migrants were living in their region of origin.[22] That year, Europe had the largest number of international migrants, at 87 million.[23] Seventy per cent of all migrants born in Europe resided in another European country, with nearly half of those having moved between Member States of the European Union.[24]

For the purposes of estimating the number of individuals impacted by changes in or overlapping tax residence, the number of 281 million migrant individuals needs to be adjusted, as it is likely to be both an under- and an over-estimate. It is an underestimate in that it is a static picture that includes only those individuals who do not live in the jurisdiction of their birth at the time of testing. It does not take into account multiple moves; an individual moving from home jurisdiction A to jurisdiction B and subsequently to jurisdiction C will only be counted as a migrant once, even though he or she could have acquired two additional tax residences without having lost tax residence in his or her jurisdiction of origin. The estimate also does not count as a migrant anyone who has returned to his or her jurisdiction of origin, even though he or she could be a tax resident in both the jurisdiction of migration and the jurisdiction of origin even after returning to the jurisdiction of origin. Individuals who move for economic opportunity, employment, or education, and who in fact make up the majority of migrants, may engage in more than one move in their lifetime, either back to their jurisdiction of origin or to a third jurisdiction. By contrast, it seems plausible that refugees and those moving for family reasons are more likely to move only once in their lifetime. None of these moves, which over time could give rise to dual or multiple residences for tax purposes, is captured by the 'snapshot' migration statistics.

Furthermore, the free movement of labour rules of the European Union and the European Union's attempts to harmonise domestic tax laws mean that intra-EU migration, about 35 per cent of the total number of migrants in Europe and

---

[17] ibid 6.
[18] ibid 7.
[19] ibid 6.
[20] ibid 6.
[21] ibid 7.
[22] ibid 21.
[23] ibid 8.
[24] ibid 21.

11 per cent of the total population of migrants in the world, should be considered a distinct category of migration for tax purposes. On the one hand, there are limitations within the European Union on the rules that a member jurisdiction can apply to outbound migrants. On the other hand, the absence of normal visa requirements means that EU migrants are probably more likely than most migrants to move back to their jurisdiction of origin or, alternatively, to another EU country, perhaps repeatedly, and thus to be under-counted in estimates of individuals subject to more than one tax residence.

At the same time, the migration statistics represent something of an overcount. In particular, minors without independent means (ie, the majority of minors) are unlikely to be subject to taxation in any jurisdiction, let alone multiple ones. By the time they are likely to be paying taxes, they are more likely to be residents of only one jurisdiction.

It is also important to note that there are few reliable statistics that could shed light on the number of individuals who could be tax residents in another jurisdiction without migrating. In particular, there are no reliable statistics on multiple citizenships, and it would be even more difficult to estimate how many people might be domiciled in another jurisdiction under that jurisdiction's law.

III. Residence Rules in Three Different Jurisdictions

There is a very wide range of national approaches to residence. The three jurisdictions discussed here, the United States, Canada, and the United Kingdom, are, of course, not representative of the approximately 190 national level tax jurisdictions in the world. They do, however, present an interesting study of three jurisdictions that started with the same (common law) approach but have diverged. Furthermore, all three take a mixed approach to determining residence for tax purposes.

A. United States

The US Internal Revenue Code (the 'Code')[25] provides that tax residence in the United States for federal income tax purposes is triggered in one of three ways:

1) Citizenship: Alone in the world, the United States considers citizenship an independent basis for taxation; an individual is liable to taxation on a worldwide basis if he or she is a US citizen, regardless of any other connection to the United States.[26] And because US citizenship can be acquired by operation of

---

[25] Internal Revenue Code of 1986, as amended, codified as Title 26 of the United States Code.
[26] 26 US Code s 7701(a)(30).

law by a fleeting presence at birth[27] or birth abroad to a US citizen,[28] taxation by the United States on a worldwide basis can arise without the individual having any substantive connection to the country.

2) Legal Permanent Residence: An individual admitted under the immigration law to permanent residence in the United States (a holder of a 'Green Card') is a tax resident,[29] even if he or she no longer lives in the United States but has not formally lost or given up that status.[30] By contrast, other visas, even long-term ones, do not automatically make the holder tax resident in the United States.[31]

3) Substantial presence test: The substantial presence test[32] is a day counting test. Under the substantial presence test, to be resident in the United States for federal income tax purposes, an individual must be present in the United States for 183 days in the tax year, calculated as follows: at least 31 days in the current year and a total of 183 days over a three-year period, with each day in the current year counting as a full day, days in the previous year counting as one-third days, and days in the year before that counting as one-sixth days.[33] A day counts as a day of physical presence in the United States if the individual is present in the United States at any point in the day.[34] Days are disregarded under certain circumstances, eg, if the individual was unable to leave the United States because of the COVID lockdowns.[35] In addition, physical presence in the United States as a diplomat or student is not counted.[36] The regime also allows for split years in the year of arrival and departure.[37]

An individual will not be treated as meeting the substantial presence test if he or she was present in the United States for fewer than 183 days in the calendar year, has a tax home in a foreign country, and can establish a closer connection with that foreign country.[38] The Treasury Regulations provide that a tax home is the individual's regular or principal (if there is more than one regular) place of business and must be maintained for the entire year. If the individual has no regular or principal place of business, either because of the nature of the business, or because the individual is not engaged in carrying on a trade or business (for example, because

---

[27] 8 US Code s 1401(a).

[28] 8 US Code ss 1401(c) and (g).

[29] 26 US Code ss 7701(a)(30) and 7701(b)(1)(A)(i).

[30] 26 US Code s 7701(b)(6)(B); 26 Code of Federal Regulations ss 301.7701(b)–1(b)(2) and (b)(3).

[31] See 26 US Code s 7701(b)(1).

[32] 26 US Code s 7701(b)(1)(A)(ii); 26 Code of Federal Regulations s 301.7701(b)–1(c).

[33] 26 US Code s 7701(b)(3)(A); 26 Code of Federal Regulations s 301.7701(b)–1(c)(1).

[34] 26 Code of Federal Regulations ss 301.7701(b)–1(c)(2)(i) and 301.7701(b)–3(a).

[35] 26 US Code s 7701(b)(3)(D); 26 Code of Federal Regulations s 301.7701(b)–3(a)(2); Revenue Procedure 2020-20.

[36] 26 US Code s 7701(b)(5); 26 Code of Federal Regulations s 301.7701(b)–3(b)(1).

[37] 26 US Code s 7701(b)(2); 26 Code of Federal Regulations s 301.7701(b)–4.

[38] 26 US Code s 7701(b)(3)(B); 26 Code of Federal Regulations s 301.7701(b)–2.

he or she is an employee), then the individual's tax home is his or her regular place of abode in a real and substantial sense.[39] The Regulations also state that a closer connection to a foreign country can be established based on the facts and circumstances of the case, including but not limited to:

(a) the location of the individual's permanent home;
(b) the location of the individual's family;
(c) the location of personal belongings owned by the individual and his or her family;
(d) the location of social, political, cultural or religious organisations with which the individual has a current relationship;
(e) where the individual conducts his or her routine personal banking activities;
(f) where the individual conducts business activities (other than those that constitute his or her tax home);
(g) the jurisdiction in which the individual holds a driving licence;
(h) the jurisdiction in which the individual votes;
(i) the country of residence designated by the individual on forms and documents; and
(j) the government forms and documents filed by the individual.[40]

The first two rules for residence, citizenship and permanent residence, are status-based. By contrast, the substantial presence test depends on physical presence in the United States and is a largely mechanical day counting test, except to the extent that the individual seeks to invoke the closer connection exception, which involves a traditional facts and circumstances evaluation of a range of factors that establish a connection to a jurisdiction other than the United States. Thus, the United States uses primarily legal status (citizenship or permanent residence) and physical presence in the country to determine tax residence; it uses connecting factors only to exclude some individuals from residence.

Before the current regime was put in place,[41] the Code did not define resident or non-resident. The Regulations described a resident as a person 'actually present in the United States who is not a mere transient or sojourner' and clarified that '[w]hether he is a transient is determined by his intentions with regard to the length and nature of his stay'.[42] The Regulations proceeded to discuss the effects of various intentions and purposes. This regime led, unsurprisingly, to considerable litigation, sometimes getting into excruciating detail about the facts and circumstances of an individual's life, including his or her living arrangements, employment, social activities, investments, driving licence and foreign tax status, among other things.[43]

---

[39] 26 Code of Federal Regulations s 301.7701(b)–2(c).
[40] 26 Code of Federal Regulations s 301.7701(b)–2(d).
[41] Deficit Reduction Act of 1984, Public Law 98–369, s 138.
[42] 26 Code of Federal Regulations ss 1.871–2(b) and 2(c).
[43] See, eg, *Park v Commissioner*, 79 TC 252, 286 (1982), affirmed without published opinion, 755 F.2d 181 (DC Cir. 1985).

It is clear from the legislative history that the US Congress intended to replace the highly subjective test then in use with a more objective test, even as it acknowledged that some foreigners would become residents where they had not been before, and vice versa.[44] However, by choosing to provide for the closer connection exception to US tax residence, the US Congress declined to completely eliminate the need for detailed facts and circumstances determinations.

B. Canada

Canada provides an interesting but different example of a mixed approach to the tax residence of individuals. Canada considers a bundle of factors originally derived from the common law and also has deemed residence provisions. The Income Tax Act (the 'Act')[45] uses the term resident more than 400 times, but it does not define it anywhere, except to say that 'resident' includes a person who is 'ordinarily resident',[46] a term that is itself not defined. The Act also provides that a person who sojourns in Canada for 183 days or more during the year,[47] members of the Canadian armed forces[48] and Canadian diplomats, and Canadian and provincial employees[49] are 'deemed residents' of Canada. The Act does not define 'sojourn'. To understand the terms 'resident', 'ordinarily resident' and 'sojourn', one must look to the common law and the interpretation of the Canada Revenue Agency (the 'CRA'). The Act also contains one deemed non-resident provision: an individual will be deemed to be a non-resident of Canada at a particular time if, at that time, although otherwise resident in Canada, the individual is considered to be resident in another country under an income tax treaty between Canada and that other country.[50]

The leading case in this area is *Thomson*.[51] The case dealt with the Income War Tax Act,[52] which had language similar to the language in the Income Tax Act. The taxpayer, a Canadian who had moved abroad, argued that he was only sojourning in Canada and that because he had not reached the 183-day limit, he was not taxable in Canada on his worldwide income.[53] The Supreme Court of Canada rejected this argument and held that he was resident in Canada during the year in question. Having previously left Canada, over a period of seven years, he spent almost half the year in Canada with his family and servants in a house he owned in New

---

[44] Joint Committee on Taxation, JCS-41-84, 'General Explanation of the Revenue Provisions of the Deficit Reduction Act of 1984' (1984) 463–464.

[45] Income Tax Act, RSC, 1985, c 1.

[46] Income Tax Act, s 250(3).

[47] Income Tax Act s 250(1) (a).

[48] Income Tax Act s 250(1) (b).

[49] Income Tax Act s 250(1) (c).

[50] Income Tax Act s 250(5).

[51] *Thomson v. Minister of National Revenue*, [1946] SCR 209, 2 DTC 812.

[52] Income War Tax Act, 1917, 7–8 George V, c 28.

[53] *Thomson* (n 51) 214.

Brunswick.[54] The Court held that residence is 'chiefly a matter of the degree to which a person in mind and fact settles into or maintains or centralizes his ordinary mode of living',[55] and Thomson's ordinary residence was 'where in the settled routine of his life he regularly, normally or customarily lives'.[56]

These definitions of residence and ordinary residence have left the practical determination of tax residence to a facts and circumstances analysis. The CRA position is laid out in an Income Tax Folio.[57] Basing itself on the opinions in *Thomson*,[58] the CRA states that '[t]o determine residence status, all of the relevant facts in each case must be considered, including residential ties with Canada and length of time, object, intention and continuity with respect to stays in Canada and abroad'.[59] It then proceeds to list the factors that make one 'factually resident' in Canada. (The CRA refers to residence based on these factors as factual residence, as opposed to deemed residence based on presence in Canada for at least 183 days or service in the Canadian armed forces or government.) The most important factor is residential ties,[60] with significant residential ties being the individual's:

(a)   dwelling place or places;
(b)   location of spouse or common-law partner; and
(c)   location of dependants.[61]

Secondary residential ties include:

(a)   personal property in Canada;
(b)   social ties with Canada, such as memberships in Canadian recreational or religious organisations;
(c)   economic ties with Canada, including employment by a Canadian employer and active involvement in a Canadian business, as well as Canadian bank and other financial accounts;
(d)   landed immigrant (permanent resident) status or appropriate work permits in Canada;
(e)   hospitalisation and medical insurance coverage from a Canadian province or territory;
(f)   a driving licence from a Canadian province or territory;
(g)   a vehicle registered in a Canadian province or territory;
(h)   a seasonal dwelling place in Canada or a leased dwelling place;
(i)   a Canadian passport (ie, Canadian citizenship); and
(j)   memberships in Canadian unions or professional organisations.[62]

---

[54] ibid 216.
[55] ibid 225 (Rand J).
[56] ibid 231–32, (Estey J).
[57] Income Tax Folio S5-F1-C1, Determining an Individual's Residence Status.
[58] ibid paras 1.5–1.7.
[59] ibid para 1.8.
[60] ibid para 1.10.
[61] ibid paras 1.11 and 1.13.
[62] ibid para 1.14.

Generally, secondary residential ties must be looked at collectively in order to evaluate the significance of any one such tie. Generally speaking, a single secondary residential tie with Canada is not sufficient on its own to lead to the determination that an individual is factually resident in Canada while abroad.[63]

Other residential ties that have been considered by Canadian courts and by the CRA include the retention of a Canadian mailing address, post office box, or safety deposit box; personal stationery, including business cards, showing a Canadian address; telephone listings in Canada; and subscriptions to Canadian newspapers and magazines. These residential ties are generally of limited importance, except where there are other residential ties.[64]

Whether the individual is entering or leaving Canada matters. The CRA considers whether there is evidence that an individual's return to Canada was foreseen at the time of his or her departure. If so, it will attach more significance to the individual's remaining residential ties with Canada in determining whether the individual continued to be a factual resident of Canada subsequent to his or her departure.[65] It also considers the individual's compliance with the departure tax on deemed capital gains of Canadians becoming non-resident.[66] However, the fact that an individual establishes significant residential ties abroad will not, on its own, mean that the individual is no longer resident in Canada.[67]

The date of departure is the date on which the individual severs all residential ties with Canada, which will usually coincide with the latest of the dates on which:

(a)   the individual leaves Canada;
(b)   the individual's spouse or common law partner and/or dependants leave Canada (if applicable); or
(c)   the individual becomes a resident of the country to which he or she is emigrating.[68]

For individuals entering Canada, the same general factors apply. In addition, acquiring landed immigrant status and provincial health coverage will generally make the individual tax resident in Canada.[69]

A factual resident of Canada, considering the various residential ties listed above, cannot be deemed a resident of Canada. Thus, the factual residence determination must come first. The distinction between factual and deemed residence is non-trivial. Among other things, because an individual who is deemed to be resident in Canada is not factually resident in Canada, he or she will not be resident in a particular province for provincial tax purposes.[70] In addition, an individual

[63] ibid para 1.14.
[64] ibid para 1.15.
[65] ibid para 1.17.
[66] ibid para 1.18, see Income Tax Act, s 128.1.
[67] ibid para 1.21.
[68] ibid para 1.22.
[69] ibid para 1.25.
[70] ibid para 1.30.

who is factually resident in Canada for part of a year is only taxed on his or her worldwide income for that part of the year; in other words, the year is split for tax purposes. By contrast, an individual who is deemed to be resident in Canada is liable for tax on his or her worldwide income for the entire year.[71]

The day counting procedure for deemed residents under the 183-day deemed residence rule is complicated because it is based on the language in the Income Tax Act about sojourning. Thus, for example, a distinction is made between sojourning and commuting, even though both involve physical presence in Canada.[72]

To assist taxpayers in determining their residence status, individuals leaving Canada can file Form NR73, Determination of Residency Status (Leaving Canada), and those entering Canada can file Form NR74, Determination of Residency Status (Entering Canada) to request a residence opinion from the CRA. However, the CRA's opinion is not binding on the CRA and may be subject to a more detailed review and a request for supporting documentation at a later date. In some circumstances, individuals leaving or entering Canada may apply to the Income Tax Rulings Directorate for a ruling on tax residence.[73]

C. United Kingdom

Until 2013, the United Kingdom determined residence for purposes of the individual income tax on the basis of a complicated system of residence and ordinary residence that was in turn dependent on highly developed, if not completely consistent, case law.[74] The Finance Act 2013 put in place a Statutory Residence Test (the 'SRT') for the 2013–2014 and subsequent tax years.[75] The SRT is a highly complex set of tests for determining the tax residence in the United Kingdom of individuals. In order to be resident in the United Kingdom, an individual must either satisfy the 'automatic residence test' or the 'sufficient ties test' for the tax year (6 April to 5 April for individuals).[76] The 'automatic residence test' is in turn satisfied if at least one of the 'automatic UK tests' and none of the 'automatic overseas tests' are satisfied.[77] In addition, the 'sufficient ties test' requires that the individual not satisfy any of the automatic overseas tests.[78] Thus, an individual who satisfies any of the automatic overseas tests will not be resident in the United Kingdom,

---

[71] ibid para 1.32.

[72] ibid para 1.33.

[73] ibid paras 1.54–1.56.

[74] For a detailed discussion of the previous UK regime for determining residence, see J Schwarz, *Booth and Schwarz: Residence, Domicile and UK Taxation*, 21st edn (London, Bloomsbury Publishing, 2022) ch 4.

[75] Finance Act 2013, s 218 and Sch 45. For a detailed analysis of the UK Statutory Residence Test, see Schwarz (n 74) ch 2.

[76] Finance Act 2013, Sch 45, paras 3–4.

[77] ibid para 5.

[78] ibid para 17(1)(a).

regardless of any other circumstances; someone who does not satisfy any of the automatic overseas tests and also does not satisfy any of the automatic UK tests or sufficient ties tests will also not be resident in the United Kingdom for tax purposes.

The automatic overseas tests are:

(a) the individual was resident in the United Kingdom for one or more of the preceding three years, spent less than 16 days during the year in the United Kingdom and did not die during the year;[79]
(b) the individual was resident in the United Kingdom for none of the preceding three years and spent less than 46 days in the United Kingdom during the year;[80]
(c) the individual worked primarily overseas and took no significant break from overseas work, worked in the United Kingdom for less than 31 days and spent less than 91 days in the United Kingdom during the year;[81]
(d) the individual died during the year, was resident in the United Kingdom for neither of the two preceding years and spent less than 46 days in the United Kingdom during the year;[82] and
(e) the individual died during the year, met the third automatic overseas test above for both of the two previous years and meets the third automatic overseas test for the year, modified to consider only the period during which he or she was alive.[83]

The four automatic UK tests are:

(a) the individual spent at least 183 days during the year in the United Kingdom;[84]
(b) the individual had a home in the United Kingdom, spent at least 30 days during the year in that home, and, during a 91-day period of which at least 30 days fell during the tax year, spent at least 30 days in that UK home and either had no home overseas or spent less than 30 days at any such home;[85]
(c) the individual worked full time in the United Kingdom;[86] and
(d) the individual died during the tax year, was a UK resident by virtue of meeting the automatic residence test during each of the previous three years and, when he or she died, had his or her home in the United Kingdom or had homes in the United Kingdom and overseas but did not spend more than 30 days in the overseas home and was not there when he or she died.[87]

---

[79] ibid para 12.
[80] ibid para 13.
[81] ibid para 14.
[82] ibid para 15.
[83] ibid para 16.
[84] ibid para 7.
[85] ibid para 8.
[86] ibid para 9.
[87] ibid para 10.

Under the 'sufficient ties test',[88] tax residence in the United Kingdom depends upon whether or not the taxpayer was a resident of the United Kingdom during any of the previous three years and also upon the number of days the taxpayer spent in the United Kingdom during the year. It is also affected by whether the individual is leaving or arriving in the United Kingdom. An individual who was resident in the United Kingdom during any of the previous three tax years and is leaving the United Kingdom needs to satisfy between one and four UK ties, depending on how long he or she was present in the United Kingdom, to be UK resident.[89] An individual who was not resident in the United Kingdom during any of the previous three tax years and is arriving in the United Kingdom needs between two and four UK ties, depending on how long he or she was present in the United Kingdom, to be UK resident.[90] The UK ties are:

(a) a family tie, namely a spouse, partner or minor child in the United Kingdom;[91]
(b) an accommodation tie, specifically whether he or she has a place to live in the United Kingdom for at least 91 days during the year and does indeed stay there;[92]
(c) a work tie, namely working at least three hours a day for at least 40 days in the year in the United Kingdom;[93]
(d) a ninety-day tie, ie, presence in the United Kingdom for more than 90 days in the year;[94] and
(e) for an individual who is leaving the United Kingdom and was a UK resident during any of the three previous years, a country tie, namely that he or she spent the greatest number of days in the United Kingdom.[95]

As a practical matter, an individual who is present in the United Kingdom for at least 183 days will be resident in the United Kingdom, as it is impossible in that case for him or her to satisfy any of the automatic overseas residence tests. If the individual is not present in the United Kingdom for at least 183 days, he or she has to consider, in the following order:

(a) whether he or she satisfies any of the automatic overseas tests, in which case he or she is not UK resident; if not, the individual must consider:
(b) whether he or she satisfies any of the automatic UK tests, in which case he or she is UK resident; if not, the individual must consider:
(c) whether he or she has the required number of ties to the United Kingdom under the sufficient ties test.

---

[88] ibid para 17(1)(b).
[89] ibid para 18.
[90] ibid para 19.
[91] ibid paras 31(2)(a), 31(3)(a), 32 and 33.
[92] ibid paras 31(2)(b), 31(3)(b) and 34.
[93] ibid paras 31(2)(c), 31(3)(c), 35 and 36.
[94] ibid paras 31(2)(d), 31(3)(d) and 37.
[95] ibid paras 31(2)(3) and 38.

The automatic residence tests, ie, both the automatic overseas test and the automatic UK test, mix physical presence and workday day counts, together with other considerations such as whether or not the individual died in the year and where he or she has a home. The sufficient ties test relates primarily to subjective factors related to traditional concepts of domicile that hearken back to case law.

IV. Justifications for the Taxation of Individuals

The determination of residence needs to have a normative basis. In the cross-border context, fairness between states is important, particularly where the relationship is between developed and less-developed ones.[96] However, the taxation of individuals should be based first and foremost on fairness for individuals. To the individual, redistribution is not very important – the important thing is how much he or she will have to pay, and at what administrative and procedural cost. Most taxpayers will not be able to defend themselves against the consequences of double taxation on the basis of residence; the international tax system therefore should be designed to minimise its occurrence as much as possible.

To determine the 'correct' approach to residence, including at what point residence for tax purposes should be considered to commence or terminate, the justification for taxing individuals must be decided. All definitions of tax residence are ultimately attempts to establish a connection between the individual and the jurisdiction that justifies taxation by that jurisdiction.

Taxation of individuals is generally seen to be justified on either an ability to pay or a benefits basis. The ability to pay theory is generally considered to be the more contemporary approach. This approach, which has been around for about a century,[97] argues that those who have a greater ability to pay should pay more.

Directly related to the ability to pay theory is the principle of vertical equity. This principle states that those with more should contribute a greater percentage of their income. This is the theoretical basis for progressive taxation. The principle of horizontal equity is its first cousin, and states that similarly situated individuals should be taxed similarly.[98] Although these two principles are broadly accepted as the basis for how to tax individuals, neither has anything to say about who should be taxed.

---

[96] See T Shanan & D Narotzki, 'Taxation of Cross Border Migrations – Re-Evaluating the Allocation of Tax Collection of Immigrants Between Home Country and Host Country' in I Lindsay & B Mathew (eds), *Fairness in International Taxation* (Oxford, Hart Publishing, 2024).

[97] See, eg, MS Kendrick, 'The Ability-to-Pay Theory of Taxation' (1939) 29 *The American Economic Review* 92.

[98] See RA Musgrave, *The Theory of Public Finance: A Study in Public Economy* (New York, McGraw-Hill, 1959) 159.

This leaves us to seek other justifications for the taxation of individuals. Some connection must be established between the state and the individual that warrants the taxation of the latter by the former. A range of possible bases for taxation have been suggested over the years.

Political allegiance has been put forward as a justification for taxation, in which case citizenship is a suitable criterion. However, even a century ago, the four economists noted that

> [a] citizen of a country living abroad is frequently held responsible to his own country, though he may have no other ties than that of citizenship there. His is a political fealty which may involve political duties and may also confer political rights. It may well be that the political rights are such as to imply a political obligation or duty to pay taxes.[99]

> In modern times, however, the force of political allegiance has been considerably weakened. The political ties of a non-resident to the mother-country may often be merely nominal. His life may be spent abroad, and his real interests may be indissolubly bound up with his new home, while his loyalty to the old country may have almost completely disappeared. In many cases, indeed, the new home will also become the place of a new political allegiance ... In the modern age of the international migration of persons as well as of capital, political allegiance no longer forms an adequate test of individual fiscal obligation. It is fast breaking down in practice, and it is clearly insufficient in theory.[100]

Today, political connection, ie, citizenship, may be thought of more usefully for tax residence purposes in terms of its constituent parts, including the unlimited right to live in or return to the jurisdiction and the right to vote in its elections. To the extent that tax residence can be justified on the basis of citizenship, it should be on the basis of the right to live in the jurisdiction and participate in its political life, not on some inchoate connection between the state and the individual that is reminiscent of the traditional link between sovereign and subject. Where this right to live is not actually exercised by the individual, is there sufficient justification for taxing him or her on a worldwide basis?

A related approach to political connection is the membership theory of taxation, which argues that an individual should be subject to taxation if he or she is a member of the society imposing the tax.[101] However, this definition is circular and simply brings us back to a discussion of what constitutes membership in the society, ie, which points of connection justify taxation, as reflected in residence, ordinary residence, permanent home, domicile and nationality.[102]

The inadequacy of political connection and membership in society as bases for taxation leaves us with the benefits theory of taxation. The benefits theory of

---

[99] GWJ Bruins, LNL Einaudi, ERA Seligman and JC Stamp, 'Report on Double Taxation', League of Nations Document EFS 73 F 19 (1923) 19.

[100] ibid 19.

[101] C Garavan, 'The Membership Theory of Taxation' (2023) 51 *Intertax* 290, 303.

[102] ibid 305.

taxation, although intended to provide a justification for taxation, also implicitly sets out who should be taxed, namely those who benefit from the state imposing the taxation.[103] Furthermore, this definition provides us with a conceptually simple basis for taxation, even if it is not always easy to operationalise.

The approach of the benefits theory makes intuitive sense and seems fair, both as a justification for taxation and as a mechanism for determining who should be taxed. If '[t]axes are what we pay for civilized society',[104] then taxes are basically a payment for public goods. It follows that those who benefit from those public goods should pay taxes, while those who do not should not. The problem then becomes how to implement the principle. Which benefits should be considered to give rise to an obligation to pay taxes, and at what level? What degree of benefit from public goods justifies taxation, and how should generally available state-provided goods and services be ascribed to individuals?[105] The implicit, underlying question is, what degree of participation in the society justifies taxation, and in particular the imposition of taxation on a worldwide basis that is normally associated with residence? It is thus possible to consider receipt of benefits an indicator of membership.

All of these approaches seek to establish a connection between the individual and the state, on the basis of political, social or economic factors, that justifies taxation. Ultimately, however, none of them provide a comprehensive answer to this question, as evidenced by the wide variety of national approaches.

V. Towards a More Uniform Approach to Residence

The tests employed by the United States, Canada and the United Kingdom outlined in the previous section employ all the main types of tests available. The United States uses citizenship and permanent residence as independent bases of taxation, and Canada uses permanent residence as a generally dispositive factor in determining the residence of inbound individuals. All three jurisdictions have used domicile, ie, intention, in the past, although it remains today only as a vestigial aspect of the US and Canadian determinations of residence. And all three use day counts, from the simple Canadian 183-day test to the United States' more complicated three-year moving window test and the United Kingdom's incredibly complex bundle of tests.

The use of citizenship as an independent basis for taxation is problematic. The differences in the grant or acquisition of citizenship suggest widely different attitudes towards citizenship, which means it is a poor measure of sufficient

---

[103] ibid 293.

[104] *Compañía General de Tabacos de Filipinas v Collector of Internal Revenue* 275 US 87, 100 (1927) (Oliver Wendell Holmes, Jr, dissenting).

[105] See, eg, Musgrave (n 98) 66–67.

connection to a jurisdiction. It is not a proxy for residence, as the existence and number of expatriate citizens prove. Furthermore, to the extent that multiple citizenship is accepted, citizenship is no longer exclusive. And citizenship as an independent basis for taxation quickly comes into conflict with other bases of residence; US citizens abroad are almost always subject to residence-based taxation in at least two jurisdictions. It is therefore inappropriate as a criterion for tax residence if we are trying to limit the occurrence of dual tax residence.

Day counting, at least in the Canadian and US versions, is simple and easily administrable, by both individuals and tax administrations. It is also a reasonable proxy for the substantive connections in most thick residence tests. However, like any bright line test, the Canadian and US tests create opportunities for planning. They also create 'cliff edges' that are difficult to justify – why, for example, should someone who sojourns in Canada for 180 days be treated differently (potentially) than someone who sojourns for 185 days?

Thicker conceptions of residence, such as the Canadian factual residence test and the closer connection exception to US residence, comport better with basic notions of fairness and horizontal equity. They do, however, suffer from two important weaknesses. The first is that they create uncertainty, for both individuals and tax administrations; it is clear from the respective legislative histories that both the United Kingdom and the United States were driven by this complexity and the resulting disputes to move to their current regimes. The second is that, by their very expansiveness, which makes them better measures of actual connection to a jurisdiction, they increase the chances of dual or even multiple residence.

Conceptually, the idea of overlapping claims to residence-based jurisdiction is not problematic. On the contrary, in today's world, it is not unusual for an individual to have sufficient connections that justify taxation in more than one jurisdiction. A scalar definition of residence[106] would reflect this reality,[107] and this non-binary definition of residence would open up the possibility of different levels of taxation in each of the jurisdictions with which a dual or multi-resident individual has a sufficient connection to justify taxation.[108] It would also eliminate the cliff edge, and the accompanying problem of horizontal inequality, inherent in day counting regimes.[109]

Unfortunately, scalar residence does not by itself answer the all-important question of the criteria for determining that someone is resident, to whatever degree, in a jurisdiction. And how do we allocate taxing rights between jurisdictions with overlapping claims? Scalar residence leaves the practical question of how to tax those who are 'partially resident' to the politics of international relations, because such a system would have to be widely adopted to avoid overlapping

---

[106] See D Elkins, 'A Scalar Conception of Tax Residence' (2022) 41 *Virginia Tax Review* 149.
[107] ibid 178.
[108] ibid 181.
[109] ibid 176–177.

residence-based jurisdiction. As with the proposals for replacing transfer pricing with formulary apportionment, it is difficult to imagine how such a system would ever be agreed and put into place.

In the absence of a practical alternative to a binary conception of residence, at least for individuals, we are left with our traditional, exclusive conception of residence and a strong need to make the system predictable and administrable for individuals and tax administrations. Of the available alternatives – citizenship, domicile, thick definitions of residence, and day counting – only day counting offers the possibility of a matrix of domestic residence regimes with minimal overlap between jurisdictions. The day counting regime should not be limited to a simple in-year test, which would be too easy to plan around, and the threshold should not be too low, to avoid too many possibilities for multiple residence. It should have a three- or at most four-year lookback period, which would balance the need for simplicity against the need to limit manipulation of the rules. Alternatively, greater resilience against tax planning could be introduced by adding one or two additional elements. For example, a reasonable residence test could provide that an individual is resident in the jurisdiction if he or she: (a) is physically present for at least 183 days in the year; or (b) is physically present for at least 91 days in the year and is either a citizen or has the right to reside in the jurisdiction indefinitely. Such a residence rule would be clear and easy to apply while still acting as a reasonable proxy for specific connections to the jurisdiction.

VI. Conclusion

Residence, the basis for the taxation of individuals, is an intuitively justifiable basis for taxation, but one whose detailed definition and practical application are very difficult to specify. Various approaches are used by different jurisdictions, which refer to citizenship or immigration status, domicile, thick conceptions of residence, and/or physical or working presence in the jurisdiction. None of these four categories, let alone the specific variations used by different countries, is clearly normatively and practically superior. Furthermore, the resulting patchwork of approaches results in complexity and considerable overlap for cross-border individuals. In the absence of consensus around a normative approach to residence, jurisdictions should move towards modified day counting regimes to provide clarity and certainty to both individuals and their own tax administrations.

INDEX

www.ingramcontent.com/pod-product-compliance
Lightning Source LLC
LaVergne TN
LVHW010728060325
805169LV00003B/52